D1474962

Miniature Crafts and Their Makers

Miniature Crafts and Their Makers

Palm Weaving in a Mexican Town

Katrin S. Flechsig

THE UNIVERSITY OF ARIZONA PRESS   TUCSON

In Memory of Arthur O. Flechsig

The University of Arizona Press
© 2004 The Arizona Board of Regents
All rights reserved

∞ This book is printed on acid-free, archival-quality paper.
Manufactured in the United States of America

09   08   07   06   05   04   6   5   4   3   2   1

Library of Congress Cataloging-in-Publication Data
Flechsig, Katrin.
Miniature crafts and their makers: palm weaving in a
Mexican town / Katrin Flechsig.
p.   cm.
Includes bibliographical references and index.
ISBN 0-8165-2400-9 (cloth: alk. paper)
1. Mixtec Indians—Industries—Mexico—Chigmecatitlán.
2. Mixtec Indians—Mexico—Chigmecatitlán—Rites and ceremonies.
3. Mixtec baskets—Mexico—Chigmecatitlán.   4. Palm frond
weaving—Mexico—Chigmecatitlán.   5. Miniature craft—Mexico—
Chigmecatitlán.   6. Chigmecatitlán (Mexico)—Social conditions.
7. Chigmecatitlán (Mexico)—Economic conditions.   I. Title.
F1219.8.M59F54   2004
972'.480049763—dc22
2004010393

Attention by itself is an enlarging glass.

—Gaston Bachelard

Contents

Illustrations

Maps

Tables

Figures

Color Plates

Plate section follows page 134.

PLATE 6 Woodpecker and *ita tsiní* flowers suspended from the Corpus
Christi altar of the Hermandad de Guadalupe

PLATE 7a *Tlachiquero*, lithograph by Claudio Linati, 1828

PLATE 7b *Tlachiquero*, probably from the 1960s

PLATE 8 Palm and plastic baskets (*ika*) to hold candy for Las Posadas

Preface

This book is about a journey to the "backstage" of craft production, the counterpart to the public face of crafts the tourist in Mexico encounters in the city market. I first saw miniature basketry from Santa María Chigmecatitlán while living in Mexico City in 1987. Following a tip from a book by the eminent folklorist and illustrator Alberto Beltrán (1979), I had gone to the Zócalo, Mexico City's central plaza, on Corpus Christi Sunday to look for pieces for my expanding collection of miniatures. A young woman sitting on a cloth, her hair in a long braid down her back, was selling miniature palm people, animals, and baskets. I bought several and she told me she was from Chigmecatitlán, in the state of Puebla. Little did I imagine that years later I would rack my brain trying to remember her face, wondering if she was someone I had met again while spending nearly a year doing ethnographic fieldwork in that town.

I arrived in the town of Chigmecatitlán, Puebla, in October 1995 as a graduate student from Austin, Texas, undertaking dissertation research. I lived there for ten months doing participant observation among artisans and returned for a three-week follow-up in June and July 1997. In graduate school, Susan Stewart's *On Longing: Narratives of the Miniature, the Gigantic, the Souvenir, the Collection* (1993) had provided the theory that was needed to elevate my longtime captivation with the miniature to a topic of academic inquiry. My objective in this book is to try to understand the meaning of miniature crafts "on the ground" in one particular community, and, ultimately, to contribute to a cross-cultural anthropology of the miniature.

The practical inspiration for this book was Gabriel Moedano's (1970:x) prescriptive comment: "Only a study of the producers of miniatures, their world view, the socio-economic environment in which they work, the uses and functions of miniatures, as well as their intended market, can demonstrate the truth or falsity of the multiple interpretations that have been made about them." Marta Turok's (1988a:194) advice that "the popular arts phenomenon is not isolated from the general problems of farming, industry, commerce, and tourism" also influenced my approach. Accordingly, I locate the crafts of Chigmecatitlán within several social and cultural contexts, including manufacturing (Chapter 2), local history (Chapters 3 and 4), religion (Chapter 5), design and technique (Chapter 6), and selling (Chapter 7).

One of the reasons for choosing Chigmecatitlán as a research site was that few anthropologists had visited that remote community. The Puebla portion of the Mixteca has been little studied in comparison with the Oaxaca portion, the Mixtec heartland. Those anthropologists who have gone to Chigmecatitlán, however, supplied valuable background for my research. Leonardo Manrique (1964), linguistic anthropologist with the Instituto Nacional de Antropología e Historia (INAH), visited briefly in 1959 and wrote a short article focusing on population. Klaus Jäcklein (1974, 1978) and Erdman Gormsen (1977) of the Puebla/Tlaxcala Project also provide data about the region. Jäcklein's superb research on sixteenth- and seventeenth-century archives for his ethnohistory of the Popolocas of Tepexi, Puebla, is useful for Chigmecatitlán history. I am indebted to Hortensia Rosquillas for calling my attention to Jäcklein's work. Martha García and Marco Antonio Hernández (1986) wrote an unpublished paper based on their field research as students at the Escuela Nacional de Antropología e Historia (ENAH). I am grateful to García, anthropologist and reporter for Indian affairs for the newspaper *La Jornada,* for generously sharing with me her notes and information on Chigmecatitlán. Another ENAH student, José Antonio Ochoa (1993), wrote a thesis on musical bands in Chigmecatitlán, and researchers from the Summer Institute of Linguistics visited the town briefly in June 1996 to conduct a language survey and hold a Mixtec writing workshop.

My research methodology consisted of discussions and interviews with palm and raffia weavers about their work. Interviews took place at artisans' homes. Tirso Anzures, a local window and door maker and bricklayer, functioned informally as my assistant, setting up interviews and translating between Spanish and Mixtec when necessary. Conversations also took place spontaneously in passing at the market, at a fiesta, or in the town hall library. I took notes on my informants' responses, copying crucial phrases verbatim. Back at my house, preferably on the same day, I wrote detailed descriptions of our conversations. In addition to my observations in the town, I sought out commercial locales in Mexico City and Puebla to trace the destination of palm crafts from Chigmecatitlán.

Many people contributed to writing this book. I would like to give special thanks to Brian Stross and other anthropology faculty members at the University of Texas at Austin: Ward Keeler, Pauline Turner Strong, and Samuel M. Wilson. The writing has also benefited from conversations with Andrew Causey, Boyd Dixon, R. Neill Hadder, Michael Hironymous, Kathleen Murphy, De Ann Pendry, and David Samuels. Tom Wendt, Plant Resources Center, University of Texas, and Phyllis G. Flechsig aided with botanical identifications.

I would like to especially thank my parents, Arthur O. Flechsig and Phyllis G. Flechsig, for their support including visiting me in Chigmecatitlán in 1996.

In Mexico City, Gabriel Moedano graciously served as my Fulbright adviser. I also greatly appreciated the help of Dolores Ávila, Guillermo Contreras, and Margarita Estrada and family. Thanks to the INAH, Subdirección de Etnohistoria, especially its Subdirector Cristina Suárez, for permission to photograph the palm collections of the Museo Nacional de Antropología. Museum researchers Efraín Cortés Ruiz, María Eugenia Sánchez Santa Ana, and Sergio Torres Quintero, as well as curatorial assistant Julián Cruz, were all very helpful. Efraín Cortés Ruiz via Catalina Rodríguez generously provided an unpublished text on palm weaving.

In Chigmecatitlán, my deepest appreciation to my friends, especially Antonio Álvarez, Tirso Anzures, Flavio Gallardo, Luz María García Contreras, Delia Mejía Rosas, J. Severiano Méndez Hernández, Pedro Pineda, and Basilia Sánchez. I am grateful to municipal presidents Wilfrido Cortés Herrera and Gonzalo Martínez Rodríguez, and to his wife Catalina Arizpe, for permitting my research in Chigmecatitlán. Thanks to Sue Hugghins, Inga McKendry, and Diane Veld of the Summer Institute of Linguistics in Oaxaca for their insights into the Mixtec language.

My field research in Chigmecatitlán was partly funded by a Fulbright Grant. A University Fellowship from the University of Texas at Austin funded nine months of writing. All translations are by the author unless noted in the bibliography.

Abbreviations

AGN	Archivo General de la Nación
BANFOCO	Banco Nacional de Fomento Cooperativo
CNC	Confederación Nacional Campesina
CONASUPO	Compañía Nacional de Subsistencias Populares
DIF	Sistema Nacional para el Desarrollo Integral de la Familia
ENAH	Escuela Nacional de Antropología e Historia
FONART	Fondo Nacional para el Fomento de las Artesanías
INAH	Instituto Nacional de Antropología e Historia
INI	Instituto Nacional Indigenista
NAFTA	North American Free Trade Agreement
PAN	Partido Acción Nacional
PRD	Partido Revolucionario Democrático
PRI	Partido Revolucionario Institucional
SEDESOL	Secretaría de Desarrollo Social
UNAM	Universidad Nacional Autónoma de México

Miniature Crafts and Their Makers

The Lilliputization of Mexico

Santa María Chigmecatitlán is a town in the desert of southern Puebla, Mexico, where people make delicate crafts so small a marching band could fit in the palm of one's hand. The town occupies a parched landscape from which the ancient Mixtecs wove palm goods as tribute to the dominating Aztecs in their capital of Tenochtitlan before the Spanish conquest in 1521. The modern Mixtec Indians of Chigmecatitlán weave colorful miniature crafts from strips of palm or plastic for a market composed of urban dwellers of the major Mexican cities whose nostalgia for an authentic Indian past is amply confirmed by these enchanting handmade objects.

Chigmecatitlán is one of more than one hundred towns where artisans produce miniatures, for Mexico is a miniaturist country par excellence. Rare is the craft-producing town that does not harbor at least one artisan or family who has found a niche creating small-scale versions of the local craft specialty.

When I began fieldwork in Chigmecatitlán in 1995 I expected to trace woven palm miniatures ultimately to the ancient Mixtec ancestors of the current inhabitants. Many writers have speculated that the abundance of tiny crafts in Mexico is a pre-Hispanic legacy in light of the thousands of diminutive artifacts dug up at Mexico's archaeological sites. But, shortly after my arrival, the townspeople informed me that, far from making miniatures since the sixteenth century, *they* had only made miniatures since 1965. My research into the "why" of miniature crafts had to consider postmodern factors such as tourism and the construction of national identity.

Pietro Bellasi's (1983, 1985) analysis of the phenomenon of "Lilliputization" in Switzerland provides a productive starting point from which to explore Mexico's "obsession with miniaturization" (Oettinger 1990).

Bellasi contends that tourist attractions such as the miniature town Swissminiatur on Lake Lugano present a rural image of chalets, chateaus, and toy railways that disguises the massive size of industrial reality in Switzerland. Reduced scale, according to Bellasi, affords a refuge from the impersonal and menacing vastness of historical, political, and natural cataclysms perceived as being beyond human control.

Like Switzerland, Mexico has cultivated a picturesque image of Indian peasants and rural countryside that has persisted throughout the twentieth century (Oles 1993; Ramos 1962:102–103) despite competing images of turmoil in Mexico's history such as the violence of the Mexican Revolution, mass industrialization in the 1950s and 1960s, and the current financial, political, ethnic, and environmental crises that have engulfed the country since the 1990s.

Pedestrians in Mexico City's historic center are likely to find themselves gazing on the Aztec past as Lilliput. Pigeons whose ancestors arrived with the early Spaniards dwarf a scale model of Lake Texcoco sculpted in bas-relief on the ground outside the museum of the Templo Mayor, the Great Temple of the Aztecs. Here, on one corner of the downtown Zócalo, throngs of Mexicans and tourists congregate to the throbbing drumbeats of dancers reenacting the Aztec revival movement known as *Mexicanidad*. The model replicates in miniature the contours of the vanished lake at this very site that surrounded the former Aztec city of Tenochtitlan at the time of the Spanish conquest.

Wandering away from this model, visitors confront an array of diminutive items among the merchandise for sale on the sidewalk. Here a woman from Chigmecatitlán is selling palm miniatures on the pavement near the model of Lake Texcoco. Does the presence of Indian people and crafts in the metropolis prove the continuity of the past, or are they, too, part of the reconstruction of myth?

MEXICAN CRAFTS AS SYMBOLS OF IDENTITY

Handmade crafts played a role in building a national culture in the prolifically creative aftermath of the Mexican Revolution of 1910. The post-Revolutionary government of the 1920s through 1940s sponsored cultural programs that recuperated the Indian past and rediscovered Indians and *campesinos* in the present (Albers 1970, preface; Atl [1922]1980:21; Bonfil Batalla 1996:53; García Canclini 1993:43; Morales-Moreno 1994:171; Novelo 1993:31–40; Novo [1932]1989:417; Oles 1993,

2002; Pomar 1980; Toor 1939; Vázquez Valle 1989). As Victoria Novelo (1993:32) lucidly puts it:

> *In the search for nationalism, the discovery of a Mexican culture was imperative. To that end, the guiding concept was that all Mexicans were united by a common racial and cultural heritage. The Indians and some of their cultural manifestations became a motive for pride. The non-Indian minority of the country had to learn to love that which was their own, that which was authentic, fusing it with some of their values and customs so that from this union, something truly national would be born.*

The Mexican government embraced the richness of native crafts in its plan to unify the divided country around new nationalist themes. Manuel Gamio, the first director of the Anthropology Bureau in 1917, proposed that "Mexicans could be united by the same cultural patrimony," including crafts (Kaplan 1993:103–104). Mexican Indians were seen as living successors of pre-Hispanic civilizations and their handmade crafts as a continuation of the patrimony of antiquity (cf. Errington 1998:161–62). Mexican artists and intellectuals such as Dr. Atl (Gerardo Murillo), Miguel Covarrubias, Jorge Enciso, Frida Kahlo, Roberto Montenegro, and Diego Rivera enthusiastically promoted popular arts and crafts hand-in-hand with American and other foreign émigrés including Anni Albers, Anita Brenner, Jean Charlot, René d'Harnoncourt, Frances Toor, and Edward Weston. Their colleague, writer Katherine Anne Porter ([1922]1993:171), wrote in 1922: "Of late, the Mexican students, writers, painters, the vivid group which makes up the National University life, has discovered anew the principles of design in this neglected native art. They have realized that in those undeciphered characters on temple walls is buried the history of the lost races of Mexico. With admirable humility they have set themselves, unreservedly, to the task of re-discovery."

These artists and writers helped establish an appreciation for regional crafts among the Mexican elites who previously had espoused things European, preferably French. Landscape painter Dr. Atl in 1921 pronounced the popular arts "next to revolutionary fervor, what is most Mexican about Mexico" (Martínez Peñaloza 1972:18; Pomar 1980:IX). Porter (1970:356) wrote, with equal vigor, in 1923, "It would be difficult to explain in a very few words how the Mexicans have enriched their national life through the medium of their native arts. It is in everything they do and are." An excerpt from a travel guide distributed to guests at the chic Hotel Genève in Mexico City's Zona Rosa in the 1930s similarly identifies the "soul" of Mexico with its popular arts: "POPULAR ARTS OF MEXICO.—Only four simple words, but of what significance. In them is expressed the entire artistic soul of a people. Synonymous with the most exquisite beauty and idealism, they reveal the quiet and patient spirit of the Mexican Indian" (Poyo 1939:5). Crafts thus became a symbol of national identity in the search for authenticity and "*lo nuestro*" (what is ours), in implicit opposition to what is European and North American.

The same artists and intellectuals assembled significant collections, public and private, of folk art for preservation and display. The close-knit in-group of Mexican painters and American and other foreign writers, in collaboration with officials of the Mexican government, was directly responsible for making craft collections fashionable in the eyes of museum-goers in the 1920s and 1930s.[1]

In Mexico, the first major exposition of Mexican popular art ("Exhibición de Arte Popular") was inaugurated by President Álvaro Obregón in September 1921 at #85 Avenida Juárez in Mexico City as part of the centenary celebration of Mexican independence (Martínez Peñaloza 1972). Young painters Jorge Enciso and Roberto Montenegro assembled the objects, and Dr. Atl wrote the catalogue, revised in 1922 as *Las artes populares en México*. As Oles (2002:19) suggests, the collectors' identity as artists focused public appreciation of popular crafts on aesthetics, while at the same time the context clearly demonstrated that they were to be valorized as political expressions of the Mexican nation. The collection, which included "very rich lots of artifacts of palm," was apparently later split in two and sent to Brazil and Argentina for exhibition there.[2]

Katherine Anne Porter initiated an exhibit of Mexican popular art in Los Angeles in 1922 and wrote *Outline of Mexican Popular Arts and Crafts* (Porter [1922]1993) as its catalogue raisonné. The exhibition was organized through the Secretaría de Industria, Comercio y Trabajo. Painter Xavier Guerrero was designated as its director. The show included more than 1,800 pieces, which were later scattered among the Mexican consulates (Martínez Peñaloza 1980).

U.S. Ambassador to Mexico Dwight D. Morrow conceived another exhibition of "applied" and fine arts, for which organizer René d'Harnoncourt borrowed folk art pieces from the private collections of Morrow, Miguel Covarrubias, Fred Davis, Jorge Enciso, William Spratling, and others of the artistic crowd. The exhibit traveled from 1930 to 1931 to eight U.S. cities. Toys; miniature carvings in ivory, bone, stone, and wood; and miniature maquettes (mock-ups or models) were included (American Federation of Arts 1930; see also Danly 2002).

A "Museo de Artes Populares" opened in 1934 at the Palacio de Bellas Artes in Mexico City. Roberto Montenegro began assembling the collection, which included toys, in 1930 at the behest of Moisés Sáenz, Undersecretary of Education. The brief catalogue (Montenegro 1948) in Spanish, English, French, and Italian reflects the international audience for Mexican folk art.

In addition to museum collections, folk art shops known as "curio shops" blossomed on Avenida Juárez in Mexico City. Surveys of Mexican crafts were published, cataloguing and celebrating the deservedly exalted reputation of Mexican crafts (for a bibliography of Mexican crafts, see Turok 1988b).

The notion that Mexican crafts are an essential motive for national pride and identity is now taken for granted in Mexico. A recent policy statement by a government bureau continues the trend: "Mexico's cultural identity is determined in essence by its rich origins and traditions. One of its chief manifestations is its crafts" (SECOFI [1991]:5).

Miniatures were singled out from the beginning in these exhibits, shops, and publications as a significant category of Mexican popular art. Anthropologist Frederick Starr (1899) of the University of Chicago included miniatures in one of the earliest works on Mexican crafts, his *Catalogue of a Collection of Objects Illustrating the Folklore of Mexico*. Dr. Atl proved even more influential in establishing the miniature as a respectable genre with his seminal *Las artes populares en México,* the first Mexican book on popular arts, published in 1921 and revised in 1922 (Martínez Peñaloza 1980). Thereafter it was nearly de rigueur for books on Mexican crafts to incorporate a section on toys and miniatures.[3]

MAGICAL MINIATURES

If miniatures are analogues of a thing, what we do to the miniature, we symbolically do to the thing. This is the classic principle of imitative or homeopathic magic Sir James Frazer (1922:11) elucidates in *The Golden Bough* under the rubric "Like produces like" (his Law of Similarity): "Thus, among the Esquimaux boys are forbidden to play cat's cradle, because if they did so their fingers might in later life become entangled in the harpoon-line. Here the taboo is obviously an application of the law of similarity, which is the basis of homoeopathic magic: as the child's fingers are entangled by the string in playing cat's cradle, so they will be entangled by the harpoon-line when he is a man and hunts whales."

The Mexican government introduced miniature models into Indian communities as a heuristic tool in the 1920s, mobilizing young people in cultural missions to fan out from the metropolis into various towns in the interior with the goal of "forming a true national soul," in the words of the Secretary of Public Education, J. M. Puig Casauranc (SEP 1927: XXII). The missions, proposed in 1924 and implemented in 1926 under President Plutarco Elías Calles, sought to improve the level of teaching by rural schoolteachers through workshops led by middle-class instructors from the city. The curriculum dictated that rural teachers construct scale models of the ideal school and enter them in contests. The rationale for the diminutive buildings was to provide the teachers with "the modern concept of the Rural and Urban School" and a notion of "how the ideal school should be" (SEP 1928:173). Memoirs of the missions (SEP 1927, 1928) contain photographs of complete tabletop models of schools, which often include detailed landscaping and outbuildings. These models were the symbolic adjunct to teaching Spanish as "the national language."

This use of the miniature as a didactic method is familiar to any elementary school teacher in the United States. It also illustrates the universal use of miniatures as a kind of imitative magic, an attempt to control the future, in this case by focusing the previously heterodox national gaze on a unified goal modeled in miniature. In a broad sense, an architect presenting a scale model is persuading the client to proceed with the project by envisioning it in full size. The cultural missions used miniatures not to re-create what was, but to prescribe what ought to be, in this case to "try to fill the unfathomable chasm that heretofore separates the Mexican organization in its upper classes and in its peasant classes" (Puig Casauranc addressing members of cultural missions in 1925; SEP 1927:XXII).

The central government's magical or prescriptive use of miniatures is similar to a local custom that anthropologist Elsie Clews Parsons (1930) describes among the Zapotec Indians. On New Year's Eve, she writes, people from several towns near Mitla, Oaxaca, stack up pebble models, known as petitions or "*pedimientos,*" of things they hope to obtain in the coming year. Parsons (1930:38) provides sketches of some of these ephemeral models; one, for example, depicts a "house, cook-shed, sheep-corral, tethered animals, sow with litter, chickens roosting, fruit trees, corn-shack, money." Michael Duke (personal communication, 1997) observed a similar use of crude miniature houses on the ground at Huatulco, Oaxaca, where people erected them when the "brother" of Santa Cruz Huatulco answered their prayers. "I have little doubt," Parsons (1930:44–45) writes, "that the contemporary practice among some of them of reproducing in miniature the objects of their desire is the survival of an ancient habit of mind."

The Huichol, as Frances Toor recorded in the 1940s, attached small objects to prayer arrows as imitative magic. "Many of the symbolical objects made in miniature to offer to the gods are attached to the arrows; for example, a tiny pair of sandals to express a woman's prayer for a husband or merely to symbolize the stomping in the dances intended to call the attention of the gods; or tiny deer traps asking for success in the ceremonial hunt" (Toor [1947]1985:71–73).

These practices may represent the pre-Hispanic use of miniatures as iconic symbols to communicate with deities or they may be syncretic—that is, a blending of Catholic and indigenous beliefs.

PRE-HISPANIC USES OF THE MINIATURE

The perceived connection between pre-Hispanic and modern miniatures has enhanced their coinage as appropriate symbols of national identity. *Why* Mexico is a miniaturist nation may have as much to do with tourism and commerce as with ancestral heritage, but the traditional approach has been to look at the two major wellsprings of Mexican culture, indigenous and European, for evidence of miniatures. Lately, scholarly interest in the Afro-Mestizo heritage has reestablished the "Third Root" of this family tree (see Moedano 1996), but thus far I have seen no major evidence of African influence on Mexican miniatures.

Small replicas of full-sized objects are ubiquitous in the archaeological substrate of Mexico. Clay figurines from the Preclassic were practically littered across the landscape at various sites (Horcasitas and Heyden, in Durán 1971:420).[4] A group of Olmec stone statuettes found at La Venta, Tabasco, are among the best-known Preclassic-period anthropomorphic figurines (Coe 1984). Miniature buildings, dishes, and animals of pottery and stone have been found at Classic sites including

Teotihuacán and Monte Albán and Postclassic sites including Tzintzuntzan, Dzibilchaltún, and Lake Chapala (Andrews 1961; Rubín de la Borbolla 1974:252; Starr 1897).

The exact function of the thousands of tiny artifacts excavated at Mexico's archaeological ruins continues to intrigue researchers. Were they toys or ritual objects? (cf. Babcock, Monthan, and Monthan's [1986:7–8] assessment regarding archaeological Pueblo pottery miniatures in New Mexico). The debate over toy versus ritual in Mexico has focused on discoveries of doll-like figurines with jointed limbs as well as animals on wheels.[5] The latter have particularly fascinated researchers because ancient Mexicans never used full-sized wheeled carts for transport. Michael Coe (1970) maintains that the jointed dolls and wheeled animals were toys. He and others conclude, however, that the vast majority of pre-Hispanic miniature relics were ceremonial, though their exact function is elusive (Albers 1970; Hernández 1950; Matos Moctezuma 1993; Rubín de la Borbolla 1974:252; Sayer 1990:105).

The early Spanish chroniclers have shed light on the indigenous use of miniature objects shortly after the conquest (Burgoa [1674]1934; Durán 1971; Motolinía 1973; Sahagún 1969). Sixteenth-century Dominican friar Diego Durán frequently alludes to the Aztec ceremonial use, which he regards as infantile, of anthropomorphic and zoomorphic figurines representing supernatural beings: "The caves, shrines, places of sacrifice, and temples [in the hills] were filled with little stone and clay idols" (Durán 1971:416; note in brackets by Horcasitas and Heyden). The Aztecs also utilized miniatures as symbolic sacrificial offerings to such supernatural beings: "The offerings presented were in accordance with the [importance of the] gods. They were so insignificant that they were no larger than a small gourd for the gods to drink from, tiny bowls, plates, pots, little beads, incense, rubber, and feathers" (Durán 1971:258; note in brackets by Horcasitas and Heyden).

One of the best descriptions of miniatures in pre-Hispanic times comes from the *Florentine Codex*, compiled in the sixteenth century by Fray Bernardino de Sahagún. His native informants record that the Aztecs placed little tools in the fists of newborn babies during a naming ceremony: bows, arrows, and amaranth shields for boys; spindles, skeins, shuttle, and batten for girls (Sahagún 1969, Book 6, Part 7, Ch. 37, p. 201). Durán (1971:124) similarly describes this Aztec rite, especially connected with "sons of the lord and rulers":

If the newborn was a male child, the priests themselves washed him; and when he was bathed, they placed a tiny sword in his right hand and a small shield in the other. The child went through this rite four days in a row while the parents offered oblations for his sake. If it was a girl, after bathing her four times, they placed in her hands miniature implements for spinning and weaving, together with woven cloths. Other children received quivers of arrows around their necks and bows in their hands. Children of the common people received the symbol [of their future profession] according to what had been prognosticated by the sign under which they were born. If [the child's] signs indicated that he was to be a painter, a brush was placed in his hand; if a carpenter, he was given an adz; and the others [were treated] in a similar fashion" (Durán 1971:124–25; notes in brackets by Horcasitas and Heyden).

According to the Museo Nacional de Culturas Populares (1995), "This custom is still practiced by the Popolucas of the state of Veracruz and the Maya of Yucatán" albeit with full-sized implements (cf. Anguiano 1982:26; Toor [1947]1985:116–17).

The pre-Hispanic Mixtecs reputedly excelled at exquisite detail in art, or what we might construe as miniaturist skills. Covarrubias (1957:311), for example, writes of the ancient Mixtecs: "In general it can be said that they were little concerned with monumental art, but concentrated on the decorative and precious, with an emphasis on highly developed techniques and fine craftsmanship," an assessment that Caso (1940:25), Dahlgren ([1954]1990:274), and Spores (1967:16) endorse. Their unanimity likely reflects archaeologist Alfonso Caso's well-publicized discovery of gold jewelry and delicately inscribed bones at the Late Postclassic Tomb 7 at Monte Albán, Oaxaca, which became the best-known representatives of ancient Mixtec art in miniature (Caso 1932; illustrated in Coe 1984:140, 141).

The pre-Hispanic screenfold books known as the Mixtec and Borgia Group codices are themselves superb examples of miniaturist art.[6] Unfortunately, codex iconography sheds no light on the ancient use of small-scale objects in the Mixtec area because size implies conceptual importance rather than relative scale under their pictorial conventions (Miller 1975:xi). It is thus impossible to gauge the size of the multiple offerings to deities depicted in the codices.

TABLE 0.1. Miniatures Associated with Popular Catholicism

Date	Celebration	Associated Miniatures in Mexico	Chigmecatitlán Crafts
January 6	Epiphany or Three Kings Day	Children receive presents in shoes; plastic figure of the Christ child hidden in King's cake.	
January 28	Day of the Holy Innocents	"A common practice is to promise a person something desirable and then fulfill with a miniature and worthless object of the kind promised. If one borrows a good and serviceable article, he may repay with a small and useless one, etc." (Starr 1899:98).	
February 2	Candlemas	Statues of the Christ Child are dressed, e.g., as the Santo Niño de Atocha with hat, cape, basket, gourd, throne.	White baskets for the Niño de Atocha to hold.
After Fat Tuesday	Carnival		Formerly, finger traps (*pescanovia, espantasuegra,* or *tsko konda'a* 'animal that swallows the finger').
5th Friday after Ash Wednesday	Friday of Sorrows	Altars were formerly arranged with sprouted clay animals from Santa María Atzompa, Oaxaca.	
5th Sunday after Ash Wednesday	Palm Sunday	Woven palms sold in church atriums for blessing at mass.	No palm woven for Palm Sunday.
	Holy Week		Toys to sell in Mexico City.

Date	Celebration	Associated Miniatures in Mexico	Chigmecatitlán Crafts
6th Saturday after Ash Wednesday	Holy Saturday	Papier-maché Judas figures sold in markets.	
Thursday, 60 days after Easter	Corpus Christi	Children dressed as "*inditos*" carrying baskets or crates with produce and household items photographed against backdrops. *Mulitas* and other toys sold outside the Metropolitan Cathedral in Mexico City.	Toy *petate* mats, fire fans, hats, baskets for children to carry. *Mulitas* and other toys.
November 1-2	All Saints' Day, All Souls' Day	"Playthings include skeleton miniatures of many kinds, miniature ofrendas stacked with food, small coffins" (Pettit and Pettit 1978:132).	Baskets made to hold incense, candles for graveyard offerings. Formerly, palm *mulitas* and solid cane (*otate*) baskets.
December 12	Day of Guadalupe	Children dressed as "*inditos*" attend mass.	
December 16-24	Posadas	Statues of Joseph with Mary on a donkey carried in procession to the houses. Nativity scenes.	Baskets for the "*colación*" or sweets offered to guests.
December 25	Christmas	Christmas tree decorations for export.	Nativity scenes and "*posaditas*."

Source: Anguiano 1982; Charpenel 1970; Pettit and Pettit 1978; Starr 1899; Toor 1985.

MINIATURES IN POPULAR CATHOLICISM

The use of miniatures as a medium of communication with the supernatural in Mexico after the Spanish conquest parallels in many ways their use before the conquest. Prior to the eleventh century, Spanish Catholics revered saints' relics (i.e., bones) as opposed to images, but after the eleventh century, images were introduced (Christian 1981:21). The

Orthodox Christian tradition of representing saints holding miniature churches or cities in their hands, because they either built the cities or defended them, is a thousand years old (personal communication, Fr. Charles Brown, 1997; Fr. Robert Williams, 1998). Although Erasmian influence and reforms in the late sixteenth century led the official Catholic Church in Spain to disapprove of idolatry (Christian 1981:162), popular religion continued to emphasize the immanent location of sacredness in tangible representations of Christ, the Virgin Mary, and the saints. Sixteenth-century missionaries conveyed this loyalty to icons to their Indian converts in the Spanish colonies, who were themselves already iconophiles or "lovers of images" (Turner and Turner 1982).

The Catholic ex-voto or *milagro* is an important manifestation of miniature artistry. Votive art is dedicated to a deity "in payment of a benefit received," according to María del Carmen Medina San Román (1997:107). She concludes that votive art is as old as humankind (Medina San Román 1997:107). In Spain, votive art in the form of small, stylized bone or bronze female figurines dates back to a Celtic habitation in the third or fourth century B.C. Zoomorphic offerings were also found, including "more than two hundred naturalistic representations of horses"—early analogues to Mexico's familiar milagros (Medina San Román 1977:107). Medina San Román points out the important link between ex-votos and pilgrimage; ex-votos are therefore likely to be small and portable (though Marion Oettinger discusses large votive art, some of which is "rented" at pilgrimage shrines in Brazil; Oettinger 1992:38–41).

The tradition of milagros may be more widespread and popular in Mexico than elsewhere in Latin America (Egan 1991:31). Martha Egan (1991:7) finds that while Native American and African-American cultures also influenced the practice of pledging milagros, it most directly stems from Iberian Catholicism. Believers dedicate small metal charms representing a part of the body, an animal, etc., to a saint as a symbol of gratitude for divine intercession in a crisis.

Religious jewelry is another form of Catholic miniaturia. Egan (1993) documents the exquisite craftsmanship of reliquaries, or religious lockets, which proliferated in Mexico in the seventeenth through nineteenth centuries. They encased sculptural reliefs and paintings of holy figures enshrined behind a pane of transparent mica.

The cult of saints has promoted the use of tiny things in Mexico. A dollhouse-sized figure of the lay Franciscan San Pascual Bailón, patron saint of cooks, is displayed in a small glass case on the wall of the kitchen of the restored Santa Monica convent in Puebla (cf. Giffords 1991:118; illustrated in Moedano 1988:119). The saint stands in his own miniature kitchen amid a ménage of cooking utensils that goes far beyond the requirements of hagiography.

The popular phrase *quedarse para vestir santos* (to be left to dress up saints), expressing the lot of an unmarried woman, suggests that lacking real babies, claustral spinsters must settle for playing with religious statuettes. A statue of the "Niño Doctor," a guise of the Christ Child believed to have healing power, originally harbored by a sect of nuns and now revered in a church in Tepeaca, Puebla, sits like a baby doll in his niche. His scaled-down doctor's bag and white uniform embroidered with a hospital emblem conflate the sacred with the cute.

Nineteenth-century Catholic nuns wrote miniature books in the convents in their spare time (Charpenel 1970:3). "The little nuns of the city of Puebla, who for so long created so many admirable miniatures, have stopped making them" (Charpenel 1970:10). The witty Scottish observer Fanny Calderón de la Barca (1940:507), who lived in Mexico in the mid-nineteenth century, wrote on the odd miniaturist tendencies of nuns in Valladolid (now Michoacán): "The nuns, it is said, are or were in the habit of harnessing [fleas] to little carriages, and of showing them off by other ingenious devices."

NANOTECHNOLOGY

Miniaturization in the twentieth and twenty-first centuries responds to the pressures of modernity. Baudrillard ([1968]1996) sees the development of ever more compact gadgetry as expressing a dual movement between capitalist society's tendency to expand at the same time as products are miniaturized. As the world population grows, there is less space per individual, leading to the frenetic invention of products to expand the extension of the brain (Baudrillard [1968]1996:51) while keeping them sized for the body. The cellular phone, Game Boy, Palm Pilot, and Walkman are mediated worlds available for personal consumption like before them, the miniature book (Stewart 1993). And for the denizens of cramped urban spaces, dollhouses satisfy the ersatz dream of a spacious bourgeois Victorian existence. The American-style dollhouse is of limited importance in Mexico but remains a strong motive for American visitors to Mexico to seek out miniatures.

VIRTUES IMPUTED TO THE MINIATURE

In a study of New Mexican wood carvings, Briggs (1980:147) writes that "The appeal of the carvings to outsiders derives partially from the images' perceived encapsulation of the characteristics of the carvers and their society." If miniatures are the epitome of handcrafts (Glassie 1993:826; Stewart 1993:68), the patience, skill, ingenuity, and playfulness attributed to Mexican artisans in general are magnified in miniature crafts.

Patience

The patience that Mexican Indian artisans exhibit in their frequently tedious and delicate work is a well-worn truism, apparent in such statements as "The Mexican artist is a miniaturist par excellence; patient and clever, he forgets about time" ("Arte Popular" 1954, cited in Charpenel 1970:5). Or, as Alexander von Humboldt wrote in 1809: "The Indians have a tireless patience for little knick-nacks worked in wood, bone, and wax" (Esparza Liberal 1994:76).

Skill

The skill evidenced by the manufacture of pre-Hispanic miniatures persuaded writers in the 1920s through 1940s that manual virtuosity had somehow been transmitted to the hands of modern Mexican Indian craftspeople (López Domínguez 1983:13). The cliché of the Indian artisan's "capacity for minute detail" (Castro Leal 1940:16) pervaded nationalist rhetoric about the miniature. For instance, Dr. Atl ([1922]1980:39) unscientifically attributes the Mexican Indians' "prodigious manual ability" to "a specific characteristic of the Indian race." The glorification of Indian artisans, essentialized in their "skilled hands," made its way into official policy, as a 1958 speech by future president Adolfo López Mateos shows (Huitrón 1962, cited in Novelo 1996:193): "The Mexican is endowed with ingenuity and skill that allow him to make any object beautiful. This innate capacity should be transformed into an economic force." Praise for the skilled hands of Mexican workers, especially women, continues as a stereotype in discourse about *maquiladoras,* the assembly plants in Mexico on the U.S. border (De Ann Pendry, personal communication, 1998).

Ingenuity

Ingenuity and its related qualities of cleverness, invention, and resource-fulness, expressed as the Mexican artisan's "ability to make so much with so little" (Barbash 1993:37) is a third characteristic commonly attributed to miniaturists. "The inventiveness and perseverance of the Mexicans in creating these miniatures is inexhaustible," writes Dörner (1962:53; see also Atl [1922]1980:40; Castro Leal 1940:16, López Domínguez 1983:15; Poyo 1939:5). Foreigners traveling in Mexico often notice this ingenuity born of scarcity, a "recycle, re-use" mentality in a land where waste is a sin. We Americans implicitly posit Mexican resource-fulness in counterpoint to our own wastefulness (Kassovic 1996).

It is easy to see the recourse to small scale as an economizing response to scarcity and rationing. As an announcer quipped at a concert in Mexico City, when the band revealed small fiddles and harps from the Huasteca Potosina, "*¡Es la carestía, mano!*" (That's austerity, brother!), referring to Mexico's economic environment. Indeed, Mexico's current economic crisis and unemployment, which have waxed even more critical since the 1990s, may be fostering the traditional microscopic crafts of poverty. Similarly, Bellasi (1985:233) attributes Switzerland's "great watchmaking tradition and micromechanics in general" to a "total absence of raw materials."

However, the theory that scarcity encourages miniaturization does not always hold up. A shortage of plant material due to overharvesting or burning sometimes causes crafts to get *bigger*. The Seri of Sonora have responded to a dwindling supply of dead ironwood by carving larger figures, which they consider a more efficient use of the remaining wood (Ryerson 1976:133). And the destruction of the *copalillo* tree in the villages around Arrazola, Oaxaca, has caused wood for carvings to be trucked in but has not led to reduced size; instead, carvings are larger than they were in the past (Barbash 1993:37–38). Miniaturization, in turn, often occurs in conditions of superabundance and wealth.

Playfulness

With their fanciful, frivolous, and impractical connotations and child-size dimensions, miniatures convey joy to the eye of the beholder, as photographer Edward Weston (1973) noted in his daybook in 1925 while working in Mexico City: "On the trastero I have placed my new juguetes—toys, a crimson spotted dog, a leopard, a couple of viejitos, and pigs with bursting bellies. I never tire of the juguetes, they are invariably spontaneous and genuine, done without striving, fancied in fun." These characteristics seem to reflect back on their makers, who are thereby endowed with a reputation for innocent naiveté. René d'Harnoncourt (1928:110) conjures up a composite of the Mexican toy maker in his classic sketch of "Pancho el Juguetero":

> *Pancho is the only artist I know of who literally lives up to the famous maxim, "Art for Arts sake." He has the good fortune to supply a public that does not concern itself as to the utility of his products nor as to whether they are in fashion, the worst handicap to the phantasy of an artist. His customers are the Indians, who never outgrow their desire for something to play with. It may be graceful, funny or grotesque, but as long as it stimulates the imagination, it fulfills the only purpose of a perfect toy.*
>
> *Sometimes Pancho tries to work with a purpose in view aside from that of the pure pleasure of creating; but neither his clients nor he himself take his efforts toward efficiency seriously. He makes fancy savings banks, but they are often too small to hold even a centavito and the slit in the larger ones is almost always too narrow to pass a coin. His water pitchers do not pour, and their miniature size shows clearly that he did not intend them for use. Thus Pancho is the most independent artist in the world. As no one expects him to limit his phantasy by considerations of utility and the material quality of his creations, he is absolutely free to fashion a quaint world after his own will and fancy.*

The portrayal of the typical toy maker as having great freedom of expression and enjoyment of his or her craft is appealing but hardly the norm. Renato Rosaldo warns, in his foreword to García Canclini (1995: xiv), "To imagine that the artist produces without regard for the market is as foolish as to suppose that the market fails to take the nature of artistic product into account."

A PASSION FOR SMALL SCALE

Middle-class Mexicans collect miniatures to such a degree that it has been termed "a national pastime" (Pettit and Pettit 1978). Toy collecting probably gained legitimacy among adults when artists and intellectuals began to collect them in the 1920s; as noted above, Edward Weston was attracted to the cheap handmade toys he saw on his outings to the "*puestos*" and purchased as many as he could to photograph in his studio. In their simplicity and humor he found "an inexhaustible source of pleasure" (Weston 1973:157). As Novelo (1993:46) perceptively points out, collecting crafts in Mexico has nationalist overtones. Frida Kahlo's doll and miniature collections, carefully preserved in her blue house in Coyoacán, continue to set an example of taste fifty years after her death. The parents of the burgeoning new generations of alienated modern Mexican children growing up under NAFTA, lacking the social consciousness of the generation of 1968, see nostalgic Mexican handmade toys as an antidote to cultural memory loss.

Mexico is not unique in its use of scale models in public display nor in the quantities of small-scale objects available for sale. But Mexico is unusual in the attention paid to the miniature by writers attempting to capture the spirit of "Mexicanness." Miniatures encode qualities seen as quintessentially Mexican. The legendary virtues of the Mexican artisan, considered to be inherited from pre-Hispanic ancestors, are crystallized in the miniature object. These virtues include patience, manual skill, ingenuity, and playfulness. That miniature making requires superb dexterity, concentration, and patience—beyond the extent justified by any monetary reward—is a commonplace in discourse about Mexican popular art. Ingenuity, resourcefulness, the ability to do much with little: these are stereotypical Mexican attributes with which we are all familiar. And there is admiration, yet paternalism, in the assessment that miniaturists are the most lighthearted of artists because the things they make are for the pleasure of children. The happy-go-lucky spirit of play and fantasy ascribed to miniatures has resulted in the projection of a childlike naiveté on makers and consumers of miniatures alike.

The impact of Roman Catholicism on the Mexican miniature is often underplayed in favor of pre-Hispanic origins but deserves greater recognition. It is clear that a range of meanings, from ritual to playful, can be imputed to the custom of dressing saints and votive practices. Metaphorically speaking, both religious and secular uses of the miniature attempt to control lived experience through the manipulation of reproductions.

All of these meanings and stereotypes coalesce in the miniature. Therefore miniatures have proliferated in Mexico partly because they are considered—by writers, curators, store owners, tourists, collectors, and parents—as compact symbols of Mexicanness. Ever since intellectuals steered good taste away from the France-enamored upper class with whom it had resided since the Porfiriato, crafts have stood for what is authentic and worthwhile in Mexican culture.

Miniatures, which exaggerate the characteristics of crafts in general (Stewart 1993), are seen as particularly appropriate markers of qualities of Mexican artisan-campesino-Indians. For consumers, the "Lilliputization of Mexico" offers a safe retreat from the ugly and uncontrollable advance of Mexico into modernity and postmodernity (García Canclini 1995).

CHAPTER 1

Chigmecatitlán from a Distance

From a distance, Santa María Chigmecatitlán, Puebla, is a speck of a church tower and a tiny puff of smoke across the profound gorge of the Atoyac River. The river's millennial flow has exposed geological strata in the cliff face, diagonally traversed by threads of human footpaths zigzagging up from the riverbed to the town high on a plateau. The symbolic landmark of the Mixteca-Puebla region is the snowcapped Pico de Orizaba, which rises Fuji-esque as seen from the main highway between the city of Puebla and Chigmecatitlán. Two more volcanoes, Popocatépetl and Iztaccíhuatl, are visible from the precipice at the edge of town, where blue wooden crosses mark the paths that ascend from the river. Beyond the volcanoes lies Mexico City.

Chigmecatitlán is the northern outpost of the culture area of Mexico known as the Mixteca, focused on western Oaxaca but overlapping into the adjacent states of Puebla and Guerrero. In southern Puebla, the Mixtecs share territory with historically Náhuatl, Popoloca, and mestizo communities (Ravicz and Romney 1969). Mixtec-speaking Chigmecatitlán borders with Náhuatl-speaking Huatlatlauca just across the river gorge to the north and Mixtec-speaking Santa Catarina Tlaltempan less than four kilometers to the south. Chigmecatitlán's relative detachment from the Mixtec core fosters a sense of insularity in the woven palm art for which it is known.

THE PAST

The recorded history of Chigmecatitlán is sketchy and almost silent about the origin of palm weaving. Local foundation narratives recount that the town was founded in the seventeenth century by a group of Mixtec discontents who migrated north from San Pedro y San Pablo Tequixtepec in the district of Huajuapan de León, Oaxaca.[1] These local

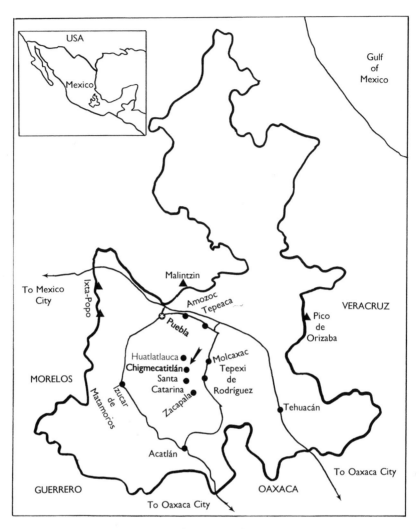

MAP 1 State of Puebla.

histories maintain that the founders split off from Tequixtepec around 1646, carrying a canvas of the Immaculate Conception of Mary on a thirty-year trek in search of a territory where they could live autonomously, finally founding Chigmecatitlán. The site of the future town was signaled to the founders by the omen of a dog among the reeds and secured from the landowner via the intervention of a young girl named María. The current townspeople venerate a dark colonial painting of the Virgin under a sacred mesquite tree every year on December 8, her saint's day.

Documents in Mexico's national archives, however, attest to the town's prior existence in the sixteenth century. Archaeological remains also prove pre-Hispanic occupation, if not long-term settlement. These artifacts may be related to an earlier, non-Mixtec people. Ruined floors near the river below Chigmecatitlán's Barrio San Antonio are ringed by scattered pottery shards, flakes, and occasional blades of translucent green obsidian. The riverbanks have been disturbed by erosion, but the stones are still in place. Townspeople used to go down to the ruined foundations by the river to search for gold, despite the belief that finding gold brings bad luck. Now almost nobody is interested. Pre-Hispanic pieces that have been found here have been mistreated, broken, or discarded. It is rumored that in the mid-1980s human skulls, a large decorated vessel, and a large piece of obsidian from an earlier habitation were unearthed on the plateau by people digging the foundation for a brick wall. The skulls that turned up were duly reburied in the municipal cemetery until the municipal president put a stop to the excavating—what is the point of digging up more and more skulls?

Popular lore glosses the Náhuatl name Chigmecatitlán as 'Dog Among the Reeds,' a derivation town officials have adopted.[2] The Aztecs imposed Náhuatl names on many of the towns under their control before the Spanish conquest in 1521. Linguist Nicholas Hopkins (personal communication, 1994) translates Chigmecatitlán as *chiqui* 'basket' + *mecatl* 'twisted' + *tlán* 'place of', i.e., 'Place Where Baskets Are Twisted.' This derivation fits Chigmecatitlán's fame as a center of basket weaving, but ultimately the name and origin of the town are still open to interpretation.

NATURAL SETTING

The Mixteca-Puebla region was once an inland sea and is now a prime cretaceous fossil-hunting area laced with underground rivers (Kathryn Josserand, personal communication, 1994). The resulting limestone soil leaves car wheels covered with a talc that clings like cement when wet. The area presents an aspect of arid steppe with desert vegetation including columnar cacti, small white mammillarias, yuccas, tillandsias, terrestrial bromeliads (*Hechtia*), rosette agaves (*Agave verschaffeltii*), "*mala mujer*" (*Cnidoscolus*), and white morning-glory trees (*Ipomoea cuernavacana* "*cazahuate*").

At the edges of town, low stone walls divide plowed, rocky cornfields shaded by an occasional craggy mesquite ("*tnundía*"). Blue morn-

FIGURE 1.1 Local fan palm, *Brahea dulcis* (H.B.K.) Mart., is rarely used for weaving.

ing-glories trail over the walls adjacent to the Marian parish church. Cultivated plants in the churchyard and town square include palm and rubber trees, Italian cypress, jacaranda, and plumeria. Low fan palms scattered among the ravines at first glance appear to provide the material for the crafts for which Chigmecatitlán is renowned, but the artisans prefer dried palm brought from out of state, formerly by mule train or burro, now by truck.

A few giant fig trees (*Ficus cotinifolia* H.B.K.) and the smaller *Ficus petiolaris* H.B.K. ("*higuera*" or "*tescalama*") grow out of a cliffside spring at a lower altitude where the namesake dog among the reeds is said to have caught the founders' attention. In the Atoyac river bed 250 meters below the town, bald cypress trees ("*tnuyuku*"), significant in the preconquest Mixtec codices, thrive as does a vine known as *pankululu* with a seedpod whose fuzz, it is said, can blind a person.[3]

The town, located on the Santa Catarina mesa at 1,500 feet above sea level, has a semi-arid climate. Wind and dust prevail for half the year, December through May. In this dry season, occasional wind storms that can last twenty-four hours whistle eerily through the asbestos-sheet roofs of the houses. The locals comment, "Hay norte en Veracruz" (There's a norther in Veracruz). Some people allege that dust devils (*tkiachi*) can lift a person or a house; when they see one approaching, they throw holy water at it to make it subside. The faithful carry bottles of water to church to be blessed by the priest on the first day of each month, storing it on their home altars to ward off evil.

The wind is thought to make scorpions emerge from their hiding places in the rocks. One of the first words I learned in Mixtec was *tsiduma* (*tsi*, affix for 'animal' + *duma* 'tail'). If people kill a scorpion, they burn it to keep from attracting more. Other wildlife, such as the lizard, snake, turtle, dove, mouse, and rabbit (*ch'ko'o*, *ko*, *tsio shtkuí*, *kulutsi*, *tsní*, and *tsidoo*) also appear in the repertoire of miniature palm crafts. As for domestic livestock, the 1990 town census counted just thirteen cows, ten pigs, and twenty-one goats. Dogs run loose, scavenging for food and water in addition to their diet of tortillas and an occasional bone.

Summer is the rainy season, when palm is pliable and doesn't need dampening. The town receives an average annual rainfall of 700 mm or 28 inches (Ochoa 1993:30). The roads become rivulets and the stones in the roads seem to come alive as frogs and toads rebound from the drought.

AGRICULTURE

Chigmecatitlán, like most Mixtec communities, practices fragile subsistence agriculture supplemented by emigrant activities and palm weav-

FIGURE 1.2 Palm scorpions on small mats, Huatlatlauca, Puebla. Photograph by Hortensia Rosquillas, 1998.

ing (Ravicz and Romney 1969:372). Cultivable land amounts to only 8 percent of the town (Ochoa 1993:42) and is held not as *ejido,* or communal, land but as private property.

Farmers cultivate with digging sticks, oxen and plows, or tractors, depending on their wealth. They plow their fields in May, plant corn from June 15 to July 15 (immediately after the June 13 fiesta of San Antonio) to coincide with the start of the rainy season, and harvest one exiguous crop per year from November to February. Crops are *de temporal,* that is, they rely on rainfall, not irrigation, although down in the wetlands bordering the Atoyac River a few farmers grow semitropical crops such as avocadoes and papayas. The large seed corn is especially adapted to the dry climate. The cornstalks are intercropped with bean plants whose tendrils twine around them, as well as squash and chiles. Once harvested and dried, the corn is soaked overnight, and in the brilliant mornings women and girls take the corn to be ground at a mill, dangling plastic buckets from their arms, later patting out oversized golden, oblong tortillas.

COMMUNICATIONS

When archaeologist Carmen Cook de Leonard (1953:423) visited southern Puebla in 1951, Chigmecatitlán lay between two parallel north-south roads: the Pan American Highway from Tepeaca through Tecamachalco to Tehuacán, and another highway from Izúcar de Matamoros through Acatlán to Petlalcingo. In the 1940s a man named Belisario Carmona from the city of Puebla, a *compadre* of the local priest Esteban Jiménez Palacios, first opened up the dirt road to the Puebla highway. The Carretera Intermixteca, Puebla 455, linking nearby Tepexi de Rodríguez with Tepeaca and San Juan Izcaquixtla, was built in 1992. From Chigmecatitlán it takes one hour by bus to reach the paved highway, another two hours to the city of Puebla (*Tensio'*), and two more hours to Mexico City (*Ñu Koyo*). Tepexi de Rodríguez (*Ñu Kavá*), the nearest large town and district political headquarters, is an hour and a half away.

The town has only one telephone, with irregular hours and service. For a fee, the telephone lady sends a child on a bicycle to summon the call recipient, who lingers at the phone office for the caller to dial again in fifteen minutes.

Several families own television sets; soap operas (such as *Esmeralda* in 1996) are popular. Returning emigrants bring in boom boxes for parties and video recorders to film large public spectacles like the communal theater of the Pastorela on December 28 or the processions of Holy Week and Corpus Christi in the spring and of the Assumption of the Virgin on August 15.

Public announcements are broadcast in Spanish and Mixtec over two loudspeakers: one in the town hall and a private one owned by palm artisans Patricia Flores and León Pérez (these are pseudonyms, as are most names used in this book). Announcements cost five pesos and include notices of electric bills to be paid in the town hall, school registration, vaccinations, church processions, fresh shrimp for sale in the market, and lost and stolen items. Some messages pertain to palm weavers: "Pick up artisan ID cards"; "Artisans' group meeting at 6:00 p.m."; "The dye salesman is here."

The loudspeaker broadcasts are heralded by recorded theme songs: "*Que le maten el pollo*" (Kill the chicken) when chicken is available; a children's song for kindergarten affairs. Health campaign announcements, political slogans, and religious propaganda are also posted or painted on the walls of buildings. Trucks occasionally make the rounds of the town, bringing in construction sand, propane gas, metal bedsteads, water barrels, or oranges, which the driver hawks from a loudspeaker attached to the truck.

LANGUAGE AND ETHNICITY

Most Chigmecatitlán residents speak Mixtec as a first language and Spanish as a second language. Mixtec, in the Oto-Manguean family, accounts for 7 percent of the Indian language speakers in Mexico after Náhuatl, Maya, and Zapotec (INEGI 1993:13). The earliest baptismal and marriage records, kept continuously in the parish church since 1766, record the ethnicity of the townspeople as "Yndio" and "Yndia" only, in contrast with more diverse towns nearby that occasionally include "Mulato," "Mestizo," and "Español" as ethnic categories. The town has been nearly uniformly Mixtec at least since early colonial times, as evidenced by a record of "Santa María Mixtecos" along with its neighbor "Santa Catalina Mixtecos" in 1743.[4]

Chigmecatitlán still identifies strongly with Mixtec in comparison with other communities in the region that are close to abandoning their native language altogether. *"Aquí no les da pena hablar mixteco"* (Here

TABLE 1.1 Rate of Monolingual Speakers in Chigmecatitlán
(of 1,015 people five years and older)

Mixtec
20%

Spanish
12%

Unspecified
0%

Mixtec and Spanish
68%

Source: INEGI 1996.

they are not ashamed of speaking Mixtec), said one man, contrasting Chigmecatitlán with its "sister" towns of Santo Domingo Tonahuixtla, Puebla; and San Pedro y San Pablo Tequixtepec, Oaxaca, where Spanish has overtaken Mixtec as the local language. In Chigmecatitlán the cordial greeting "*kuani?*" and response "*da kuan,*" equivalent to Spanish "*adiós,*" are exchanged when passing on the street. Address is formal; all adults are designated with the respectful titles "Don" or "Doña," and the "*usted*" rather than the "*tú*" form is used with all but the closest friends.

The ability to speak the local version of Mixtec is the marker that separates townspeople from outsiders. One researcher has described the local speaking style as emotionally reserved and "low key (almost silent)" (Ochoa 1993:48; cf. Ravicz and Romney 1969:396). When I discussed this with some of my informants, they said the researcher's presence affected the impression he received. People are loquacious and can talk for hours, but there is not much to say when outsiders are around. Mixtec is often couched as a secret code of underdogs. At least three times I heard people, including the municipal president, say that Mixtec is useful for communicating clandestinely. The stories they adduced featured countrymen outwitting powerful, Spanish-speaking outsiders. In one story, two vendors selling crafts in a Mexico City store negotiate the price between themselves in Mixtec in front of the shopkeeper. In another, two men in jail conspire on their testimony in Mixtec. In the third, a husband warns his wife in Mixtec to be careful because they are about to be robbed.

Results of the 1995 nationwide population count (INEGI 1996) showed that the younger a child is, the less likely he or she is to speak an Indian language. Likewise, the local language situation in Chigmecatitlán is changing as more children grow up outside the town. One artisan expressed his anxiety about his fellow townspeople's lack of interest in Mixtec culture: "There needs to be an indigenous consciousness. People should be organized and not lose traditions from here: our language, our crafts. But people leave for the city for a year or two years—their children are born outside and they no longer speak Mixtec."

Chigmecatitlán has three schools: Jardín de Niños (kindergarten) Dr. Atl, Escuela Primaria (Primary School) José María Morelos y Pavón, and Telesecundaria (Tele-Secondary) 352 Héroes del 5 de Mayo, where lessons are broadcast by satellite from Mexico City. The primary school principal banned the speaking of Mixtec at school. Only a handful of the primary and secondary school teachers are native to the town; most teachers are rotated in from outside and are not Mixtec.

According to Stephen Marlett of the Summer Institute of Linguistics (personal communication, 1996), in the Mixteca "all is separation." He believes that for historical reasons each town has maintained its dialect distinct from that of its neighbors. Chigmecatitlán and its own neighbor Santa Catarina speak different versions of Mixtec. This diversity has led to the current discussion in Mexico over whether ethnicity should be considered at the town level (Gabriel Moedano, personal communication, 1996). The fragmentation of Mixtec causes problems for programs intended to preserve Indian languages, such as sending teachers who speak Mixtec or preparing textbooks in Mixtec—they would have to be specific to that town's particular dialect.

Most official discourse is in Spanish. Josserand (1983:467) writes, "Throughout most of the Mixteca, dialects are different enough to hamper communication, and all official communication has been obligatory in Spanish for hundreds of years." The municipal government's yearly report is given in Spanish, for example. However, after workers from the Summer Institute of Linguistics held a workshop on reading and writing Mixtec, the sixth-grade graduation speech in 1997 was read in Spanish and Mixtec, which elicited surprise.

The townspeople's clothing style distinguishes them subtly from other communities. Most women middle-aged or older dress conservatively with their trademark dark *rebozos* (or shawls) draped over their heads and hanging loose on either side to protect them from the sun. Unlike their Nahua neighbors, women do not wear hats. A second rebozo is used to carry a baby on the back. Older women usually wear a gathered skirt, flowered or solid, below the knee, with an unmatched blouse worn untucked over it, and sometimes an apron. Younger women wear shorter, tighter-fitting skirts or dresses above the knee. Little girls usually wear dresses or school uniforms. Among the keys, scapulars, and medallions that women wear strung on yarn around their necks are small folding scissors for trimming palm.

Men middle-aged and older dress in trousers and a plain, woven shirt, often long-sleeved and white. They frequently wear white hats woven out of artificial palm. Younger men wear T-shirts, baseball caps, and sometimes other U.S.-influenced styles such as long hair in a ponytail or an earring in one ear.

ARCHITECTURE

The town exhibits a compact settlement pattern distributed in five sections or wards. The Fifth Ward, also known as the Barrio San Antonio, differs slightly in character from the rest of town: it has its own church, more emigrant residents, and a tougher atmosphere. Ochoa (1993:195) considers the Barrio San Antonio to be where the wealthiest live, based on their brick and cement-block houses. Traditionally *los del Barrio* have been considered a separate group. It used to be that people from the central part of town did not go back and forth between the center of town and the Barrio San Antonio at night.

The dominant structure in town, with its dual domes and two unmatched bell towers, is the Catholic church of the Immaculate Conception of Mary. It is feminine in feeling, painted in soft pastels, with stucco curlicues molded around its triple-arched portal. The architectural dominance of the church marks the centrality of Catholic religiosity to the cultural life of the town. In addition to the parish church and the barrio church of San Antonio, there is a hilltop chapel to Our Lady of Guadalupe; a modernist wayside shrine, also to Guadalupe, on the road out of town; smaller oratories such as one to the Holy Cross; and dozens of blue crosses marking spiritually significant parts of town. Cement bleachers constructed in 1995 abutting the back of the parish church seat an audience for the Pastorela on December 28, a dramatic spectacle that culminates in the lowering of a three-year-old child, acting the role of an angel, between two planks on ropes from the roof of the church. A cement shelter known as "Herod's Palace" is a permanent fixture in the proscenium, also used in this annual public drama.[5]

Diagonally across the plaza from the parish church lies the high-ceilinged, cavernous town hall, with "Palacio Municipal de Chigmecatitlán" painted in colonial-style letters across the upper facade. In addition to the office of the municipal president, it houses a library and a jail cell. The jail is rarely occupied but was used in 1990 to hold men accused of drinking past curfew. In the center of the plaza between the church and the town hall are a two-story bandstand and creaky swing set. The lower floor of the bandstand was converted in 1996 into a small museum to display Chigmecatitlán crafts. Facing the church is the municipal basketball court, which doubles as an outdoor dance floor.

Mixtec house compounds consist of two or three separate one-room

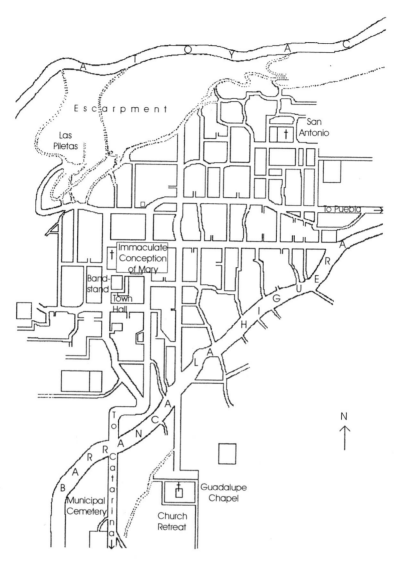

MAP 2 Santa María Chigmecatitlán, after a map by Pedro Mendoza Zaragoza, municipal president's office, 1994.

buildings surrounded by a limestone corral. Houses demonstrate a historical progression from reed to stone to cement block, all three styles still in use. In the past, most houses were constructed either of reed, known as *carrizo* (*Arundo donax* L.; Foster 1967) or brush, known as *basura* or *mi'i*, cemented with *tierra blanca*, or white earth. Cook de

Leonard (1953:434) considers this cement to be one of the most important features of southern Puebla. The traditional reed house, whose pitched roof and crevices allow smoke to escape and keep the air cool, may serve for cooking and sleeping. The pitched roofs are thatched with palm that must be purchased; it does not grow locally. People whitewash their homes with inexpensive local lime. An outdoor cooking shelter with reed walls may be used to dye palm.

A newer, flat-roofed, stone or concrete-block house may be used for receiving guests, as an altar room, and for storage, but it can be stifling in the soporific May afternoons. The late husband of one of the most respected artisans, Vicenta Chávez, is credited with teaching townspeople to build stone houses. She recalled that as they were building, the men would recite an Angelus or the Lord's Prayer at noon, three o'clock, and seven o'clock in the evening.

However, some of the stone houses appear to be older. An evangelist doctor, who had come from Puebla to practice medicine here, said his rented stone house was 120 years old. It was rumored to contain frightening sounds and voices, and at first people would ask if he heard anything. During the Mexican Revolution it was presumably common to hide gold under the floor for safekeeping. Before the doctor's arrival, people would briefly rent the house under the pretext of opening a store and dig in search of gold. When the doctor moved in, he found telltale holes in the floor.

People sleep on palm mats or on metal bedsteads with designs painted on the headboards, bought from an itinerant furniture truck. Some use indoor hammocks slung on the house beams, possibly an influence from the Gulf Coast, where many residents have migrated. Many objects, even children's plastic baby dolls, are nailed to the walls for storage. A few families own *cuezcomates*—palm-thatched corn cribs—in disrepair in their yards. There are no sweat baths (*temascal*), common to much of the rest of the Mixteca.

UTILITIES

Few houses have indoor plumbing; some have privies sheltered by reed fences or concrete-block walls. Many people use the backyard or corral as a bathroom. The street corners of the main plaza are preemptively posted "*No hacer del baño*" (No urinating). Painted on one wall of the open-air market was a faded anti-cholera message: "Put diarrhea in its place," including a painting of a modern toilet.

The only significant source of water is a natural spring known as "*las piletas*" that seeps from the limestone aquifer halfway down the steep cliffs of the Atoyac River where the giant fig trees grow. In the past, men, women, and children carried water up on their backs at 3:00 a.m., before the sun was too hot, in three-handled clay jugs known as *llo* made in Huatlatlauca. Water was first pumped up to street-corner fountains in the 1940s. Nowadays most households have chlorinated water piped to their yards. Water pressure alternates between the center of town and the Barrio San Antonio, so homes have running water every other day for about three hours a day in the morning.

People customarily bathe at least once a week. Formerly, men and women washed in separate areas at the spring at 5:00 a.m.—when the water is said to come out warm—at a continuously trickling, aquifer-fed shower on the men's side and two tanks on the women's side, also used to water livestock. It is believed that if one takes a hot bath and goes out in the cold, one will catch a cold. It is also considered risky to bathe in hot water in warm weather. In the past, women would scrub laundry with tierra blanca or Octagon soap on Saturdays at the Atoyac River, where many still descend to wash sheets and blankets.

The majority of the houses now have electric power, which fluctuates during the day. The norm is one bare lightbulb and one electrical socket per room.

Garbage is burned, tossed into a vacant lot, or discarded in a ravine on the edge of town, where animals consume it. The municipal government appoints a council member in charge of sanitation who sends a truck to collect trash every few weeks and dump it outside of town. Yards are littered with layers of accumulated pot shards and rubber sandal soles, the detritus of years of dumping the trash out back.

FIESTAS

It has been estimated that there is almost one fiesta per week in Chigmecatitlán (García and Hernández 1986:16). During certain seasons (Holy Week, June, August, and December), the fiestas are celebrated with such density that they overlap. Each saint has a corresponding *mayordomo* and *mayordoma* as well as two *hermandades,* each *hermandad* with a *presidente* and *presidenta*. All four sponsors (mayordomo, mayordoma, presidente, and presidenta) hold fiestas in their houses for the saint of their devotion (cf. Ochoa 1993:200). "The position of mayordomo is covered by people who don't live in the community, and in most cases they are men of commerce," according to García and Hernández (1986:13). They add that most mayordomos are of higher economic status than the average member of the community (García and Hernández 1986:14). Fiestas are occasions for commensality; everyone is fed, and many bring containers to collect their "*itacate*" or take-home portion.

For emigrants, the fiestas appear to constitute Chigmecatitlán as a spiritual stronghold, a place from which to make commercial forays, a place to come home to. Although the returning emigrants tend to behave like tourists in their own town, playing loud music from their trucks, drinking heavily, and going on excursions to bathe at the old bridge on the Atoyac River, they are mainstays of the fiesta system. They are the prime sponsors of the expensive fiestas to patron saints. According to Padre Abraham Barragán (March 16, 1921–March 5, 1996), "when [emigrants] arrive in their hometown they are immediately integrated into the civil or religious association to which they belong" (Paisanos de Tequixtepec 1994:6).

Such festivals of reciprocity are economic leveling devices that keep any one person from becoming too rich (Wolf 1959:216–18). Ochoa (1993) suggests that mayordomos must work outside of town to afford the outlay for fiestas. In other words, fiestas are central to village life, and people must emigrate in order to sponsor them. Religious fiestas may also be a means of reinforcing cooperative social relations, as Ingham (1986:47) remarks. García and Hernández (1986:16) point out group identification as another consequence of the fiestas. They see the festival calendar as something that maintains Chigmecatitlán's identity in the face of the disruptive factors of high emigration and "civilizing" innovation (García and Hernández 1986:16; Ravicz and Romney 1969:373).

HEALTH

A state-funded medical clinic, founded by Servicios Coordinados de Salud circa 1989 through the efforts of local townspeople, is staffed by a yearly rotation of student clinicians from the University of Puebla performing their social service. However, the town is often without a doctor on weekends when the clinic resident leaves.

The main health complaints are diarrhea and acute respiratory ailments. Accidents and alcoholism are also frequent problems, as are chronic diseases such as high blood pressure and diabetes. The limbs of older women are often visibly curved from osteoporosis, which affects their hip joints.

Alcoholism is a significant public health problem, especially for men. A cantina, which women are not supposed to enter or even look into, stands in the plaza. Men tend to drink heavily for short periods such as at year's end. They customarily drink *aguardiente,* or distilled cane spirits, known as *ndudi* in Mixtec, to fortify themselves and gain courage. For example, the electrician drank before climbing up on the church belfry to hang Christmas lights. Construction workers drink beer after plastering to counteract the effect on the lungs of breathing thinner and plaster.

In 1995 several people contracted mosquito-borne dengue fever. An official from the health agency Salubridad visited each week, walking from Zacapala, on the main highway, through Santa Catarina to Chigmecatitlán to test the municipal water tanks for the eggs of the mosquito that transmits dengue and to spray the town.

Women who undergo labor at the clinic bring their families along. They give birth without anesthesia but usually have relatively rapid deliveries, according to the clinic resident, since they work so much and are in good shape. The afterbirth was traditionally buried in the yard. Patients frequently give the doctors gifts of palm crafts, which are displayed in the consulting office.

FOOD

An open-air market under a corrugated roof houses five or six stalls where people buy rations of eggs, tomatoes, tomatillos, green chiles, onions, and crackers. The market also shelters a small shrine to the Virgin of Guadalupe in a glass enclosure. A man from Veracruz sells shrimp cocktail weekly; his stall also functions as a bar, serving beer, toasted ham-and-cheese sandwiches, and peanuts he roasts himself. A weekly outdoor market or *tianguis* on the plaza on Sundays is attended by out-of-town vendors selling a slightly larger supply of goods, including more fruit, seed corn, plastic buckets, pottery, and utensils. Mom-and-pop stores with shelves stretching up to the ceiling dispense canned and packaged food. Bread rolls are available on Sundays from a basket in the town square, and churchgoers buy ices from a cart after Sunday mass. Fresh meat is also available from a butcher on Sundays, which, since most houses lack refrigeration, is hung from the rafters to cure. A government program supplies ultrapasteurized milk at a reduced price to parents of schoolchildren. There are, however, fifteen families in town whose children are considered malnourished; some people eat just one meal a day. The pressure of poverty encourages people to weave small baskets and other crafts to exchange for food.

POLITICAL LIFE

The town belongs to the Puebla State Regional District of Tepexi de Rodríguez and Federal Electoral District 5 of Acatlán de Osorio (García and Hernández 1986:10). Local political parties (PRI, PRD, PAN, and Frente Cardenista) are only loosely affiliated with their respective parties in Puebla and Mexico City. People tend to vote PRI "*por tradición y por acuerdo*" (by tradition and by accord), i.e., to avoid clashing with the governor or *diputado,* assuming they are members of the PRI. Recently the ascension of the PRD has caused internal political rifts and broken the PRI's monopoly (Ochoa 1993:49).

The municipal president is elected and appoints other council members, including those in charge of the CONASUPO (a government-subsidized food store), education, health, potable water, and sanitation. Voting in state and local elections held in November 1995 took place at a vacant house on the corner of the plaza. Neither the PRI nor the PRD candidate actually lived in Chigmecatitlán. Both candidates promised to pave the dirt road into town from the main highway.

One of the main tasks of the municipal president is to apply for and secure funding from state and national sources—often in the form of construction materials or loans. The president may be a liaison for artisans to receive government aid for crafts. In that regard, some of the townspeople concede, "we are better off than other indigenous people."

"Why?"

One reason: "*Es municipio único.*" Because Chigmecatitlán is the sole community in the municipality, it does not take time for money to be allocated to outlying towns.

By some reckoning, life in Chigmecatitlán is more comfortable than it was in the past. Government programs like Solidaridad, a project of exiled former president Carlos Salinas de Gortari, have provided attractive honeycomb pavers for the streets around the town center, bricks to build latrines, and electric street lights. Until the lights were installed a few years ago, a woman told me, there was a haunted vacant lot where the sound of babies crying was heard at night (cf. Ingham 1986:192). As one resident told me, the standard of living is rising in Chigmecatitlán: "Even though the quality of life in Mexico City has gotten worse in the past fifteen years, in Chigmecatitlán life has gotten better. Now we have electricity, gas, and running water. My grandmother tells me when she was young, people had just one change of clothes. A man would bathe in the river while his wife washed his clothes, and he would put them right back on. Now people have two suits of clothes."

CHAPTER 2

Palm Weaving as a Microindustry

My first impression of Chigmecati-
tlán, when I got out of the car after a dusty, five-hour drive from Mexico
City with a friend, was of a ghost town at high noon. The blinding white
streets were desolate. The only sign of life was a group of bricklayers
remodeling the town hall who stood drinking beer in the shade of the
bandstand. I inquired for the municipal president, and a man in a white
cowboy hat detached himself from the group. In the coolness of the
town hall, he listened intently to my proposal to study miniature crafts
and agreed to help me find a house in which to live. "People don't rent
houses here," he cautioned.

"*I* wouldn't stay here," my Mexico City friend warned as we circled
around the barren town later. "You'll die of loneliness." But the solitude
of the place attracted me; there was a stark, ethereal beauty in the blank
whiteness of the tumbled-down stone walls and the view of the distant
Popocatépetl and Ixtaccíhuatl volcanoes from the bluff at the edge of
town. The quiet was a relief after the depressing string of towns on the
way, along a highway crowded with blaring diesel trucks and edged
with uprooted agaves and the corpses of mangy mutts. Chigmecatitlán
is not on the way to anywhere, except to Santa Catarina Tlaltempan, the
other Mixtec town with which it shares a plateau high above the Atoyac
River. On any given day, only about ten vehicles drive in.

Another anthropologist told me her city friends likened Chigmecatitlán to Comala, the surreal town of the dead in Juan Rulfo's 1955 novel
Pedro Páramo. "This is Comala! It's pure Rulfo," she said. "Someone appears out of nowhere and asks: 'Who are you?' It's a town of old people,
women, and children."

Over the months, it dawned on me that the town appeared deserted at noon because most people are sitting indoors weaving palm
at that hour. Families stay inside to avoid the midday sun that reflects

off the caliche roads, whitewashed houses, and limestone corrals, and clouds the opaque blue eyes of the oldest people. A frequent comment is *"quema mucho el sol"*—the sun is really burning. *"Hacer sombra"*—to put up a shade tarp—is the informal term for having friends over. Palm fronds must be woven indoors in the damp, away from the shriveling solar glare.

One might spend several days in Chigmecatitlán and not realize that this town is the source of a multitude of intricate woven palm figurines instantly recognizable to the outside world as Mexican popular art. It is an art reserved for external sales and largely hidden away. Except for telltale clues—raffia clippings trampled in the dirt, hanks of dyed palm slung on nails behind the market stalls, toy mules spilling out of a cardboard box in a dark corner of a house—there is scant evidence of craft production. No signs advertising *"artesanías,"* no wayside souvenir stands, no colorful displays expose the crafts to public view. A short-lived museum exhibiting local crafts under the bandstand was closed by the municipal president a month after it opened in 1996. "What do we need a museum for?" Chigmecatitlán is not a tourist town.

Nevertheless, local officials estimate that anywhere from 30 to 90 percent of the population of 1,104 weaves palm. Virtually everyone can at least fashion two strips of palm into a ball or *kitsindú*. Most people are part-time artisans who also farm or work as bricklayers. For some families, crafts are the sole source of income; for others, crafts supplement money their relatives earn working outside of town (García and Hernández 1986:8). Artisans sell their crafts to their relatives and neighbors, who resell them in the city.

A DAILY ROUTINE

Weaving takes place within domestic space. The practice of palm weaving seems to absorb all the available time for hand work. Carmen González, who weaves miniature purple mariachis, exemplifies the palm weaver's daily routine. Accompanied by her siblings at her home workshop, she showed me a small mayonnaise jar full of tiny mariachi torsos with one arm longer than the other, like those of fiddler crabs, meant to grasp a musical instrument.

Methodically, she begins weaving at 4:00 or 5:00 p.m. after finishing her homework from the *telesecundaria* and does not stop until 9:00 or 10:00 at night. Fluorescent light emanated vaguely from a tube on the ceiling, but she said she does not necessarily need to see her work. She often listens to the radio. Working assembly-line style, making a dozen of a single component, she turns out two dozen miniature mariachi musicians a week. The local evangelist doctor had recently commissioned 3,000 pieces at 3.5 pesos (about 46 cents) each, which she estimated would take a year and a half to complete.

Fishing for some kind of narrative that would "animate" (Stewart 1993) and give meaning to the miniature figurines, I asked, "What do you think about when you're weaving?"

Everyone laughed.

"The money." The money, she said, would be spent on ordinary living expenses.

Like Carmen González, most people weave out of economic necessity. Artisans speak about the crafts prosaically as "merchandise" devoid of the magic that consumers may see in them.

A SHRINKING TOWN

Chigmecatitlán's apparent desolation is partly the result of emigration. Based on parish records from 1770 to 1950, Manrique (1964) estimates that the population peaked around 1855 and has declined ever since. The exodus in the past few decades is unmistakable; Chigmecatitlán has lost 48 percent of its inhabitants since 1940 as villagers have dispersed to other parts of Mexico, especially to the southeastern states of Veracruz, Tabasco, Campeche, and Chiapas. In the 1940s, industrialization transformed the life of campesinos all over Mexico, and the countryside emptied as they converged on the cities in search of jobs (Turok 1988a:28). Some say people in Chigmecatitlán started leaving town to sell candy in the 1940s; others that they started leaving in the 1960s after several years of drought.

The abandoned houses of Chigmecatitlán are evidence of this displacement. Their bricked-up doorways and boarded-up windows present impassive faces to the street, with no cracks of light showing under the doors at night, except when their owners return in throngs to participate in the Catholic feast days of June, August, and December. The town holds a powerful spiritual sway over those who leave. Sky-blue or sea-green grillwork *protección* at the windows—the symbolic colors of the town patroness, the Immaculate Conception of Mary—guards the houses from theft during their owners' prolonged absences.

TABLE 2.1 Population of Santa María Chigmecatitlán

Year	Number of Inhabitants	Change	
		Absolute	Relative
1930	2,060		
1940	2,116	56	2%
1950	1,907	-209	-9.87%
1960	1,995	88	4.6%
1970	1,803	-192	-9.6%
1980	1,586	-217	-12%
1990	1,165	-421	-26.5%
1995	1,104	-61	-5%

Source: Censos Generales de Población y Vivienda, cited in Ochoa (1993:31); INEGI 1995.

My borrowed house, which was lent to me in exchange for renovating it, had been boarded up for twenty years after the family who owned it was killed on the highway. I heard repeatedly how the parents, two sons, and their dog died in a car accident on their way from Huatulco, Veracruz, to visit their daughter, who had lived in my house. "I buried three of them in the cemetery one day and the fourth the next day," the plumber digging my septic tank told me. I went to look for their graves

FIGURE 2.1 An unoccupied house of Chigmecatitlán.

in the sandy municipal cemetery on the road to Santa Catarina but did not find them.

When people emigrate, they rarely sell their houses or land, but hang onto them as economic, familial, and sentimental patrimony. They often invest in them, enlarging them and replacing their reed-wattle or limestone walls with cinder block. Rare is the house without piles of sand, bricks, gravel, and bags of cement waiting until enough money accumulates to resume building. Some relatively affluent community members who have made money selling "*fayuca*" (black market goods, often electronic equipment) are building two-story concrete-block houses to stay in when they return for the major religious festivals. One artisan told an anecdote that poked fun at these nouveau-riche homeowners:

> *The people in the fancy house on the road out of town live in Jalapa and sell fayuca. They held a fiesta at Christmas for the Niño Jesús and said everyone was invited, but they had carpeting, so all the guests had to take off their shoes. People went because they were curious to see the inside of the house, and took off their shoes, but when they were getting ready to leave no one could find their shoes.*

García and Hernández (1986:6) estimate that 45 percent of the population of Chigmecatitlán is "floating," or dwelling in town only part-time. People consider their relatives who live outside the town as bona fide members of the community and seem bothered that government censuses only count those actually present in town. The municipal president's office informed one reporter, for instance, that there were "five thousand inhabitants who reside there and five thousand outside" (Paisanos de Tequixtepec 1994:6).

Chigmecatitlán diverges starkly from the pattern in the rest of the Mixteca in that very few residents have headed north to the United States. Migration to northern Mexico and the United States has depleted entire communities throughout the Mixteca (Kearney 1996); one writer estimates the population of Mixtecs in Baja California alone at sixty thousand (Golden 1996). But unlike in other communities, few people from Chigmecatitlán have gone north. Villagers recalled at most ten inhabitants who had gone to the United States to work. One man disliked Texas because "you can be sued for beating a dog."

I asked artisan Jacinto Flores what accounted for the marked difference between Chigmecatitlán and other towns. "People are in business, they are traders," he explained. "They prefer a sure thing. Going to the

United States is not a sure thing. In contrast, in Zacapala half the town lives in the United States. They also go there from Catarina; it's easier because they're next to Zacapala [on the main highway]."

People leaving Chigmecatitlán historically tend to become *comerciantes* (traders, merchants, sellers). Visiting in 1957, Leonardo Manrique (1964:203) observed that "a large percentage of males regularly leave town to sell their merchandise in often far-flung places." Many leave to sell fayuca; others to sell candy, which they buy at La Merced market or Xochimilco in Mexico City and resell in various towns in the southeast (Ochoa 1993:45).

THE AGRICULTURAL CRISIS

An agricultural crisis that no longer permits subsistence on the land is the main cause of the diaspora from Chigmecatitlán. The Mixteca area of Puebla is one of the poorest agricultural areas in Mexico. It suffers from "a prolonged dry season of up to eight months, low-quality soil, insufficient technical assistance, deficient marketing, low crop yields, lack of agro-industry, all of which have fostered poverty, malnutrition, and social backwardness, only mitigated by the high level of migration" (Jiménez Merino 1995). The desert zone Chigmecatitlán occupies is characterized by "permanent drought and an agricultural infrastructure that is practically nonexistent" (García and Hernández 1986:4), referring to a lack of tractors, fertilizers, and irrigation. Only a couple of people own tractors; most families plow the small, hardscrabble plots adjacent to their houses with borrowed oxen or burros.

One dusty day in April, as I drove out of town, I noticed the solitary tree known as *tnuzina'an*,[1] bare as usual, beside a lean-to shrine out by the *jagüey* or pond (*ñu xavé*). Two weeks later, the tree had suddenly leafed out in perfect timing for the water petitioning ceremony on May 15, day of San Isidro Labrador. The longtime priest having recently died, a priest was brought from Tepeaca to lead the noon procession carrying the image of San Isidro, patron saint of campesinos. People attribute the start of the annual rainy season to this water petitioning ceremony. One resident narrated this tale about the jagüey:

> *An old man told me this. I don't remember his name. There used to be a lot of turkeys in the pond. Back then there was water. The town had riches. The people were either afraid or stupid. They wanted to chase the turkeys away. Those in back saw the turkeys splash the water with*

FIGURE 2.2 *Jagüey* or pond on the road out of town.

FIGURE 2.3 Two large peacocks (*pavos reales*) and flowers with a dove. INAH, Colecciones Mestizas, Puebla, Box 18. *Left,* No. 31734(63); *center,* No. 31759(63); *right,* No. 31735(63). Height of peacocks 3½ inches; height of flowers 5¾ inches.

their wings as they ran away. They scared the turkeys off and since then the town has been without water.

The story attempts to explain a riddle: why did the founders of Chigmecatitlán situate the town in such an inauspicious place, on an arid mesa without water? Local farmers fantasize about irrigation for their corn. They point to nearby El Rosario Xochiteopan, where the water table is only five meters below the surface and water can be drawn from wells. But according to Jiménez Merino (1995), the dams that would have to be built to bring irrigation to the Mixteca-Puebla region would not warrant the expense because of the thinness and poor quality of the soil.

Some people say the ground used to be more fertile when they were younger. Then there were cattle; now there are only goats. When Tirso Anzures was a boy in the 1960s, his father, a campesino, would get up every day at 4:30 a.m. Tirso would take him his breakfast of coffee and tortillas in the fields. Now they hardly bother with planting corn because it will be stunted from lack of water, and they sold his father's herd of goats. That's why so many people have left their land to go peddle fayuca in the southeast, in Veracruz, Tabasco, or Chiapas.

Land is frequently inherited by the youngest son, known as the *xocoyote* or *"Benjamín de la casa,"* a pattern typical of the Mixteca (Ravicz and Romney 1969:389). It is also common for land to be distributed among all the children, leading to smaller and smaller farm plots. Lack of farmland forces some of the population out.

Reverse emigration has also occurred. The acute financial crisis that has afflicted Mexico since December 1994 has driven some emigrants back to Chigmecatitlán, where they can live rent free. One young woman, for example, owned a small store in Coatzacoalcos, Veracruz, but when unemployed petroleum workers turned to commerce, they drove the existing storekeepers out of business. She asked a cousin to look after her shop while she and her ailing mother came back to stay with relatives in Chigmecatitlán. Their only income is what her mother makes weaving palm flowers.

WEAVE OR LEAVE

In the context of emigration due to the decline of agriculture, those who remain in town have few sources of cash other than weaving palm (cf. Espejel 1978:11; Zaldívar Guerra 1975:16). Government programs like Solidaridad provide infrastructure but no jobs. A candy factory in Chigmecatitlán's Barrio San Antonio employs about twenty men and women making *alegrías* (amaranth cakes) and *palanquetas* (nut brittle) to sell in Campeche and Tabasco. The only other paid occupations are municipal president, secretary, treasurer, secretary of the DIF, librarian, council member, farmer, bricklayer, carpenter, plumber, electrician, shopkeeper (general store, *tortillería*, fruit and vegetable stand, bread bakery, pharmacy, butcher stand, cantina, barber shop), telephone or loudspeaker operator, photographer, priest, teacher, doctor, nurse, and musician.

Communal labor, or *faena,* is used for repairing the road; people were paid 30 pesos a day. For repairing the CONASUPO, the workers received only beer.

Women are central and men and children peripheral to palm weaving (Ochoa 1993:40). Indeed, one assembly meeting of miniaturist weavers was attended solely by women. Men in Chigmecatitlán sometimes frame their participation as "helping their wives," although men are often accomplished artisans in their own right. Cross-culturally, mat making and basket making are "swing" activities assigned to either gender, according to Murdock and Provost's (1973) survey of labor patterns by gender among 185 world cultures. Women's dominance in Chigmecatitlán palm weaving is partly due to their greater numbers in the overall population (women outnumber men by 22 percent in the 1995 count; INEGI 1996).

According to Jacinto Flores, women turn to palm weaving because there is no work available that pays better. Men can work as bricklayers or council members (although municipal president Gonzalo Martínez Rodríguez named several women to the town council). One woman I talked to corroborated Don Jacinto's opinion: "*Soy más artesana que ama de casa. Si no hago esto no gano nada*" (I'm more of an artisan than a housewife. If I weren't doing this, I would earn nothing). Jacinto Flores also pointed out that palm weaving permits women to work at home while looking after their children. This concurs with Murdock and Provost's survey. They propose that women are often assigned work compatible with caring for young children—jobs close to home that are not dangerous and that can be interrupted and resumed at any time. According to Marín de Paalen (1976:40), women predominate in Mexican miniatures in general. Maleness is associated cross-culturally with bigness (Gilmore 1990:110).

POVERTY MADE ME DO A LOT OF THINGS

To ask people why they wove palm was to dredge up sad memories of poverty and deprivation: "*Por la pobreza empecé a hacer muchas cosas*"; "*Eramos muy pobres*"; "*El hambre es canija: por eso empecé a tejer*"

(Poverty made me do a lot of things; We were very poor; Hunger is vicious: that's why I started weaving). Cook's (1993:60) statement referring to Oaxaca—"simply put, craft production in present-day capitalism serves peasant-artisans as a means for meeting their ubiquitous need for cash"—applies equally well to Chigmecatitlán.

One afternoon in July, I met Pastor Flores, known for weaving tiny animals, who was sitting outside on the stoop of his house. His wife was recuperating from a serious illness in Villahermosa, Tabasco, but he was currently in town working as a watchman in the municipal president's office and serving as a mayordomo, or sponsor, for the Catholic feast of Carmen. Don Pastor recalled how he was obliged to weave miniature palm animals to earn money for food as a child in the 1930s.

> *Poverty made me do a lot of things. I made little tiny squirrels, dogs (police dogs with their ears pricked up and dogs with floppy ears), rabbits, scorpions, mice, sheep, rings with names on them, alligators, monkeys, peacocks, a lot of stuff.*
>
> *I was a little kid when I started weaving. I was about eight or ten years old. My father abandoned the family and my eldest brother didn't live with us. They were paying ten centavos for a dozen little animals. It took six dozen little animals to buy a liter of corn. We ate once a day at 3:00, me and my mother and siblings.*

If people didn't have to weave for the money, I was told, most would not weave at all. The situation of basketwork in Chigmecatitlán is close to Andrés Medina's (1975:9) depressing appraisal of most Mexican artisans' relationship to their work: "it allows them to survive and it often becomes a heavy yoke from which they would gladly be liberated."

MODES OF PALM CRAFT PRODUCTION

Modes of palm craft production in Chigmecatitlán coincide with Turok's (1988a, after Novelo 1976) neo-Marxist model of four modes of craft production in Mexico, all of which may exist simultaneously in the same town.

1) Household production
2) Small capitalist workshop
3) Independent master artisan's workshop
4) Manufacture (factory, cottage industry, or microindustry)

Craft production in Chigmecatitlán falls into the first and second categories, household production and the small capitalist workshop. Few people are in a position to accumulate capital, except perhaps some of the major comerciantes, or dealers.

Household Production

Household production is the most common pattern in Chigmecatitlán and throughout rural Mexico (Turok 1988a:109). Declining ownership of cultivable land leads to increased craftmaking to supplement the money sent by youths who have emigrated. Children learn the craft through long years of observation and apprenticeship. Work takes place in the family home. Artisans sell their goods directly to the "popular classes" at small fairs outside town or indirectly through traders who come to their door to pick up merchandise. There is a range of degrees of "proletarization and marginalization" within household production; some families only *maquilan* or produce components for other families to assemble (Novelo 1976; Turok 1988a).

A family that makes old-fashioned *china* and *charro* dolls exemplifies the household form of production. Basilio Herrera, his sister-in-law and neighbor Celina Zamora, and her sister Laura Zamora form a unit based on consanguinal and affinal kinship. Together they plait two dozen dolls per week. When I visited them, the three were sitting on small chairs in the sisters' dark, reed-walled kitchen. Don Basilio had strands of palm in brilliant shades beside him on the dampened dirt floor under a piece of plastic tarp; he was dipping a palm strip, split off with a needle, into a tin can of water before embroidering a doll's features. Simple tools at hand on a plank on the ground included long needles clinging to a magnet, smooth sticks used as lasts to support the cylinders of the dolls' shirt sleeves and pant legs, and a piece of scored wood to gauge the dimensions of the wooden bases.

Each of the three artisans specializes in certain elements of the dolls: Don Basilio Herrera weaves the heads (centering a diamond in front to suggest a nose), torsos, and legs; embroiders the facial features and stars; twists the rope lariat; and nails the figures to the wooden bases. Doña Celina Zamora weaves the china's rebozo and the charro's serape. Doña Laura Zamora weaves the china's elaborately patterned skirt, considered the most difficult part, on a small board on her lap. They buy the hats from a female artisan.

FIGURE 2.4 Four different artisans collaborate on a pair of *china* and *charro* dolls. One makes the head (*kitsindú*), body, features, zigzag braid (*nskí*), stars (*tskimi*), rope (*yo'o*); the second makes the serape and *rebozo*; the third makes the skirt; a fourth makes the hat (*nvelu*).

Small Capitalist Workshop

Turok (1988a:112–14) estimates that a tiny fraction of the category she calls household production forms an elite that is transformed into the category "small capitalist workshop." The head of the family continues to participate as an artisan, but salaried workers are hired to complete the least skilled tasks (Turok 1988a:112–13).

Don Refugio Bello's workshop or *taller* is an example of the incipient small capitalist workshop mode of production. José Flores recalls weaving riders on mules, or *mulitas,* as a boy in Don Refugio Bello's workshop. It was a serial process with each boy making a part and receiving a wage by the hour rather than by the piece. Some parts (hats and baskets) were bought from other makers. The system retained elements of the household form of production because Don Refugio made the most demanding parts himself, his son worked beside him, and the work took place at his home—in an underground well on his property.

> *The five of us boys (Librado Beltrán, Arturo Escobar, José Flores, José Ibarra, Lázaro Ibarra) who worked in Refugio Bello's workshop sat in a* pozo *[well] two meters deep on his property in the Fourth Ward. The oldest boy, Arturo Escobar, was around fifteen. If we got cold in the well after working three or four hours, Don Refugio would give us* huauchinangos.
>
> *Don Refugio would draw a line on the ground with a stick, since he didn't have a clock, and say, "When the sun hits that line it's quitting time."*
>
> *Once, we were throwing rocks to get our ball out of a tree and we hit a chick in a flock with their mother hen. Don Refugio put the chick in a half gourd and blew on it to try and revive it, but it was dead. That day he didn't pay us.*
>
> *Each boy in Don Refugio Bello's workshop would make one part: pineapples, leaves, attach the reins, and insert the ears. Don Refugio bought the hats from a woman. He would also buy the baskets from other people, but if he couldn't find any he liked, he would make them himself. Refugio Bello and his son Mauricio Bello made the mules and dolls. Don Refugio was the only one who made the jacket. He would put eyebrows and even eyelashes on his dolls.*

The last of five or six existing underground wells for weaving palm belonged to a man named Pedro Ibarra. The former owners would climb down on a ladder to a *petate* mat at the bottom of the well and talk or even sing while making toys such as "*tenatito*" (little baskets) to sell. People wove in the wells at night with *candiles* (kerosene bottle lanterns) and would awaken the next day with smudges of soot around their noses and chins. The wells were akin to the "artificial caves" used elsewhere in the Mixteca as well as in the state of Campeche to provide a moist environment in which palm is pliant (Cortés Ruiz 1996:n.p.; Cortés Ruiz

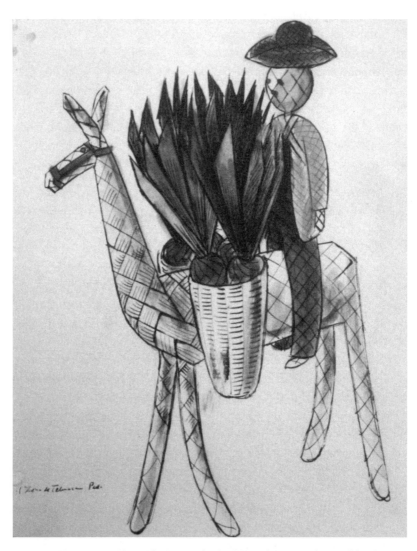

FIGURE 2.5 *Jinete* or *mulita* with pineapples by Miguel Covarrubias is like those made in Don Refugio Bello's workshop. Although the drawing is labeled "Zona de Tehuacán," the artisans I showed it to believed it to be from Chigmecatitlán. Height 10½ inches. Drawing Collection of Alberto Ulrich. Milagros Gallery (1991:56, fig. 7).

et al. 1989; Michael Hironymous, personal communication, March 1998; Hoppe and Weitlaner 1969:510–11; Marín de Paalen 1976:38; Tarazona Zermeño and Tommasi de Magrelli 1987; Turok 1988a:76). A new property owner filled in the last well before 1983 because it would flood when it rained and the chickens would fall in and drown.

The procurement of supplies for palm weaving in Chigmecatitlán contradicts the usual assumption that Mexican crafts are composed of local materials (Marín de Paalen 1976:43–44; Pettit and Pettit 1978:16; Sánchez Santa Ana 1992:11). Chigmecatitlán's need to acquire supplies from the outside world links it, albeit tenuously, with the regional and global economies.

The Palm Seller

Most artisans buy their palm from a local merchant named Alberto Vidales. Don Alberto trucks in this "good palm," *ñu va'a,* also known as *ñu Cuautla* or *ñu Yáyadu,* from Morelos. Other artisans buy palm directly from suppliers from neighboring Huatlatlauca who come occasionally to the Sunday market or tianguis. The palm originates in Acatlán or Izúcar, Puebla; or Cuautla, Morelos. Artisans in Chigmecatitlán have been utilizing this outside palm for at least fifty or sixty years; in the past, mule trains from Acatlán would arrive with no fewer than twenty burros loaded with palm sheaves.

Local Palm

Surprisingly, the native fan palm, known as *ñu kui* or green palm (*Brahea dulcis* [H.B.K.] Mart.), that grows locally is rarely used for weaving except by people from neighboring Santa Catarina (fig. 1.1). It crouches in clumps against the chalky limestone slopes at the foot of the Guadalupe chapel. One man told me he only used it to practice a new design. When I asked why, he said, "It's no good. It breaks. When you pull on it to tighten it, it breaks off" (cf. Ochoa 1993:42). Likewise the palm brought from the nearby *monte* of Huatlatlauca and Tepexi de Rodríguez breaks.

Miniature mariachi weaver Carmen González and her siblings are among the few who take advantage of the local fan palm. They harvest the fronds from the slopes on the edge of town from February to April before the rainy season and dry them indoors on a clothesline. By trial and error, Carmen learned to barely dampen the palm strips by laying them in a rectangular Tupperware container with a wrung-out rag laid on top, not touching the palm, for half an hour to an hour before beginning work; if the palm is immersed completely in water, "*se quema,*" it spoils. Palm requires dampening in the heat of April and May, but not in the rainy season of June, July, and August. Some put palm in a wet cloth folded between plastic sheeting on the floor. The local palm is noticeably shorter than palm from Cuautla and thus suitable for miniatures such as the mariachis. Carmen says *"es más blandita,"* it is softer than the Cuautla kind.

The Raffia Seller

The introduction of artificial palm, known as *rafia* or *ñu plástico,* was a major change in the palm weaving industry in the 1960s. Many weavers prefer plastic over palm because it comes already dyed in strips of uniform width, does not break off, can be worked dry, and resists fading. Raffia is available at the store of Juventino Chávez. According to Don Juventino, a chance meeting led him to bring plastic raffia to town in 1968. Someone in Mexico City commissioned him to create a matched suite of earrings, bracelet, necklace, and purse out of plastic. In his search for the cheapest source "as a way to help people in Chigmecatitlán," Don Juventino first sought a supplier in Tehuacán, where artisans from Chilacachapa, Guerrero, were already buying plastic to weave purses

TABLE 2.2 Local Retail Prices of Plastic Raffia and Thread

	Gauge	Price (100 grams)
Plastic Raffia "León"	#2	2 pesos
	#4	2.20 pesos
	#6	2.20 pesos
Plastic Thread "Polypro"	#12	3.50 pesos
	#25	3.50 pesos

Below are the weights of some objects made of plastic raffia and thread to give an idea of the cost of materials.

	Weight	Cost of Materials	Price	Cost of Materials / Price
raffia *ika* basket	7 grams	.20 pesos	.42 pesos	48%
raffia elephant	15 grams	.33 pesos	1.7 pesos	18%
raffia accordionist	10 grams	.22 pesos	4 pesos	6%
raffia saxophonist	9 grams	.22 pesos	4 pesos	6%

Note: The accordionist and saxophonist were purchased in Tepeaca and were probably double the local price. A store in Santa Catarina, whose owner also buys raffia in Mexico City, sells it at a comparable price of five pesos for 250 grams (December 1995).

TABLE 2.3 Palm versus Raffia: Advantages and Disadvantages According to Artisans

Palm

"I weave both palm and plastic but I like palm better than plastic because it's cheaper."

"Raffia is much more expensive than palm."

"Palm crafts bring a better price."

"I like palm better than raffia because I like dyeing it and it has more colors."

"I like to weave palm because of the color (my mother dyes it)."

"Plastic doesn't lend itself. I don't like to work in plastic. It doesn't work—I don't know why. It's not firm. It looks pretty but palm is better."

"Buyers want palm more than they want raffia. But it's hard to weave palm when it's hot and dry. It has to be damp. I sprinkle water on the brick floor and set my palm there and it stays damp. Early in the morning I start weaving. You have to stay indoors because if you weave outdoors, the palm dries up and breaks."

Raffia

"I weave only raffia because it's too much work to dye the palm."

"With plastic you just pick up the color you want, cut off a piece, and that's it."

"I prefer raffia because palm breaks and dries out."

"I prefer raffia because it doesn't break and doesn't have to be wet."

"Raffia is easier. With the strong winds blowing now, raffia doesn't break. But raffia doesn't sell."

"Raffia doesn't fade in the sun. But palm sells better to foreigners."

---

or bags. Eventually he located the cheapest raffia at a *jarciería*—an establishment that sells brushes and other fiber cleaning supplies on Jesús María Street in downtown Mexico City. Others began using plastic thread, *hilo de plástico,* to make baskets and baby rattles. Raffia now constitutes about 50 percent of the craft production of Chigmecatitlán.

Despite the advantages that plastic raffia offers artisans as a palm substitute, the use of raffia may ultimately be a poor economic strategy. According to Victoria Novelo (1993), artisans often seek ready-to-use materials that will save them the labor of preparing the materials. However, consumers tend to prefer natural palm. The market for crafts from

Chigmecatitlán has split into two spheres with low-end consumers buying raffia crafts and high-end consumers buying palm crafts. Ironically, raffia costs more than palm, yet raffia figurines sell for less than palm figurines.

The Dye Seller

On a hot afternoon in December, a strange car was parked alongside the otherwise deserted plaza, and a young man was conversing with a knot of local people. Jacinto Flores told me it was the dye seller and that his arrival had been announced in Mixtec on the public address system. The townspeople have been using imported aniline dyes for five generations, according to the itinerant dye seller. He drives the bumpy dirt road out to Chigmecatitlán once a month and supplies fifty other towns in the Tehuacán area, weighing out quantities of dye (*yuku*) on a portable scale.

The dye seller inherited his grandfather's *tlapalería,* or hardware store El Candado and had been in the business since he was eight years old. The store, formerly at 8 Poniente 303, Centro, Puebla, was founded in 1920 and sold "100 percent raw materials for artisans." The pigments came from Germany except during World War II, when they came from China. Such was the volume El Candado handled that a boxcar full of artists' supplies would be unloaded at his grandfather's store. In 1994 the dye seller, now the owner, closed down the locale, now occupied by a store selling sacred candles, and moved the business to his house in Colonia La Paz, Puebla. Customers did not know where to find him, so

TABLE 2.4 Dye Colors Sold by the Itinerant Dye Seller

Red	rojo	*kua'a*
Orange	anaranjado	–
Burnt orange	"chatillo"	–
Yellow	amarillo	*kuan*
Green	verde	*kui*
Blue	azul	*kui ya*
		kui antsi
Purple	morado, "camote"	*chi'i*
Magenta	rosa, "solferino"	–
Brown	café	–
Black	negro	*tnu*

he started bringing the dye to them—after the scare died down about the murder of the driver of a beer delivery truck on the dirt road to Chigmecatitlán in the late 1980s.

One of the oldest residents, Don Abraham Cortés (1907–97), reminisced about people in the past walking to Puebla to barter farm eggs for dye:

> *They would buy the dye in Puebla. They used to go to Puebla on foot. There were jumbo eggs, ranch eggs here. They'd buy eggs at two for five centavos from the ranchos and sell them in Puebla at 100 for six pesos. They'd head out with their burros on Tuesdays at 6:00 a.m. They'd spend the night in San Francisco Tzitzimihuacan [Totomihuacan = Yukuika]. They'd get there about 8:00 at night. They'd leave at 4:00 a.m., they'd arrive [in Puebla] at 9:00, 10:00, 11:00 a.m., depending on the burro they had. The eggs sold like hotcakes. Then they'd go shopping: a kilo of* picante, *a quarter kilo of dye,* cemitas,[2] *packets of tobacco. They'd leave there at 4:00 in the afternoon. On the way, they'd go through Huatlatlauca, they'd go through San Juan [Coatetelco], they'd go through Santa Marta [Yancuitlalpan], after that it was nothing but hills.*

Women are usually in charge of dyeing the palm, possibly because it is analogous to the female task of cooking. However, one man said he dyes it to avoid exposing his wife to the noxious powder; another, known for his perfectionism, dyes it himself to achieve just the right saturation. Unskilled artisans are said to leave the palm too long in the dye bath and "*se pudre*," it rots; it becomes brittle and cracks when manipulated. No mordants are used to fix the color; thus it fades rapidly when exposed to sunlight.

Nobody remembered natural dyes ever being used, though elsewhere in the Mixteca region, Efraín Cortés Ruiz (personal communication, 1996), curator of Oaxacan collections at the Museo Nacional de Antropología, observed the use of smoke to tint palm black. None of the Chigmecatitlán artisans was familiar with the technique.

Anthill Pebbles, Coyulli Seeds, Bottle Caps

The only native materials used in palm weaving—besides the rarely used native fan palm—are the noisemakers inside children's toy rattles. Palm rattles contain a pinch of anthill pebbles scavenged on the edge of town at well-worn trails three inches wide made by red ants, or *tskuñu*.

FIGURE 2.6 *Coyulli* seeds and a bottle cap are the noisemakers inside plastic raffia rattles. Materials courtesy Luis Domínguez.

Raffia rattles contain two or three native *coyulli* (*Caesalpinia cacalaco* H.&B.) seeds and a bottle cap as the sound producers.

THE ENTREPRENEUR

A young artisan turned entrepreneur is responsible for the current trend toward the miniaturization of palm figures. I met Jacinto Flores in the town hall on my first day in Chigmecatitlán when I asked the municipal president for permission to work. Though not yet thirty years old, Don Jacinto has influenced the artisans with whom he works to switch from large figures to miniatures; simplify their designs; diversify their repertoire; use palm, not raffia; apply for government loans; and penetrate elite markets. On weekends he would occasionally pause during the rounds he made by bicycle of the ten households from which he bought miniatures and discourse at length on the predicament of palm crafts in Chigmecatitlán.

Jacinto showed an aptitude for market economics from an early age. As a boy, he insisted that his mother raise prices at the family grocery in Chigmecatitlán to keep pace with inflation during the five years his father was absent in Mexico City. In Novelo's (1976) and Turok's (1988a) scheme of the evolution of craft production through stages, Jacinto verges on the "manufacture" mode of production, since he has been known to advance money to artisans, provide dyes and thread, and suggest new designs. He estimated that he and his wife collected about 1,500 pieces per month from twenty palm weavers. Jacinto brings to mind Turok's (1988a:113) musing about how certain artisans move into "the vanguard of the consumer market in their area for reasons hard to define: work? talent? luck? vision?" He is a restless entrepreneur with the professed mission of helping artisans make what sells. He says he feels a commitment to help them since many are his kin.

One day Don Jacinto looked back on how he resorted to palm weaving out of necessity. His parents had shielded their three sons from learning to weave, hoping they would choose the upwardly mobile path of "*letras*" (humanities). His impetus to teach himself to weave as a teenager recapitulates Turok's (1988a:141) mercantilist formula of making goods to exchange for money for other goods.

Jacinto was unusual, though, in that he managed to engage the support of an organization run by the ruling PRI political party, the Confederación Nacional Campesina (CNC), which provided a national outlet for his pieces and those of his family. In the 1970s, the era in which Jacinto enlisted its support, Novelo (1976:254) wrote of the CNC: "Through a special bureau in support of crafts, it participates in craft development programs among peasant-artisans. Its current project has as its principal task to foster sales and promote crafts that bear the 'mark of the campesino.'" Most importantly, Don Jacinto's association with the CNC led him to see the big picture and to interpret crafts from the point of view of intellectual audiences for crafts.

> El hambre es canija *(Hunger is vicious): That's why I learned to weave. I grew up in the midst of artisans, but I never learned to weave. My older brother and I would help by trimming the raw points off the bases of figures. For us it was a game because we'd compete to see who could trim the fastest.*
>
> *I was sent to high school in Puebla to live with my aunt and uncle, but I had desires and no spending money. I wanted to see films and buy the Marxist books that young people like. I taught myself to make a raffia doll, which was really tough, but finally I asked my aunt and uncle for pointers. I still own that doll; I use it as a pencil holder.*
>
> *In 1986 [at age sixteen], I started selling, first fayuca and then Chigmecatitlán crafts. I would take merchandise to a consignment store the CNC ran. I liked going there every week and getting money back.*

In 1986 the CNC gave me an ID card and invited me to set up an exhibition in Plaza Dorado [an upscale shopping mall], which lasted about two weeks but was not a success. The following year I sold at the Plaza de San Francisco along with my brother—I sold about 100 pieces. I was in the Feria de Puebla.[3] I started teaching palm weaving at the Dirección de Artesanías [Ex-Convento de Santa Rosa].

In September 1987 I heard about another exhibition the CNC was having at the Palacio de los Deportes in Mexico City. It didn't cost anything. I couldn't go, but I sent my parents. Never had we sold so much. We sold 75,000 pesos [i.e., 75 New Pesos] a day. The merchandise sold out in four days, and my father had to come back to town for more. From there the CNC invited my parents to another exhibition in Guadalajara, and then they sent them to Cuetzalan, to San Luis Potosí. . . .

I dropped out of college after one year of studying law. I realized I could learn more about economics outside the university.

CHIGMECATITLÁN AS A VOLKSWAGEN FACTORY

During one of our conversations over my kitchen table, the loquacious Jacinto Flores described Chigmecatitlán through the jarring metaphor of an automobile factory. His concept of the town as a profit-making corporation in which workers have different but complementary jobs and even non-artisans contribute to the system of production is consistent with Turok's (1988a:103) general model of Mexican craft towns, in which "everyone plays a part": "It's an *industry* here: Chigmecatitlán is Nissan or Volkswagen. There are people specialized in weaving miniatures, selling them, designing them, preparing food."

Sixty-five years before Jacinto favorably likened Chigmecatitlán to an automobile plant, folk art writer and illustrator Gabriel Fernández Ledesma in *Juguetes mexicanos* (1930:7) entertained the same analogy with disdain: "It is evident that in Mexico there is not a single [toy] factory organized like those of the United States and various European countries. The Yankee factories are powerful industrial gears of the commercial capitalist type. A toy factory is like an automobile factory: departments, division of labor, specialization, etc., everything that signifies economy in production and results in fabulous quantities of the 'standard' type."

Fernández Ledesma expresses the deep ambivalence of Mexican intellectuals toward the encroachment of "mechanized industries" upon "manual industries." On one hand, in the socialist spirit of the 1920s and 1930s, he glorifies the futuristic possibilities of the machine; on the other hand, he deplores American-style capitalism in which the machine crushes and subjects the worker. Fernández Ledesma (1930:4) writes: "We have seen . . . how machine civilization, at the bidding of market capitalism, debases the nobility of the mechanical function, invading the domain of the handmade object, which was never meant to be detached from its expression of intimacy." How to justify the existence of hand-made objects was the difficult task of Mexican writers such as Fernández Ledesma and Dr. Atl ([1922]1980). Intellectuals treasured crafts for their aesthetic value and reaffirmation of Mexican identity while they opposed the unequal class conditions that fostered them.

"UN LOCO SOÑADOR" [A CRAZY DREAMER]
—MOTTO ON A TRUCK IN PUEBLA

For the past ten years, local entrepreneur Jacinto Flores has been conceiving a plan to improve the livelihood of palm artisans in Chigmecatitlán. He hopes to implement an economic program that will be a "blend of traditional and modern." Jacinto's goal is "not to undo traditional forms of economy here." These traditional forms of economy embrace two main features: first, reliance on kinship to organize business transactions, and second, cooperation between artisans and sellers.

Kinship organizes both manufacturing and selling in Chigmecatitlán. "*Aquí se trabaja por familia, no por grupo*" (Here we work by family, not by group), he said, critiquing the requirement that artisans organize into groups to solicit government loans. Sellers tend to handle merchandise their relatives make. This is true both for artisans who sell directly to the public at three fairs a year and for major intermediaries such as Don Jacinto.

The second "traditional" element that Don Jacinto would preserve in his modernizing plan is the overlap between artisans and sellers. Like Turok (1988a), he sees both roles as integral to the overall crafts system. Rather than viewing sellers as exploiters of artisans, he sees them as mutually dependent, intertwined in a symbiotic relationship. In his view, their identities intersect, as illustrated below:

Artisans	Sellers
80 percent weaving	20 percent weaving
20 percent selling	80 percent selling

The modernizing elements Jacinto would impose on the traditional structure include industrialization, credit, and raising prices.

Industrialization

Don Jacinto proposes: "I would like to industrialize crafts like they did in China. In other words, each person would make a certain part of each piece. And we would know the order beforehand: 300 dozen little baskets for such-and-such a store, for example. Also, the design would be according to the taste of the consumer. A machine could be designed to weave palm."

At first I was taken aback by Don Jacinto's desire to turn Chigmecatitlán into a factory assembly line. My negative reaction to his statement that machines could be designed to weave palm put me dangerously close to the category of "the most conservative minds, in love with the primitive," who reject change (Novelo 1993:48). "This traditionalist current overvalues static aesthetics and opposes any innovation that would lighten the process of artisanal labor," Novelo (1993:48) admonishes. Cook (1993:61) describes this conflict as pitting "the material interests of artisans against consumer interests." On the other hand, as I pointed out to Don Jacinto, it is precisely the hand labor in crafts that attracts consumers in the tourist and urban market (Nash 1993:10; Novelo 1993:49, 67).

For his part, Don Jacinto acknowledged that not all artisans are in favor of industrialization. "Some people agree with the industrialization of crafts and some don't. Some are going to make the figures they want to make. For example, there's a guy out there who makes miniature figures very, very well and earns three pesos per figure. If he didn't make them quite so well, he would *still* earn three pesos per figure." This conflict can be seen as that of individual creativity versus commercialism, or the unique object versus mass production.

Credit

Jacinto Flores says people think he is rich, but he is not. He just lives on credit. The second part of his ambitious dream of modernizing the palm industry in Chigmecatitlán entails obtaining government loans. Artisans sporadically hold town meetings to organize and apply for federal and state loans. Below are some examples of credits for which artisans have successfully applied.[4]

Federal After 1991, Mexican artisans were urged to register in the "Padrón Nacional de la Microindustria y la Actividad Artesanal" (National Census of Microindustry and Artisanal Activity) and receive their *"Cédula de Artesanos"* (Artisan ID), which some people in Chigmecatitlán did as a condition to receive loans, despite their suspicions that this might make them subject to taxes.

Federal The Empresas de Solidaridad program (now FONAES, Fondo Nacional de Empresas en Solidaridad) under Mexican president Ernesto Zedillo provided interest-free loans to worker initiatives in Puebla. During 1995–96, seventy-four artisans obtained credit from Empresas de Solidaridad, according to the outgoing municipal president's report (Wilfrido Cortés Herrera, 14 February 1996).

Federal The Instituto Nacional Indigenista (INI) was another source of credit through its Fondos Regionales. The INI offered loans at 12 to 15 percent interest, payable in one or two years.

Federal In May 1996 artisans met to receive loans from Fondo de Solidaridad para la Producción (FOSOLPRO).

State The finance department (Finanzas) of the state of Puebla also offered an interest-free loan, payable in one to five years. A group could borrow up to 300,000 pesos ($40,000 U.S. in March 1996).

Jacinto anticipated that government loans would be used productively. Sellers could afford to go on sales trips to Tijuana and the United States. A group of artisans could contract with a foreign designer. A community center could be built that would contain meeting rooms, display space, and typewriters.

Loans would help stabilize artisans' income and stimulate higher prices, according to Jacinto. Currently, during months when there is a surplus of merchandise, the price drops. Inexperienced sellers without the resources to wait out periods of low prices compete among themselves and drive prices down. Loans would allow prices to rise because more intermediaries would have money to buy merchandise, creating a shortage, so prices would go up. Artisans would then sell to the highest bidder.

Raising Prices

Raising the price of palm crafts is Jacinto's third goal. "It pains me to see crafts sold so cheaply," he confessed. I was skeptical, since, as a wholesaler, he benefits from low prices. He claimed he did not feel a conflict because he was an artisan himself. To his critics, Jacinto responded: "Everyone says Don Jacinto will get money out of this. Yes, I will benefit. Will you benefit? Or will I alone benefit?"

The jump in prices was visible during the time I spent in Chigmecatitlán. In October 1995, the wholesale price per dozen miniature figures was thirty pesos ($4 U.S.). By June 1996, it was forty pesos ($5.30 U.S.). One year later, in June 1997, the price had risen to sixty pesos ($8 U.S.). The increase was widely attributed to Jacinto, who had announced at a town hall meeting of miniaturists in May 1996 that prices *could* double. As a self-fulfilling prophecy, prices immediately jumped. Jacinto told me he had raised prices in four stages: from thirty to thirty-five to forty to fifty to sixty pesos per dozen miniatures.

His aim was for an artisan to earn the same as a bricklayer, the highest-paid job. An artisan in 1996 earned 100 pesos per week, while a bricklayer earned 200 pesos per week.

By June 1997, an artisan's salary was nearly comparable to that of a bricklayer. As a result, the number of artisans fabricating miniature figurines jumped from twenty-five in May 1996 to fifty in June 1997.

NATIONAL PROJECTS TO MODERNIZE CRAFTS

Jacinto's personal vision is surprisingly compatible with official political proposals to modernize craft production nationwide. A speech in 1958 by then presidential candidate Adolfo López Mateos voiced the Mexican government's interest in stimulating and fostering crafts: "If our artisan class is fortified with sufficient credits and organization, it can, within the parameters of a household industry, become an important rung of the overall economy. Much of what the rural family produces in its free time, when agricultural tasks do not require their presence in the fields, could be organized and developed into the basis for diverse articles that

TABLE 2.5 Weekly Income from Crafts in Chigmecatitlán

Interview Date	Artisan	Item	Quantity	Price	Weekly Gross
28 May 96	A	Small wallets and baskets (*nda' cho*)	1 doz/wk*	12–24 pesos/doz	12–24 pesos/wk
16 Mar. 96	B	Miniature animals	3 doz/wk	5 pesos/doz	15 pesos/wk
25 May 96	C	Miniature herons	1–2 doz/wk	25 pesos/doz	25–50 pesos/wk
22 June 96	D	Miniature animals	4 doz/wk	15 pesos/doz	60 pesos/wk
5 June 96	E	Large fans	1 doz/wk	75 pesos/doz	75 pesos/wk
19 Mar. 96	F	Miniature mariachis	2 doz/wk	40 pesos/doz	80 pesos/wk
6 July 97	F (2nd interview)	Miniature musicians	2 doz/wk	60 pesos/doz	120 pesos/wk
8 June 96	G, H	Miniature *chinas, charros,* etc.	0–3 doz/wk	40 pesos/doz	0–120 pesos/wk
14 July 97	I	Miniature clowns, etc.	2 doz/wk	60 pesos/doz	120 pesos/wk
1 July 97	J, K, L	Large *chinas, charros*	2 doz/wk	120 pesos/doz	240 pesos/wk (div. among 3 people)

Note: All items are palm. 7.5 pesos = $1 U.S. (1996); 8 pesos = $1 U.S. (1997).
* Estimated by the author

would be in demand by our city dwellers and could be exported" (Adolfo López Mateos, in Huitrón 1962, cited in Novelo 1993:36, 1996:193).

A policy statement issued under now self-exiled former president Carlos Salinas de Gortari outlined an explicit program for the modernization of crafts (SECOFI [1991]). The document concentrates on the economic development of crafts as a "microindustry" (an apt term in the case of the miniature), in line with the Salinas government's general policy of free-market capitalist development.

The Salinas statement posits that "the use of Indian languages as the only language" is an obstacle for the modernization of artisanal activity and that most artisans are unaware of methods for determining prices. Further obstacles, according to the document, are that "the means of production are rudimentary and [work] spaces are inappropriate" (SECOFI [1991]:9). In general, the goals of the policy—"to raise the productivity of artisanal activity, facilitate the supply of raw materials necessary for its development, procure the corresponding financing, stimulate the direct marketing of artisanal products" (SECOFI [1991]:5)—are much like Jacinto's goals for Chigmecatitlán. Like Jacinto, the Salinas policy touts assembly-line–style manufacture and laments that "design and quality do not always adapt to the preferences of consumers" (SECOFI [1991]).

Novelo (1976:27, 1993:68) concludes that the Mexican government has attempted to support crafts for two reasons. First, because it sees crafts as a recourse to maintain people on the land in the face of Mexico's agricultural crisis rather than have them join the mass migration to the cities. Second, because it considers crafts, and folk culture in general, an important source and symbol of Mexican identity.

LITTLE BASKETS

The situation of palm crafts as a microindustry in Chigmecatitlán offers a counterpoint to the classic short story "La canasta" (The basket) by B. Traven (author of *Treasure of the Sierra Madre*; see also Horcasitas 1978 and Turok 1988a). This dated but still widely circulated story is set in small-town Oaxaca. In it, a greedy American businessman is nonplussed to learn from the Indian basket maker whose little baskets he would like to exploit that the price per basket would go up, not down, the more he commissioned. The basket maker in the story reasons that he would have to neglect his fields and goats to dedicate himself full time to making the ten thousand little baskets that the American covets.

> *"Besides,* señor, *there is something you don't know. I have to make these little baskets my way, with songs and pieces of my own soul. If I am obliged to make them by the thousands, there would not be a piece of my soul in each one, nor could I put my songs into them. They would all turn out the same and in the end that would be the death of my heart" (Traven 1990:31).*

The theme of the story is that capitalist attitudes are not universal—but it patronizes the Indian just as it mocks the naiveté of the American

Canasta hecha con rafia

FIGURE 2.7 *Canasta hecha con rafia* (raffia basket), drawing by Jaime Santillán Fuentes, age 13, July 1997.

businessman. This fragment evokes a romantic attitude about folk art that did not hold true in Chigmecatitlán, where baskets were treated and spoken of as commodities, not as expressions of one's subjectivity.

Nevertheless, it is relevant in a broader metaphorical sense as a warning that the massive exploitation of crafts requires careful consideration to avoid destroying the very conditions and processes that have made them attractive to the people who produce them as well as to prospective consumers. One cannot but see the parallel with Chigmecatitlán, where palm crafts are "goods whose economic value does not reflect, in many cases, the labor time and cost of materials employed in their elaboration" (SECOFI [1991]:8). The subtext of the Traven story is the lack of comprehension and conflicting goals of different groups, centered on an object of desire, the handmade basket.

CHAPTER 3

Brittle Memories: A History of Weaving Palm

Jolting and swaying in the front seat of the priest's white truck, ensconced between the young priest and his brother, I am heading to the district jail in Tepexi de Rodríguez, Puebla, to hunt for miniature crafts. The brothers encourage me to sing old Beatles songs along with them. It is an hour's drive by dirt road through the dry landscape studded with columnar cacti, terrestrial bromeliads, and rosette-shaped agaves. The priest is going to make a call from the public telephone in Tepexi; the June rains have put the only telephone in Chigmecatitlán out of service for a month.

To get to Tepexi, we pass the *ve'e te'ende* or "ruined church," a truncated mound on the right said to be guarded by a snake; the *curva del diablo* on the left, where a dirt shortcut turns off to the Atoyac River; the highway junction at La Monera, where people gather *chinche* bugs (*texca*) to be eaten boiled and salted; the Pie de Vaca fossil museum; the Centro Coordinador Indigenista Nahua-Mixteco-Popoloca (INI); and finally, the shady town square at Tepexi. I was not thinking about it at the time, but the landmarks we were passing were material reminders of Chigmecatitlán's recent and archaic past.

The priest runs off to make his phone call, his brother lounges in the truck, and I proceed to the jail under the colonnade that runs the length of the town hall. A woman embroidering behind iron bars is the sole female prisoner. The bars are hung with rectangular handbags made of colorful plastic cord and a few openwork palm hampers. I tell the guard I'm looking for palm crafts. He shows me some bags; no, I'm looking for *animalitos*. At last he produces a woven palm bird from the back room. *¡Eso es lo que buscaba!* (That's what I was looking for).

The guard calls out to one of the inmates who can be seen through an iron grille playing soccer in the courtyard, and all the men come running to watch. A slight, middle-aged prisoner brings me what he has to sell. I can barely understand that his name is Celso Sánchez Orozco, he is from Santa María Nativitas Cuauhtempan, Puebla, and he learned to weave in jail about twenty years earlier from a fellow inmate, whose name he does not remember, from Santa María Chigmecatitlán.

It is an intriguing coincidence that the weaver should be from Santa María Nativitas, a Popoloca town for which a record of palm weaving survives from 1681 in the national archives (AGN) in Mexico City: "they have farmed and cultivated the ranch lands and from the palm that grows they make mats and other things, with the proceeds of which they support themselves and deliver their tributes and alms" (AGN-Indios 27, 67, 31v–32, cited in Jäcklein 1978:127).

Knowing that prisoners often work in miniature, I had already asked people in Chigmecatitlán if they knew of anyone who had spent time in prison. Of course, that was an indiscreet question. After I came back and showed them the animalitos from the Tepexi jail, however, they recalled two men, now deceased, who had been imprisoned in Tepexi at some vague time in the past and might have taught the man to weave.

Mexican jails are environments that promote the diffusion of palm weaving (Foster 1960:94). "This is one of the activities in which prisoners are allowed to engage, nonweavers learning to weave, and weavers often acquiring new techniques" (Foster 1960:94–95). Foster (1967:124) elsewhere adds: "In both Spain and Mesoamerica basketry types are diffused through the custom of teaching prisoners to weave during their jail terms; in both areas I have encountered competent weavers who took up the trade during periods of enforced incarceration." Efraín Cortés Ruiz (1996:n.p.) specifically points to district jails in the Mixteca as centers of palm weaving.

Fernández Ledesma (1930:25) writes of prisoners weaving palm in Oaxaca in the 1920s: "The inmates of the Oaxaca jail dedicate themselves, among other work, to weaving little palm baskets, purses, cigarette cases, etc., and manufacturing brooms, baskets, and a multitude of flowers and toys. They are uniquely adept at plaiting strips of various colors to form the most expressive and humorous animals. They manufacture these toys at a very low price and their work gives them true aesthetic pleasure."

Celso Sánchez Orozco's pieces from the Tepexi jail, two rickety birds and a mule that barely stand on their own, are antique figures rarely made now in Chigmecatitlán. The birds resemble Fernández Ledesma's (1930:48) illustration of a bird from the Oaxaca City jail. Prisons are not only a milieu for craft learning but also a repository where designs from the past are frozen in time.

Where does Chigmecatitlán palm weaving fit in the broader geographical region of southern Puebla and the Mixteca? Is the town unique or similar to other places? Collectively, the town distinguishes itself from other towns by insisting that the invention of palm miniatures is a uniquely local development. Chigmecatitlán artisans see themselves, as in the Tepexi jail anecdote above, as unintentional agents for the diffusion of palm weaving into neighboring towns.

COLLECTIVE MEMORY OF WEAVING PALM

Jacinto Flores once commented that old people in Chigmecatitlán, most of whom could not read or write, had mastered mnemonic techniques with which he was unfamiliar. When he wanted to commit something to memory, he would ask his grandmother to remember it for him. Still, the collective memory of Chigmecatitlán's past was, from my perspective, materially vague and temporally shallow. The majority of the people seemed unconcerned with the town's history of palm weaving. "I'm sure what 'facts' I'm managing to capture here are just meager dregs and scrapings," I fretted in a letter to a friend. Direct data on the history of palm weaving in Chigmecatitlán—not to mention the town's very existence—is extremely fragmentary. This lack of certifiable history drove me to become a rabid positivist in my search for facts and dates, like Klaus Jäcklein (1978:103) in his equally frustrating quest for the Popoloca history of Tepexi de Rodríguez, who writes, "the current state of documentation on Tepexi obliges the ethnohistorian to be grateful for the tiniest clue that might yield information."

Various local and state bureaucrats have sporadically shared this anxiety to pin down hard facts. "Chigmecatitlán was founded in the pre-Hispanic era by Nahua groups and was conquered around 1521 by the Spaniards," a book on *Los municipios de Puebla* (1988) breezily alleges, without providing any supporting evidence.[1] The urge to codify the town's history for official purposes has resulted in oral history being written down at various times. At some point the municipal president, Franco Acevedo Barragán (1984–87 term), convened the oldest people, now deceased, to stipulate the history of Chigmecatitlán and decide on dates. A signed and sealed document in the local town hall dated 1946 affirms that the town was founded between the years 1646 and 1655 (Ochoa 1993:60). I collected several versions of the town's foundation narrative, two of which allude to the history of palm weaving.[2]

In one oral example, Don Abraham Cortés (1907–97) embeds an explanation of the origin of palm crafts within a longer narrative of the town's settlement. I heard the story from him one morning when I ran into the evangelist doctor and asked him to introduce me to his land-lord, Don Abraham, who at age eighty-nine was one of the oldest men and a town historian. He and his third wife, a palm weaver, lived in two thatched-roof dwellings up the street from me. We found the couple in their dark kitchen, where she sat eating a tortilla on a low stool next to a hearth made of three concrete blocks with a griddle made of an oil-drum lid. The dirt floor was imprinted with chicken tracks, except under the metal-frame double bed which had ragged petate mats un-derneath. The bed had an old mattress and no sheets. Don Abraham sat on the bed, with dried palm fronds, some dyed and in bags, leaning on the wall next to him. On my prompting, he launched into the story of Chigmecatitlán's founding, a fragment of which I excerpt here:

> *The first people only made hats and mats, but they looked for a way to make others: little horses, little mules. They make clowns now. Among the first settlers, the men wove hats, the women wove mats. There was a couple, Eligio Fernández and Tomasa Rodríguez.[3] The wife searched for an idea of how to weave. They bought dyes, they looked for palm. The wife started making baskets,* ndo'o. *Others started making coin purses, little wallets,* nda'cho *(Abraham Cortés, 1996).*

Later the doctor gave me a written version of the story, entitled "*Datos Importantes Fundación y Vida y Desarrollo de Santa María Chigmecati-tlán del Estado de Puebla. Pue.*" (Important Facts, Founding, Life, and Development of Santa María Chigmecatitlán, State of Puebla, Puebla), which Don Abraham had apparently typed himself.

Palm toys also figure in a second version of the foundation narra-tive, in which the people of Chigmecatitlán present toys as gifts to their long-lost "kin" in San Pedro y San Pablo Tequixtepec, the Mixtec town in Oaxaca that they consider their town of origin. A Chigmecatitlán school principal, Fidela Hernández Nava de Calixto, was commissioned to collect this foundation narrative for a work on the history of the state of Puebla (Martha García n.d.). Hernández transcribed, translated, and reordered the narrative from an oral history she elicited from a local man named Bonifacio Peregrina in 1961 (Martha García, personal communication, 1997). In the following excerpt, which ends the foundation narrative, an old man from San Pedro y San Pablo Tequixtepec visits Chigmecatitlán for the first time in 1946.

> *And that was how that old man came here [to Santa María Chigme-catitlán], and when he arrived, the first thing the people did was to take the old man to the rectory so Father Palacios could meet him. Once this was done, the people gave him a variety of toys to take back home [to Tequixtepec] and tell about the art of their sister town. The old man carried out the mission of taking the gifts made by the sister town, and when they received everything, they were very pleased and recognized the art to which the lost tribe has been devoted ever since (Bonifacio Peregrina, as told to Fidela Hernández Nava de Calixto, June 8, 1961).*

Chigmecatitlán's collective belief in itself as the site where palm toy weaving originated is a powerful paradigm. The inclusion of palm toys in the two foundation narratives demonstrates that local people consider toy and miniature weaving to be a singular accomplishment and a marker of community identity. But, contrary to local belief, there are counter-examples of palm toy weaving in many other parts of the Mixteca and beyond.

"Woven straw animals and toys," which Gilbert Chase (1931:184) implies are from Guerrero, were for sale at the Oaxaca City market in 1930. The Popolocas of San Felipe Otlaltepec, Tepexi, formerly made miniature palm animals (Jäcklein 1974:141). Palm toys are made in San Juan Teita, Mixteca, west of Oaxaca City (Sue Hugghins and Inga Mc-Kendry, personal communication, 1996). The Ixcatecan-speaking people of Santa María Ixcatlán, Oaxaca, also in the Mixteca, occasionally weave palm toy animals such as giraffes (Michael Hironymous, personal communication, 1998). Nahua speakers in Santiago Tlamacazapa, Guerrero, make medium-sized palm deer, sheep, and balls with spiral tails known as *guamúchiles*. The response of my friends in Chigmecatitlán, when I showed them pieces from Tlamacazapa, was, "They're copies of designs from here. They didn't make them before; the weave shows it. They work the palm too wet. They're not well finished."

No one knows exactly how long the inhabitants of Chigmecatitlán have been weaving palm. Unlike artifacts of pottery and stone, palm disintegrates and is rarely found at archaeological sites. It is clear, however, that palm weaving in southern Puebla is an ancient industry. Chigmecatitlán is only 106 kilometers (sixty-six miles), as the crow flies, from Coxcatlán Cave, the famous rockshelter in the Tehuacán Valley where archaeologist Richard MacNeish dug up the preserved remnants of twilled palm basketry from the Santa María phase some 2,800 years old, not to mention the primitive ancestor of corn (MacNeish, Nelken-Terner, and Johnson 1967). These normally ephemeral artifacts were preserved in burials in the dry microclimate of the cave. They are similar in shape, size, and weave to baskets still made in the area, as MacNeish et al. point out in their report on excavations in the Tehuacán Valley:

> *Although the three specimens [of woven palm] consist only of small rim fragments, I would guess that these baskets were roughly cylindrical in form and measured from 15.0 to 20.0 cm. in diameter. Palm strands, from 0.5 to 1.5 cm. wide, are woven in a two-over-two, two-under-two pattern. The twill weave is at a 45-degree angle to the rim of the vessel, and the strands are folded over and linked into the weaving and end just below the rim.*
>
> *Twilled basketry first appeared in the Santa Maria [800 BC–150 BC] period in the Tehuacán Valley, and today it is the popular type in the region (MacNeish, Nelken-Terner, and Johnson 1967:166).*

The specifications of the twilled baskets mentioned above could well describe the modern *nda'cho* from Chigmecatitlán. Even earlier was an imprint of a twilled mat or basket found on clay from the Ajalpan phase (1500–800 BC). MacNeish also found a checker-weave mat or band from the Palo Blanco level (150 BC–AD 700) and four twilled palm petate fragments from the Palo Blanco and Venta Salada (AD 700–1500) levels (MacNeish, Nelken-Terner, and Johnson 1967:167–68).

Palm mat iconography abounds in the pre- and post-conquest native screenfolds known as the Mixtec codices. A couple sitting on a mat symbolizes marriage. Palm was significant enough that the sacred tree from the south in the *Codex Vaticanus B* is a palm.[4] The palm plant perhaps epitomizes the flora of the Mixteca as seen from central Puebla.

FIGURE 3.1 Palm tree as sacred tree from the south, *Codex Vaticanus 3773* or *B*. Page 18 of codex, page 207 of book.

COLONIAL HISTORY OF PALM WEAVING

Based on indirect evidence, the Mixtecs in Chigmecatitlán have been making palm goods for at least five hundred years. This inference is derived from tribute lists and transcripts of court disputes over territory from the Spanish colonial period (1521–1821) found in the national archives in Mexico City.

At the time of the Spanish conquest in 1521, the Mixteca was divided into small *cacicazgos* or chiefdoms that channeled tribute to the

powerful Aztecs in Tenochtitlan. Chigmecatitlán belonged to the caci-
cazgo of Tepexi, the political district to which it still belongs.[5] Tepexi
was ethnically Popoloca, though it included two Mixtec towns (Santa
María Chigmecatitlán and Santa Catarina Tlaltempan) and a Nahua
town (Huatlatlauca) in its purview. The ruling elites of Tepexi adopted
the Náhuatl language (Jäcklein 1978:5). Local caciques in the sixteenth
and seventeenth centuries remained more powerful than Spanish-im-
posed local administrators (Jäcklein 1978:6). The Mixtecs in Chigmecatitlán provided tribute in goods and personal service to the caciques
in Tepexi, who in turn tributed to the Aztecs in Tenochtitlan before the
conquest and to the Spanish kings after the conquest. Records of these
tributary relationships, written down retrospectively in colonial times,
provide data on palm weaving.

In the fifteenth century, according to Jäcklein (1978:5), Tepexi was a
subordinate ally of the Aztecs under Moctezuma Ilhuicamina (= Moctezuma I, 1440–69), who was followed by Ahuizotl (1486–1502; Brotherston 1995:58). The early chronicler Tezozómoc records that Tepexi
and other towns of the Mixteca under Aztec domination received king
Ahuizotl and his armies with goods that included "palm sandals [and]
mats for their journey, to shelter from the sun and to sleep" (Tezozómoc
1878, chapter 76, cited by Dahlgren [1954]1990:192).

Chigmecatitlán is specifically mentioned in a *merced* or grant pur-
portedly from 1520, copied by scribe Joseph de Montalban in 1788
(AGN-Tierras 2697, 14, fol. 403–410; Jäcklein 1978:191, 261). It grants
Don Francisco Chicoyautzin, one of five caciques at the time of the
Spanish conquest of Tepexi in 1520 (Jäcklein 1978:7), rights to Chigme-
catitlán and its neighbor Huatlatlauca:

> *the land lots they call Chichemecatitlan and Quautlatlauca which are*
> *one behind the other crossing the Atoyac River which you shall mea-*
> *sure transverse and taking two thousand steps marking a square, of*
> *which you shall have fruition and ownership including the common-*
> *ers and families who live there (AGN-Tierras 2697, 14, 407v–408;*
> *Jäcklein 1978:263).*

Between 1578 and 1585, Spanish king Felipe II ordered written
surveys, known as Relaciones Geográficas, to be made of Spain's ter-
ritorial possessions overseas (Cline 1972). These surveys were based
on a standard detailed questionnaire and often included maps by native
artists. Two Relaciones Geográficas were recorded for Tepexi, but both

are lost.[6] There is no Relación Geográfica for Chigmecatitlán, but there is one for its neighbor Huatlatlauca. Since, as mentioned above, both towns were claimed by Tepexi cacique Don Francisco Chicoyautzin as of 1520, we may presume that industries in Chigmecatitlán were similar to those in Huatlatlauca. The Relación Geográfica for Huatlatlauca, written in 1579, informs us that before the conquest, Huatlatlauca paid tribute to its leader Ocelotzin in the form of cotton blankets, or *huipiles,* mats and baskets, among other things (Rosquillas 1986:42):

> *[T]hey were vassals in heathen times and had as their lord a leader called Ocelotzin which means jaguar and they gave him as tribute and estate, cotton blankets, huipiles, mats, baskets, and personal service; they served and planted seeds and adored an idol called Citlalpul which means star and each one had two or three wives.*[7]

We can assume the mats and baskets (*"chiquibites"*) were palm because the Relación de Huatlatlauca subsequently lists palm mats as one of the main industries:

> *the commerce and profits the natives of this province have is to make palm mats each of which is worth one* real.[8]

Therefore, we can infer that Chigmecatitlán, like Huatlatlauca, was probably making palm crafts around 1520.

One of the most important colonial documents, the *Codex Mendoza,* lists the early-sixteenth-century tribute the Aztecs demanded from various regions under their dominion. It is a crucial source of data on pre-Hispanic crafts and extractive industries. Unfortunately, Tepexi appears in the *Codex Mendoza* only as one of a group of twenty-two towns under the heading of Tepeaca, the city to the north that the Aztecs had conquered in 1466.[9] Tepexi's individual tribute to the Aztecs is not separated out (Jäcklein 1978:123). Moreover, woven palm goods are not part of Tepeaca's listed tribute, except for the mats in which four thousand loads of lime are wrapped (*Codex Mendoza,* folio 42, in Berdan and Anawalt 1997:88–89). According to Elizabeth Snoddy Cuéllar (1993:254), baskets were not considered important enough to be listed as tribute items in their own right in the *Codex Mendoza,* though palm chairs and mats were. Yet, she points out, baskets appear constantly in the pictographs as containers and measures for the rest of the tribute.

Another scrap for piecing together the history of palm weaving is a painted tribute record for Tepexi in the Museum of the American In-

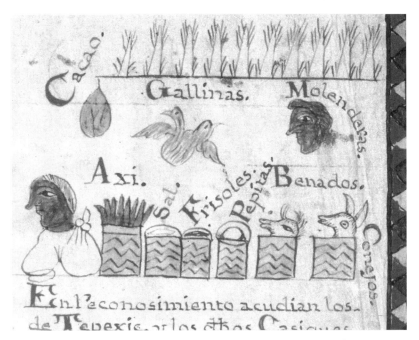

FIGURE 3.2 Detail, *Painted Tribute Record of Tepexi* (Courtesy, National Museum of the American Indian, Smithsonian Institution, Cat. 08/4482).

dian, New York (Cat. 8/4482). This parchment is thought to be a nineteenth-century copy of an original from between 1537 and 1544 (Cook de Leonard 1961:87–107; Gorenstein 1971:335–43; Jäcklein 1978:122–28). It depicts pictographically and verbally tribute demanded by Don Gonzalo Mazatzin Moctezuma, one of the five caciques in Tepexi, from the surrounding lands and barrios. Like the *Codex Mendoza,* it excludes palm goods from the tribute, except for palm chairs *(icpales).* However, it shows various bulk goods in palm containers with a twill weave designated by parallel zigzags (Cook de Leonard 1961:98; Jäcklein 1978:127). Cook de Leonard (1961:102) associates these drawings of baskets in the Tepexi tribute record with those of modern Chigmecatitlán:

> *All have the same wavy lines to indicate basketry, and are painted yellow. As a basket, this form is not made anymore in the coarse palm leaf worked in the southern vicinity of Tepexi. It is found, though, a little further north, in the Mixtec town of Chigmecatitlan, made with very fine palm leaf strips and often tinted, all in one color, or interwoven with designs.*

In the year 1581, the *corregidor* grants a later cacique of Tepexi, Don Francisco Moctezuma, grandson of Don Gonzalo Mazatzin Moctezuma, "possession of Santa María Concepción Chiquimecatitlán, including the Indians and commoners" (Jäcklein 1978:60–61; AGN-Tierras 9, 1, 6). According to Jäcklein, "the witnesses testify that Santa María had been 'since time immemorial' subject of Tepexi" (Jäcklein 1978:60–61). We know Don Francisco Moctezuma's subjects relied on palm crafts, among other industries, to provide him with tribute because of testimony from witnesses in a land dispute from the following partially burned page from 1591 referring to Tepexi:

> *that in said lands they harvest palm, wicker, reeds, turkeys, white honey, and other things with which the commoners pay their tributes, and sustain themselves, and the majority of this New Spain is purveyor of mats,* petacas, *and* chiquihuites *(AGN-Tierras 3418, n.p.)*

There is no evidence, either in the pre-conquest or colonial periods, that the palm crafts included miniatures. However, the lack of evidence is inconclusive; as Daniel Rubín de la Borbolla (1974:170) points out, colonial officials paid little attention to palm weaving in general because they (correctly) considered it an activity of old people, women, and children.

WEAVING TECHNIQUE AS A CLUE TO HISTORY

The morphology of basketry can be evidence of its history. Baskets are often classified in museum collections by the attributes of their wall construction, whether plaited, twined, or coiled (Adovasio 1977). The logic behind this classification is that weaving technique is considered stable enough to be an indicator of the ethnic group that produced it. The close

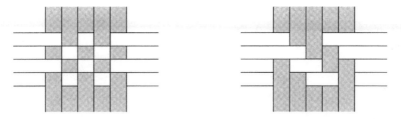

FIGURE 3.3 *Left,* simple plaiting (*"de uno en uno"*) and *right,* twill plaiting (*"de dos en dos"*).

identification of different basketry specialties with a particular region or town applies to pre-Hispanic Mexico as well as modern Spain (Foster 1960:94).

In Chigmecatitlán, plaiting and twining are present, but coiling is absent. Plaiting, the most frequent technique, is subdivided into "simple" and "twill."

In simple plaiting (1x1), also known as checker weaving, "the weaving elements pass over each other in single intervals" (Adovasio 1977:99). Simple plaiting is used to make *ika,* or market-type bail baskets, and miniatures.

FIGURE 3.4 Guide to basket types: *Upper, nda'cho, lower left, ndo'o, lower right, ika.*

FIGURE 3.5 Twill plaited palm in the *Codex Nuttall* obverse, p. 10. Courtesy of Dover Publications.

In twill plaiting (2x2), "the weaving elements in one set pass over two or more in the other set at staggered intervals" (Adovasio 1977:99). Twill plaiting, illustrated in the Mixtec codices, the *Codex Mendoza,* and the Tepexi tribute record, is used in petate mats and *nda'cho* and *ndo'o* baskets and is one of the most common basket-weaving techniques in Mesoamerica (Foster 1967:117).

Twining is used less frequently than either type of plaiting in Chigmecatitlán. It is primarily used to sew strips together when starting baskets and mats and to make *ika estambre,* a type of basket wrapped with embroidery thread, now rarely made.

It is likely that the simple-plaited ika is of Spanish origin, while the twill-plaited nda'cho and ndo'o baskets are of native origin.[10] Most miniatures are made with simple plaiting, perhaps hinting at recent ancestry.

A curious iconographic coincidence reinforces the antiquity of palm weaving in Chigmecatitlán. A distinctive knot equivalent to a "Josephine knot" or "Carrick bend" is used to bind two palm strips to start a woven palm ball. This ball, known as *kitsindú*, is used as a doll head, pineapple, necklace bead, or ball-and-stem ornament. The same knot, composed of two interlaced snakes, is found as the headdress of a woman named Seven House in a pre-Hispanic Mixtec codex, the Nuttall obverse (p. 29).[11] More evidence of this sort of convergence, however, is needed to fix the age of Chigmecatitlán crafts.

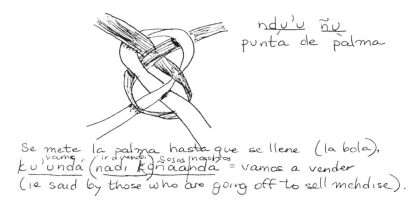

FIGURE 3.6 *Upper, ndu'u ñu, "punta de palma."* Sketch of how two strips of palm are looped together to begin to form a ball (*kitsindú*). *Lower,* the same knot in the headdress of Seven House, *Codex Nuttall* obverse, p. 29. Her personal name is "Interlaced Serpent." Courtesy of Dover Publications.

The relationship between Chigmecatitlán and its two nearest neighbors, Huatlatlauca and Santa Catarina, is reflected in the crafts each produces. Whatever the circulation of palm weaving in the region may have been in the past, in the twentieth century Chigmecatitlán has been the center of innovation, production, and dissemination of palm weaving techniques to its two neighbors. It is said that people from Chigmecatitlán married into Huatlatlauca and "*Ñu*" (Santa Catarina) and taught people there to weave. The other two towns conserve designs that the Chigmecatitlán artisans have already abandoned.

Huatlatlauca

At night the street lights of Huatlatlauca shimmer across the void of the Atoyac river canyon, reminding those of Chigmecatitlán that somehow they have never been able to gather the resources to pave the highway, while Huatlatlauca has. Now that their road is paved, a woman in Huatlatlauca has opened a display of local palm crafts in her home for visitors (Hortensia Rosquillas, personal communication, 1998).

A unidirectional relationship exists as far as the diffusion of palm weaving from Chigmecatitlán to Huatlatlauca. Jacinto Flores said people in Huatlatlauca learned to make bicyclists when a brass band from Chigmecatitlán went there for two weeks. There was a sense of pity for their lack of skill: someone from San Miguel La Barranca (Colonia Obregón, Huatlatlauca) makes bicycles and sells them in Chigmecatitlán on Sundays before All Saints' Day, but no one buys them, I was told.

One day I drove to Huatlatlauca with the kindergarten teacher and another friend across the Puente de Dios, a natural land bridge shown in the sixteenth-century map of Tepexi included with the Relación de Huatlatlauca.[12] We asked at a corner store for people who weave palm and were told that "everyone" weaves baskets. One person also weaves fine petates on commission with any name the customer wants for about 200 pesos. We were referred to Enrique Moncayo, who used to make palm bicycles.

Sr. Moncayo and his adult son Pedro brought us little chairs from his house, and we sat under a tree and talked. Sr. Moncayo, seventy-four years old and nearly blind after having a beam fall on his head at the market, said a local curer had treated his eyes with rosemary, and his children begged him to see an oculist in Tepexi, but he said pessimistically, "They just take your money. Better to save it for the casket."

His mother knew how to dye and weave petates, though not as skillfully as the people in Chigmecatitlán. He first saw woven figures at his neighbor Esperanza's. Three or four people in Huatlatlauca were already weaving figures when he started between 1945 and 1950.

> *I taught myself to weave when I used to watch the calves. I made it up out of my own head. I made necklaces [kitsindú], balls [coyulli]. I cut the palm with my machete and kept on and on and on, and it came out well. People were surprised that I learned to make a ball. Then I tried the doll [muñeco]. After days and days, it was hideous. It was about a foot high. I found the wire for the bicycle in Santa María [Chigmecatitlán]. I went to the field and cut more palm. People said I was crazy [tetzahuite] and that I did strange things. "You're making dolls, you're making wheels—you're going to make a living like that?"*

Eventually Sr. Moncayo made *tlachiquero, mulita, tirador, soldado,* and *apache* (pulque harvester, mule, hunter, soldier, and Apache), which he sold to "la dichosa Eustolia" and Don Albino Gómez in the Barrio San Antonio in Chigmecatitlán. Now he makes only bunches of flowers, which he says is "*criollo*: another guy and I invented it." His son Pedro hikes across the ravine to deliver his own and his father's work to Chigmecatitlán.

Santa Catarina

Even though Chigmecatitlán and Santa Catarina are twin Mixtec outliers positioned north of the Mixteca proper, they have not cleaved together but cultivate separate dialects and social identities. The people of Ñu, Santa Catarina, not only speak a different version of Mixtec but are considered distinct in other ways. When I showed people in Chigmecatitlán a photograph of some Santa Catarina boys posing with palm dolls, they said it was obvious from the boys' faces they weren't from here. Later another man said he could tell by the little boys' smiles that they were from Santa Catarina. This may well be true; Monaghan (1995:203) indicates that in Mixtec communities, "centuries of endogamy have given each group a distinct set of features." It was also adduced that double family names in Chigmecatitlán (that is, two supposedly unrelated families with the same last name): Cabrera, Ibáñez, Méndez, Ojeda, Pineda,

Ramírez, and Rodríguez—were different from family names in Santa Catarina: Bailón, Barrales, Escandón, Ortega, Rosete, and Zaragoza.

A sense of economic rivalry between the two towns exists, despite the fact that each refers to the other familiarly as ñu, "*pueblo.*" In the 1940s people from Santa Catarina used to be the main buyers and sellers of Chigmecatitlán merchandise. Now the tables have turned and artisans from Santa Catarina make the forty-five–minute walk to peddle their work to wholesalers in Chigmecatitlán. The picture I was painted by people in both towns is that Santa Catarina is less proficient and lags behind Chigmecatitlán in palm weaving.

"They recently started copying toys from here. They used to just work in the countryside," one man from Chigmecatitlán observed. Another woman recalled that in her childhood in the 1940s, people in Santa Catarina didn't know how to make anything but necklaces. A third said, "Before, people from Catarina didn't know anything. The [school] textbooks helped them a lot." Another man told me that until twenty-five or thirty years ago, people in Santa Catarina only made balls with stems (*tsia'ñu*) and necklaces, nothing else, not even nda'cho baskets. A Santa Catarina woman around seventy years old who wove balls with stems confirmed that she learned to weave at age thirty when she saw people from Chigmecatitlán who sold crafts; a man from Chigmecatitlán taught her.

Santa Catarina weaves whatever is in fashion: purses, earrings, cigarette cases, Don Jacinto told me. They make what sells at that moment, he said, for example, fifteen years ago, the purse that opened in two. He added (in June 1997) that he thought the people of Catarina were beginning to make miniatures.

While Chigmecatitlán is not unique in weaving toys, it is unusual. Palm weaving follows ethnicity in the Mixteca-Puebla region: Nahuas and Popolocas make mats; Mixtecs make hats (Cook de Leonard 1953:424). The Mixtecs in Santo Domingo Tonahuixtla, Puebla—a town some believe to be another offshoot of San Pedro y San Pablo Tequixtepec, Oaxaca, and therefore also Chigmecatitlán's "sister town"—weave nothing but unfinished hats (Edmundo Reséndiz, personal communication, 1996). Chigmecatitlán and its neighbor Santa Catarina are rare in not making hats like other Mixtec towns. Their divergence from the norm can not be attributed to lack of palm—Tonahuixtla is also short of palm and must import it, yet it continues to produce hats.

It brings up the question of why Chigmecatitlán crafts have branched out into multiple designs and miniaturized. I can only guess at an explanation based on the traits that distinguish Chigmecatitlán from other towns:

A lack of water necessitated an alternative to farming.

It is an island ethnically and linguistically distinct from surrounding towns, perhaps also leading to a sense of insularity in craft production.

Chigmecatitlán's (and Santa Catarina's) geographical distance from other Mixtec towns may have made them inaccessible to hat fabricators who buy unfinished hats in bulk to steam and shape.

The town is not on the main highway, discouraging emigration to the United States.

Chigmecatitlán's citizens profess an ethos of resorting to itinerant trade and looking for "a sure thing" as opposed to the insecurity of working in the United States.

The devout Catholicism of the people is conducive to the long-term integrity of the town despite high emigration to other parts of Mexico.

Buyers are available for their crafts: people from Santa Catarina historically served as intermediaries to market the goods Chigmecatitlán produced.

A TEMPORARY MUSEUM

On a chilly day at dawn on February 14, 1996, the kindergarten teacher and I dragged ourselves from our beds and over to the town bandstand under a flowering jacaranda to help install the inaugural exhibit of the new crafts museum. We had each been enlisted several weeks earlier, she because of her teaching post and I as someone who had at least been inside a museum before. Jacinto Flores, the local crafts innovator, had obtained a 13,000-peso grant from the INI in Tepexi de Rodríguez to install the museum on the ground floor of the bandstand.

Don Jacinto called a museum committee meeting on January 16, 1996, with an architect from Puebla and a few local people. His intention was to provide a space to salvage tradition and promote the internal and external diffusion of palm crafts. He calculated that the museum would be instrumental for sharing ideas between artisans unfamiliar with each other's work due to the secrecy of weaving as a private, domestic activity, as well as the closed, kinship-based system of sales. A second rationale for the project was that visitors needed a site to focus their attention on local palm crafts, until then mostly invisible to outsiders. It would be a reference point for buyers seeking out particular artisans whose work was displayed. Don Jacinto envisioned rotating exhibits that would narrate the use of each craft; for example, mulitas for Corpus Christi or *canastitas* for All Saints' Day and Christmas.

The architect, Carlos Parra, designed simple, glass-fronted display niches recessed into the thick walls of the octagonal bandstand after the windows were bricked up. The upper tier of the bandstand would still accommodate one of the three local bands playing marches, waltzes, and paso dobles during the Fiestas Patrias on September 15 and 16. Don Jacinto insisted that the new museum be painted bright tangerine on the outside and peach on the inside to stand out from the virginal white and blue of the rest of the town's buildings. The color would rapidly fade, anyway, like the rectory which used to be bright red but now was pink. "I wanted it to clash, give it a different character, make it livelier," he explained.

The director of the INI in Tepexi de Rodríguez, Edmundo Meneses Calva, visited the site of the remodeling and was reportedly impressed with the project. The INI offered the possibility of applying for further money to improve it. By the project's completion, the actual budget was 18,500 pesos:

8,000	door and exhibit cases
5,000	carpentry
2,000	paint
2,000	glass
1,500	electrical installation
18,500	TOTAL

At 9:30 p.m. on February 13, Jacinto summoned the kindergarten teacher and me to help install the exhibits; the museum had to be ready to include in the annual report of the outgoing municipal president at noon the next day. What exhibits? I wondered. By 11:00 p.m., only four of eleven invited lenders had dropped off their collections. The town elec-

trician was still installing the fluorescent light tubes in last-minute fashion. The paint had curdled, and trips were made to buy more.

The morning of the grand opening on February 14, 1996, the floor was still paint-spattered, one of the windows of the display cases had cracked while it was being installed, and the glass boxes that fit on top of the wooden pedestals had failed to arrive. With hasty efficiency and forced artistry, we plundered the borrowed bags of merchandise and improvised arrangements of large baskets and tiny nativities and marching bands on stacks of bricks we had painted in pastel colors the evening before. The new museum displayed collections lent by four vendors: Imelda Zamora, Luis Zamora, Clara Zamora, and Jacinto Flores. Each case represented a different vendor. Don Jacinto placed a live fan palm in a bucket of sand at the entrance and posted a hand-lettered sign in Spanish and Mixtec. There was no time to write display labels. Still, the effect was striking.

MUSEO	*MUSEUM*
ARTE POPULAR	*POPULAR ART*
CHIGMECATITLAN	*CHIGMECATITLAN*
EXPOSICION COLECTIVA	*GROUP EXHIBITION*
"CHIND'E ÑA' ŤA	*"SEE WHAT IS WOVEN*
NDA'A NI' VI ÑUUNDA"	*BY THE HANDS OF OUR*
	PEOPLE"
Del 14 de feb. al 24 de marzo	*Feb. 14 to March 24*

(Note: letters with an inverted circumflex (ˇ) are nasalized).

By midday, the sun was unrelenting. Jacinto, the master of ceremonies for the outgoing administration's annual report, told the assembled public, seated on wooden chairs, that the municipal president's final action was the inauguration of a museum *"para conocer su propia artesanía"* (to get to know its own crafts). Edmundo Reséndiz, personal representative of the INI director in Tepexi, added his praise for the new museum:

> With the support of the INI, a response to an impulse to do a display of the coveted crafts, better known on the northern border of our country, so the visitor or tourist can become familiar with work from here. The Program of Funds for Cultural Patrimony (Programa de Fondos de Patrimonio para la Cultura) invites you to apply for more funding

in 1996. They contributed 13,000 pesos. The temporary exhibit will remain for one month.

The entire populace was invited to view the round exhibit space.

The modest but effective museum under the bandstand attempted to provide permanence to the legacy of art flowing out of town. It is significant that the effort to preserve and display was aimed not only at filling a commercial need for a visitors' destination and orientation, but also at remedying an intrinsic need among the artisans themselves to appraise the town's art as a communal body of work. The temporary museum was a rare homegrown example of the desire to situate local crafts in their rightful place in history.

My intent in this chapter has been to elucidate some of the historical processes that have led to Chigmecatitlán's preeminence as a site of miniature palm weaving. The desire to remember and record does not always arise from within the community, however, but to satisfy the curiosity of outsiders: state publications, the school system, or anthropologists; the resulting histories circulate back into local knowledge.

To the extent that native historians have participated in these inquiries, they tend to produce a totalizing vision of Chigmecatitlán as the source of palm toys and miniatures *sui generis*. Local foundation narratives date the town to some time after 1642 or 1646, when a devout band of discontents leaves San Pedro y San Pablo Tequixtepec, Oaxaca; wanders on a pilgrimage for several years; and eventually establishes Chigmecatitlán. They weave utilitarian items at first (petates, baskets, and possibly hats), until a creator couple, Eligio Fernández and Tomasa Rodríguez, begin to weave small toys around 1895.

Archaeological and archival records imply that the town is even older than local memory would have it, that Chigmecatitlán has been occupied since at least 1520 in weaving palm goods first for the local caciques and the Aztecs, then for the Spanish crown and clergy, and now for urban Mexicans and foreign tourists.

It seems important in the auto-definition of the townspeople collectively to be known as innovators and inventors of palm crafts. Local people's reconstruction of history denies the evidence of toys in other towns. Alternative histories challenge this unilateral origin. Other sites in the region were historically active in producing diverse palm objects, but palm weaving at other sites has either declined or become focused on a single commodity such as hats or mats, while weaving in Chigmecatitlán has tended to diversify and miniaturize.

CHAPTER 4

Shrinking Crafts

One of the main purposes of my study of Chigmecatitlán was to test the hypothesis that the widespread popularity of miniature crafts in Mexico may have stemmed from the persistence of a pre-Hispanic ritual tradition. Under the spell of a romantic impulse to discern ancestral heritage in modern practice, I expected to find that the townspeople had been weaving palm miniatures since before the Spanish conquest in 1521. But my pet theory was overthrown when confronted with artisans' unambiguous statements that "*la miniatura no es tradicional*" (miniatures are not traditional). Evidence indicates that figures made in Chigmecatitlán were once relatively *large* and have only become miniaturized since the 1960s. I was therefore compelled to look for other explanations for Chigmecatitlán's shrinking crafts.

This chapter explores several episodes in the history of local crafts to suggest alternate causes of reduced scale beyond a simplistic ascription to tradition. Children's toys and play jewelry set a precedent for small scale in the early twentieth century. The influence of middlemen who stopped buying medium size, the rational calculus that miniatures are cost-efficient, and the patronage of politicians in search of the "typical" are factors squeezing crafts to ever smaller dimensions.

INVENTION OF THE MINIATURE

One couple, José Flores and Catalina Escalante, are universally credited with innovating miniatures in Chigmecatitlán around 1965. Although other miniature objects were already being made, Don José and Doña Catalina were the first to concentrate on miniature human characters. In their son's words, "Other people made large figures; they made them small." He glossed the history of the miniature this way: José Flores and Catalina Escalante were the only miniaturists forty years ago (1966);

José Flores taught his brother Celestino Flores to weave miniatures thirty years ago (1976); most artisans have been weaving miniatures for fewer than ten years (since 1986).

It was a year before I finally met the couple in a light-suffused court-yard a few steps removed from the downtown Puebla clamor of honking horns. A congenial interlocutor with a precise memory for detail, José Flores recalled, with more bitterness than nostalgia, vicissitudes in the history of miniaturization in Chigmecatitlán. Our conversations, with the intermittent presence of his wife, Catalina Escalante, sons, and daughter-in-law, took place at their cart with painted-on lettering that read *"Ricos Garapiñados."* From it they sell bags of caramel nuts outside the arched portal of the University of Puebla.

KF: Could you tell me how it was that you started making miniature figurines?

JF: I don't remember exactly what year it was that people stopped buying medium size.

Around 1960 or 1961 my wife and I got married and we moved to Córdoba [Veracruz] so I could support her. I learned to make peanut brittle, which my wife sold in Córdoba and I sold at the sugar mills around Córdoba: San José de Abajo, La Providencia, Mata de Caña, Mata Redonda, Rodríguez Tejada.

After a few years we moved back to Santa María. I don't remember exactly what year it was; it was around 1965. All I knew how to weave was baskets [ika], but I learned to make miniature tlachiqueros [pulque harvesters] from Benigno Rosas. That's all he made, miniature tlachiqueros.

There were four sizes of figures: large, medium, small, miniature.

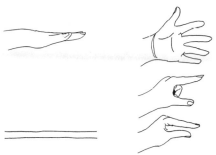

FIGURE 4.1 Size categories in Chigmecatitlán: Large (circa 10 inches), medium (4 inches), small (2 inches), miniature (1 inch).

My wife and I made mainly medium-size figures, but people stopped buying medium-size. I said to my wife, "We're going to make nothing but miniatures." She was already making piñera/piñero *and* china poblana *couples. So we had three figures: the tlachiquero, the piñera/ piñero, and the china poblana/charro.*

FIGURE 4.2 *Tlachiquero* (pulque harvester), *jinete* (muleback or horseback rider), *cazador* (hunter). Height 1 inch.

We started going to Mexico City to sell at the Zócalo—behind the Cathedral, in the Cathedral atrium, and under the arches across from the National Palace—at Holy Week, Corpus Christi, and September 16th. In Mexico City we met a man named Sabino Vázquez from San Pedro Totoltepec, outside of Toluca [State of Mexico]. He had a booth in the San Ángel market and one in the Villa Olímpica where tourists went. He ran into us behind the Cathedral. We were charging 1.30 or 1.25 pesos per miniature. He started picking them out; he wanted nothing but miniatures. He asked if he could buy our entire stock and he paid 1.25 pesos. Because of him I started making more figures, so then I had four figures: tlachiquero, piñera/piñero, china poblana/ charro, and hunter. I'd either go to his house or his sales booth and sell miniatures to him. This went on for three or four years.

Sabino Vázquez said, "Bring more, I want something new."

"What do you mean?"

"You're the artisan, invent something."

I made some little Apache Indians with arrows.

"Why don't you make me a band of musicians?"

I'm a musician, I know more or less how the instruments should go.[1] I made a wheelbarrow driver with his little pick and shovel, a water carrier.

FIGURE 4.3 Soprano sax player, Apache Indian, *carretillero* (wheelbarrow driver). Apache, height 1½ inches, courtesy of Guillermo Contreras.

My wife said, "Why don't we make a little devil?"

The horseback rider was already being made when I was little. We also made a fisherman, a baseball player. I spent three or four years selling to Sabino Vázquez. He didn't want to raise the price. One time I went to the Villa Olímpica and was leaving some merchandise with Sabino's mother. She bought what I had for twelve pesos a dozen. Then while I was still standing there, a "gringa" came by and asked the price of a figure.

"Twenty-five pesos."

The gringa said it was expensive, and Sabino's mother said, "It's just that you have no idea how hard it is to weave this; my back is killing me!"²

I felt horrible. "Why don't you raise the price a little, at least to 1.25 pesos?"

Sabino refused. Sabino Vázquez visited Santa María once; that made me happy because he saw how far it was.

It was 1987 or 1988 when I handed over all the merchandise to my son. It was at the Feria de Puebla. My sales had gone way down. One hundred and five thousand pesos [i.e., 105 New Pesos] was all I sold the whole month. I only sold well on May 1st, 5th, and 10th [Mexican Labor Day, Cinco de Mayo, and Mother's Day]. That was when I threw in the towel. I told my wife, "I'm going back to making candy."

I've suffered from everything, from palm as much as from candy.

José Flores's condition as toy maker clashes with the classic portrait of a carefree and playful artist that René d'Harnoncourt (1928:110) portrays in his sketch "Pancho el Juguetero" in *Mexican Folkways* (cf. Charpenel 1970; Hernández 1981:244). Pancho el Juguetero is motivated by the desire for creative self-expression. Don José, on the other hand, has to be pushed to invent novel figures ("You're the artisan, invent something"). Middlemen like Sabino Vázquez often suggest new figures, leaving the artisan to work out the technical structure.

The genesis of the palm baseball team is a case in point. Don José and Doña Catalina used to barter palm figurines for corn with a man named Daniel in neighboring Santa Catarina. At one point, Daniel was unable to trade with them, but another man in Santa Catarina stepped in, on condition that they make *beisbolistas*. It took a week of racking their brains. Don José practiced on the native green fan palm. "I had to deliver in a week because hunger is vicious." Don José devised the baseball glove, ball, bat, chest protector, and kneepad; his wife made the dolls, about six inches tall. The pressure on Don José to innovate or starve is a far cry from Pancho el Juguetero, who is "absolutely free to fashion a quaint world after his own will and fancy" (d'Harnoncourt 1928:110).

Pancho el Juguetero takes pleasure in creating ("he is the most contented being on earth"; d'Harnoncourt 1928:114). In contrast, Don José's back is breaking and his eyes are strained: "I've suffered from everything" (*De todo he sufrido*). He feels "horrible" when Sabino Vázquez's mother represents his aches and pains as her own as a sales pitch, not caring that he is within earshot. He is conscious of the asymmetrical power relationship that obliges him to travel to Sabino Vázquez's house and market stall in Mexico City while the trader only visits Chigmecatitlán once.

Pancho el Juguetero shrugs off economic concerns ("Money does not signify for him the equivalent of time and energy spent"; d'Harnoncourt 1928:111). Don José, on the other hand, specifically adapts his production toward what he perceives as greater profitability: "We're going to make nothing but miniatures." He resents the exploitation by the dealer, who refuses to pay his asking price. José Flores ultimately sold miniatures to Sabino Vázquez at twelve pesos per dozen wholesale; that is, he reduced his asking price of 1.25 pesos to 1 peso each. Don José and his wife also continued to sell their own work and that of their neighbors directly to the public from a cloth spread on the sidewalk at the Zócalo in Mexico City. Don José earned even less selling back home in Chigmecatitlán: nine pesos per dozen to Luz María Guajardo or her daughter Clara Zamora, who bought whatever he could not dispose of in Mexico City. The highest price Don José earned for miniatures in his career was two pesos per figure.

Our conversation was interrupted by University of Puebla students and professors buying bags of caramel peanuts, squash seeds, and walnuts for three, four, and six pesos—the current price of a miniature palm figure. José Flores's son had introduced him to government agencies such as "Artesanías" in the Ex-Convento de Santa Rosa: "we hung out with the artisans; we hung out in Celaya [Guanajuato]. . . ." It was in Celaya and San Luis Potosí, ironically, that some men taught Don José to make *garapiñado* (caramel-coated roasted nuts), which is lighter work than the *palanqueta* (solid peanut brittle) with which he had begun his career. Retired from selling miniatures, he peddled garapiñado as an itinerant candy vendor in various towns in Puebla: Izúcar de Matamoros, Ciudad Serdán, Acatzingo, and Tepeaca.

It speaks of the predicament of artisans in Mexico that the couple would rather rent a room in Puebla and sell candy from a cart than live in Chigmecatitlán and weave miniatures. After working as artisans for twenty-five years, they grew disillusioned with the low prices paid by dealers and abandoned palm weaving to return to selling caramel nuts from their pushcart outside the Benemérita Universidad Autónoma de Puebla.

Don José and Doña Catalina were crucial innovators whose success, though economically debatable, influenced other artisans to imitate them:

"José Flores showed us miniatures."

"Catalina Escalante was the one who invented them, maybe."

"Catalina Escalante was already making things *chiquito*." They also influenced sellers such as Jacinto Flores and the Zamora family to concentrate on selling miniatures.

A review of palm figures from Chigmecatitlán in museum collections confirms the astonishing impact of José Flores and Catalina Escalante on shrinking craft size. The oldest collections extant, the Roberto Montenegro and Nelson Rockefeller collections, which date from the 1930s, contain large- to medium-sized palm figures approximately seven inches and six inches tall (Oettinger 1990). Even pieces from the 1960s were much larger than the ones being made today. The same designs that were eight or twelve inches tall in the 1960s are one inch tall today.

Far from tracing the production of miniatures to their ancestors, most people I interviewed said that miniatures were not made in Chigmecatitlán in the past. Instead, men and women alike wove ordinary, utilitarian items such as those woven today all over the Mixteca. "I see it as unlikely that miniatures were made," Jacinto Flores told me. "Utilitarian things were made: baskets, mats, and hats." There is disagreement about whether hats were ever made in town; some older people have said they were not.

Nevertheless, José Flores and Catalina Escalante did not spontaneously start making miniatures in a vacuum. Although they were catalysts who boosted the manufacture of miniatures in Chigmecatitlán, precedents for small-scale figurines already existed.

Around 1895, a creator couple named Eligio Fernández and Tomasa Rodríguez invented "the finest curiosities" of palm, according to a local foundation narrative.[3] Records in the parish church of Chigmecatitlán verify the couple's marriage in 1895. They are said to have made "*te-natitos y estrellitas,*" little baskets and stars. Judging from the townspeople's recollections, their parents and grandparents worked in a range of sizes—large, medium, and small—in the early twentieth century. In addition to utilitarian size, they wove scaled-down versions of baskets, wallets, fire fans, and mats as toys for the nation's children.[4]

When Dolores Escamilla (b. ca. 1906/1916-d. 1997) was a girl, her father sold large and small ndo'o and nda'cho baskets for Day of the Dead to little girls in *Diyuko* (Tepeaca). Similar baskets are shown in a postcard view from the early twentieth century by American photographer C. B. Waite. It depicts a street vendor, apparently from Puebla, hawking three sizes of palm baskets. The townspeople also wove flat nda'cho wallets in large and small sizes. These wallets, "made into halves that slip one over the other like a pocketbook" (Porter [1922]1993:181), were probably common throughout the Mixteca. Dr. Atl (1922:204) mentions that there were various sizes of palm wallets from Oaxaca in the early 1920s, ranging from "very small, like toys, to 20 centimeters long." Ample wallets sized to hold *bilimbiques,* the large currency printed during the Revolution (Gabriel Moedano, personal communication, 1996), were made along with toy size.

José Flores credits Benigno Rosas with showing him how to weave his first miniature figure, the tlachiquero or pulque harvester. I met Benigno Rosas when he was in town serving as mayordomo for the Preciosa Sangre religious fiesta, though he now lives in Ciudad del Carmen, Campeche, and has given up weaving because palm spoils there. His children surrounded him as we talked, filtering his Mixtec to Spanish. Benigno Rosas was an orphan who learned to weave "out of poverty" around 1948, when he was five or six years old. His grandparents punished him until he learned to weave little palm ika baskets. His uncle, Alberto Ramírez, later taught him to weave middle-sized tlachiqueros. "Since they didn't sell, I started making them smaller."[5] The reduction was at the request of "people of Catarina." Many artisans mentioned the pressure to miniaturize put on them by nameless dealers from this town next door, where they speak a different version of Mixtec. When I asked whether he had ever worked down in a well, like José Flores as a boy, his deadpan reply, duly repeated by a translator, "No, I always stayed above ground," broke the serious mood, provoking a burst of laughter from the listeners.

PALM JEWELRY

In addition to toy versions of utilitarian objects such as wallets, baskets, fire fans, and mats, palm jewelry was another stimulus to miniaturize. José Flores said that Fidel Becerro and Toribio Río were already weaving jewelry from plastic filament in the 1950s. Mexican girls wear earrings hung with miniature woven stars, baskets, fans, and hats as part of their costumes for Corpus Christi and the Day of Guadalupe (December 12). On these holidays, children in many parts of Mexico traditionally attend church dressed as "*inditos*" (Indians).

Miniature leather sandals (*huarachitos*) are a side industry of Chigmecatitlán jewelry making that helps confirm Chigmecatitlán's prominence as a miniaturist town. Pedro Anzures, Benjamín Sandoval, and another man were the first to make these miniature sandals; now Alberto Vidales, Juan Sordo, and Agustín Vidales carry on the practice.

Don Alberto Vidales demonstrated one afternoon how he and his wife, Jesusa Zamora, make huarachitos and assemble them into earrings. We sat in the patio of his house behind a blue-painted gate, where he also dispenses dried palm fronds, plastic raffia, and plumbing supplies. He had ordered a hollow punch or *sacabocado* forged in Guadalajara to stamp out the sandal soles. Laying a sheet of kidskin over a round mesquite chopping block such as Mexican butchers use, he placed the sacabocado on the leather and struck it with a metal hammer to punch out a tiny leather sole. He tapped on a sharpened screwdriver to pierce four slits in the sole where the leather straps, which are plaited like palm, would be inserted. He and his wife assemble the earrings with jeweler's pliers using wire and links from a chain. They add minute red lacquer bowls from Guerrero and tiny black trays from Michoacán bought at fairs.

Juan Sordo is another maker of miniature huaraches, who learned the technique from Alberto Vidales. He has been living for eighteen years in Puebla, where he owns a modest store a block away from the University of Puebla and sells *fantasía* such as imported costume jewelry, purses, and barrettes. He made some tiny sandals as we talked in the front room of his store, while keeping an eye on the soccer game on television. The uppers are kidskin, softened in water; the soles are patent leather. Juan Sordo returns to Chigmecatitlán to stamp out the soles because he, like Alberto Vidales, uses a mesquite trunk and a sacabocado he commissioned from a town blacksmith. He showed me a box of miniature sandal lasts (*hormas*), each numbered, that he and his father whittled from *tnu skulali* wood he cut a long time ago in the Atoyac gorge below town.

Agustín Vidales, a third huarachito maker, frankly admits to copying the design to increase his stock of merchandise: "They didn't want to sell them to me because I would only buy half a gross. I took one apart to see how it was made. "*Ni modo, cuando tiene uno hambre hay que hacer*" (When you're hungry you have to do something). With the stringent standards characteristic of this artisan, he modified the pattern slightly, making the tops slanted, noting that is how real huaraches are shaped.

WHAT THE ANCESTORS LEFT US

Little palm animals—animalitos—are a possible exception to the claim that miniatures have only been made since the 1960s. Zoomorphic figures appear to predate anthropomorphic figures among palm miniatures. José Flores remembers the renowned palm weaver Vicenta Chávez making little animals "*desde que yo era chamaquito*" (since I was little). Fernández Ledesma (1930:45) comments on the prevalence of animal themes in Mexican toys: "The preferred subject matter and that most commonly used in the manufacture of our toys seems to be . . .

the representation of animals." He hypothesizes a dual influence: the daily observation of animals and also "a heritage of ancestral animal worship" (Fernández Ledesma 1930:46), the latter perhaps a reference to the *tonal* or animal spirit companion complex of many Mexican Indian groups.

The earliest weaver of tiny animals now living is Doña Vicenta Chávez. In her youth, she produced the phenomenal quantity of four dozen per day, twenty-four dozen per week. Pastor Flores, age sixty-seven, confirmed this: "Doña Vicenta Chávez, I remember, made mice, rabbits, later squirrels when I was a boy." Vicenta Chávez herself told me that she began weaving little animals when she got married around the age of eighteen, circa 1937. The first to weave palm mice was a man named Zumaria Espinosa, older than she, followed by others weaving pigs and squirrels. Doña Vicenta's late husband, who built stone houses, is credited with inventing the palm rabbit.

Some of the oldest residents, including a couple in their eighties, said they observed diminutive palm animals in their childhood. One man I interviewed even agreed with my suggestion that they might be exceedingly old: "*Es lo que nos dejaron los ancestros*" (This is what the ancestors left us). But despite the allure of this statement, it is problematic. There is disagreement among the townspeople about the age of miniature animals. Don Agustín Vidales (b. 1928) insists that in his grandparents' time and when he was a boy "*no hacían miniaturas*," not even miniature animals. The problem may lie in definitions, that is, distinguishing the miniature from the merely small.

MINIATURIZATION BEFORE MY EYES

Local entrepreneur Jacinto Flores advocates miniaturization as a strategy to increase palm weavers' income as well as his own. An occasional weaver himself, his livelihood depends on buying crafts from a cadre of local artisans and reselling them at prestigious venues such as FONART and the Sanborns chain in Puebla and Mexico City. He deals with twenty artisans and makes the rounds of his suppliers every Saturday to ensure them a regular income. He concentrates on *muñequitos* like the ones José Flores and Catalina Escalante developed, inch-high human figurines on flat bases.

He encourages artisans under his tutelage to reduce the scale of their pieces to sell more with less work. He cited the example of a man who wove bicyclists, whose wife wove clowns. The man had lived in Campeche for fifty years and in 1997 had just come back to town to wait out the nationwide economic recession. Jacinto was going to coach him on miniaturizing the cyclists. Jacinto suggested the man combine his wife's clowns with his bicycles. The clowns' features would be of thread instead of palm. The wheels would have fewer spokes. One bike would be a unicycle. The clowns would wear different hats. One would be a plain man, not a clown. The man was willing to try Jacinto's advice because "*el hambre es canija*" (hunger is vicious).

Gloria Anzures is another of Jacinto's converts, who specializes in gossamer-thin *garzas* (herons) and *guajolotes* (turkeys). Sitting in a dark room with her two preschool-age daughters nearby, Doña Gloria explained that she had made a tactical shift from raffia to palm and from large to miniature scale. She had started out at age ten or twelve making four-spoke raffia baskets with her mother, then larger eight-spoke baskets. Almost nobody bought them. On a selling trip with her mother to Ciudad Serdán, Puebla, she noticed that herons sold well, and she began to make large 3½" herons. Three years ago she switched to

FIGURE 4.4 Miniature bicyclist and unicyclist.

FIGURE 4.5 An artisan and her daughter with miniature herons.

miniatures: "With just two palms I can make a miniature heron, including the base." She weaves whenever she has time, making six to eight herons per day, one to two dozen per week, if she concentrates. I asked what she thought about while weaving miniatures. "*Ojalá que termine rápido*" (I hope I finish fast).

Doña Gloria's pragmatic statement reveals the effectiveness of Don Jacinto's strategy of streamlining, which responds to her interest in saving time. Such bald statements efface the mystique that has been constructed in the metropolis about the miniature and scrawl over it with the graffiti of resigned practicality. Her pragmatic motivation was worlds away from the dramatic and magical speech Ochoa (1993:44) quotes from two Chigmecatitlán artisans in his thesis on musical bands:

> *We, as players in bands, have created little palm figures [monitos] because we feel they are a part of ourselves. Those little men, they walk at night all around María (name used for the town), they make their way into the churchyard and start playing their instruments; afterwards they head for the cemetery and make music at daybreak for the deceased who were musicians in life. Later we sell those elves [duendes] out of necessity, and afterwards we weave more and more so the dead people will never go without hearing their sound. But the ones we sell will never play music again, because they play only for us.*

In this speech, the palm toys appear to have a potential life before and after the action frozen in tableau, like the imaginary life of the inhabitants of a dollhouse (Stewart 1993:54). I never heard anyone talk about the miniature with that kind of personified intimacy during my months in Chigmecatitlán.

DELUSIONS OF SMALL SCALE

Down in the basement of the Museum of Anthropology in Mexico City, where ethnographers work behind a guarded checkpoint, the INAH houses its woven palm collections. The large pieces in storage from Chigmecatitlán testify to the recent shrinking process and a concomitant movement to simplicity. The elaborate detail expended on large figures from the past is illustrated by my notes on three riders, accessioned in 1963, in the INAH collection:[6]

> *The jinetes have saddles. Wear ties. There are three pineapples in each side basket. Animal has sewn palm eyes and nostrils; man has sewn thread eyes, eyebrows, nose, mouth. Rider holds reins. One wears a jacket (they wear three kinds of jackets) and has a different kind of fruit along with the pineapples.* Conclusion: *These figures had more elaborate details than the ones now.*

The sewn thread eyes and mouth are the only facial features that the current miniature rider retains. Scaling down is "an act of condensation" (Albers 1970, preface, n.p.). It is evident that miniature figurines in Chigmecatitlán are not isomorphic with large figurines, but highly edited versions of their referents, mere sketches that imply much in abbreviated form.

To consumers, miniatures appear to require greater care and patience to weave than larger crafts, but the appearance of perfection is misleading. According to Jacinto Flores, it takes greater skill to make large-scale figures *well* than to make miniatures. Imperfections in a little figure will not be noticed, he said. This is due to the Lilliputian principle that minification reduces defects (Jacobs 1953:5). Gulliver reflects, during his voyage to Brobdingnag,

> *I Remember when I was at Lilliput, the Complexion of those diminutive People appeared to me the fairest in the World; and talking upon this Subject with a Person of Learning there, who was an intimate Friend of mine, he said that my Face appeared much fairer and smoother*

FIGURES 4.6-4.7 A comparison of a small and large *china* blown up to the same size shows that they are not isomorphic. *Left,* one-inch china. Skirt contains seven rows. Rebozo is one strand of palm. Price: three pesos. *Right,* ten-inch china. Skirt contains forty-eight warps by fifty wefts. Rebozo contains five warps by forty-eight wefts. Price: eight to ten pesos.

> *when he looked on me from the Ground, than it did upon a nearer View when I took him up in my Hand, and brought him close, which he confessed was at first a very shocking Sight.*

I asked an artisan who had worked in both large and small scale which was harder. "It's more work to make large things. It's more repetitions. The palm has to be wide and long to make something big. With miniatures, I barely start and I'm finished." A teacher listening to our conversation commented that it seemed as though the opposite were true.

Miniaturization physically involves two parameters: the width of the palm and the number of strands or repetitions. Jacinto Flores's followers thus reason that paring a figure down to essentials saves both materials and labor. In economic terms, miniatures bring in 50 percent more money per day than large dolls.

| Large china | 8 pesos each x 2 per day = 16 pesos/day |
| Miniature china | 3 pesos each x 8 per day = 24 pesos/day |

Another advantage of size reduction is that smaller pieces do not require the skeletal underpinnings large pieces do. Artisans just learning to make miniatures are unsure of how well supported structurally the figures need to be. Jacinto assures them that miniatures do not need to withstand much stress of handling, since customers tend to grasp them delicately. Moreover, Jacinto recommends that artisans weave only two strands per leg, rather than the standard three of larger figures. And, he told me, all miniatures are woven *de uno en uno* (checker weave), which is easier than the traditional *de dos en dos* (twill weave).

Not everyone in Chigmecatitlán heeds Don Jacinto's advice to simplify. Agustín Vidales is the exception, a purist whom Don Jacinto admires as "a true artist" whose "work is very fine." Agustín Vidales invests extra effort in his miniatures without earning more. When I went to see Don Agustín, he was watching the soccer game on television, the blue and yellow harlequin legs he was plaiting scattered on the floor under his chair. He held one up to show that it was made with his trademark eight palms, while other people's are made with only six.

"It doesn't look the same. With eight it looks different. Even though you work quicker with six palms. Okay, so I'm crazy!" He began with medium size, but "I always liked working thin" which he considers more difficult, although he says "my eyesight is tired."

Not everyone is capable of producing miniatures, Don Jacinto admitted. "If you don't have the talent to make miniatures, you won't be able to make them." Take, for example, Basilio Herrera, Celina Zamora, and Laura Zamora, the trio who make large, medium, and small china and charro dolls. "People want smaller ones," they told me. A buyer named Don Erasto came from Catarina looking for miniatures, but they could not make them: "We're used to making big ones." Or consider Librado Beltrán, who, when I asked what size crafts he makes, answered: "Don Jacinto wants them smaller, but I can't do it." Or León Pérez, who said other people make fun of him and say his work is "all thumbs"; why can't he do finer weaving? He replies, "I can't make them any bigger or smaller."

Jacinto Flores's mother says he is a perfectionist who would complain, "This is ugly!" when he didn't like her figurines. She would cut off their heads out of spite. They explained later that the heads were disproportionate to the bodies and could be redone. When I mentioned this story, one artisan remarked that the first thing Jacinto notices in a group of miniatures is one that is not right, e.g., a face that needs redoing. Jacinto's particular sense of scale leads him to distinguish "imitation miniatures" from the real thing. He rejected a small *ranchero* on my shelf. "This is ugly. I wouldn't sell it."

Exactly how scale is determined, though, is idiosyncratic. Unlike miniatures in the United States and Europe, which adhere to conventional scales for commercial and aesthetic reasons (Cooper-Hewitt Museum 1983:10), miniature scale in Mexico is inexact and arbitrary. People gauge size by the joints of their fingers; as with Tom Thumb, the hand is the measure of the miniature (Stewart 1993:46). "*Es al puro tanteo*" (It's pure estimate) (Léon Pérez, June 1997).

POLITICS OF THE MINIATURE

Government officials have intervened in Chigmecatitlán's turn toward the miniature. It was at the request of the first lady of Puebla that José Flores and Catalina Escalante first wove a miniature nativity in the 1980s, an event that was in turn the catalyst for creating other reduced-scale figures. Governor Mariano Piña Olaya's wife had founded Arte Popular-DIF Puebla, a folk art shop in the city of Puebla at 5 Oriente 3.[7] José Flores recounts:

> It was during Governor Piña Olaya's term [1987–93]. The governor's wife asked for crafts to sell in the DIF. She asked my son for a nativity which she wanted to sell in the store; they already had pottery ones. My son asked my wife to make one. The first one she made was medium-sized.
>
> "The nativity is very pretty but why don't you make it in miniature?"
>
> It was easier for us to make large things. To form the little face was very hard for us. Working on the little angel was very hard for my wife. Figuring out how to make the wings was extremely hard. And all the figures were different; we discarded lots of figures while we were searching. The nativity took one to two months working every day. The Christ Child, we had no idea. He had to be even smaller than the other figures. I made Joseph with the lily. We copied the comedia on December 28th and the nativity in church.

The nativity motif reinforces urban consumers' perception of popular religiosity in Mexico, but in fact, the naturalistic clay or plastic nativities most Mexican families set up are unlike the abstract ones they produce for export. In the words of Jacinto Flores, "The nativity was made to sell." As Victoria Novelo (1993:81) aptly remarks, "When asked the origin of such-and-such a craft style, the name often shows up of some functionary, well known in intellectual circles, who came up with the idea." She also says, dryly, "directors of official crafts agencies and shop owners have turned out to be good creators of traditions" (Novelo 1993:46). In the case of the miniature palm nativity, the first lady not only suggests the theme but also requests that it be made smaller, presumably based on her feeling for the qualities that constitute typical Mexican crafts.

Palm crafts mediate the interaction between politicians and townspeople on the rare occasions when candidates for political office come to Chigmecatitlán on election campaigns. Politicians' visits are virtually the only instances when crafts are publicly displayed. The candidates put on necklaces of palm beads like Hawaiian leis in a demonstration of symbolic solidarity with the artisans.

The municipal president paid little attention to local crafts at the outset of his term of office in February 1996 but was forced to become involved after the governor of Puebla, Manuel Bartlett Díaz, proclaimed his enthusiasm for the miniature. In preparation for Governor Bartlett's imminent visit to Chigmecatitlán in June 1996, the municipal president asked Doña Imelda Zamora, the head of a group of women artisans, to organize a crafts exhibit on the town square in honor of the governor's visit. The municipal president had shortsightedly closed the new palm crafts museum inaugurated by his predecessor. Meanwhile, the artisans allegedly wrote the governor a letter asking him "to support artesanías in our town, since it is our livelihood and the municipal president doesn't support us." When Governor Bartlett arrived, he brought a substantial monetary contribution for Chigmecatitlán in the form of a 300,000-peso check (100,000 pesos according to another version of the story). He and his entourage wore the accustomed necklaces of palm beads. The governor reportedly was delighted by the tiny crafts and went from table to table picking out pieces, which he was given on the spot as gifts. Furthermore, he purchased numerous crafts and asked the municipal president to continue to supply him periodically with miniatures, which is why the municipal president is now in the miniatures business. One palm weaver said she heard they were buying at the town hall, but "they only want miniature," which she doesn't know how to make.

I asked artisans why Governor Bartlett wanted miniatures. They suggested that they were gifts for friends and dignitaries. My interpretation is that his appreciation for miniatures confirms the importance of Mexican folk crafts as cultural capital. I speculate that the fame of miniatures as meaningful exemplars of artistic heritage and cultural identity reinforces the traditional legitimacy of the PRI old guard to which Governor Bartlett belongs. Also, of course, they represent the most picturesque of Puebla's image for export.

SELECTING FOR THE MINIATURE

Chigmecatitlán has distinguished itself among surrounding towns in Puebla and throughout the Mixtec region as a specialist in the miniature. Exactly why that occurred is open to question. Whether the region was once knee-deep in similar craft production and only Chigmecatitlán retained it, like water in a tidepool, is unknown.

Rather than size changes in a single direction, there might have been oscillations of size in the past (Pauline Turner Strong, personal communication, 1997). Ethnomusicologist Guillermo Contreras (personal communication, 1997) agrees; he gives the analogy of the musical instrument known as the *jarana*. Until 1925 the jarana was small, according to archival sources; it became larger in the nationalist period (1920–40), partly to make the sound bigger. Then it shrank again under the influence of the modern, such as compact cars in which huge instruments could not be transported, and microphones which amplified smaller sounds.

It is worth considering whether the increase in tourism in Mexico since the 1970s has constituted pressure to miniaturize. Gill (1976:108) alludes to "the frequently noted miniaturization of a craft or art when it reaches a stage of overt commercialism" (cf. Babcock, Monthan, and Monthan [1986:19] on Pueblo pottery souvenirs). Susan Stewart (1993:144) writes on the miniaturization of baskets under the influence of tourism, "They have moved from the domain of use value to the domain of *gift,* where exchange is abstracted to the level of social relations and away from the level of materials and processes." In theory, such crafts begin life as functional objects but become decorative symbols when transferred to a new environment as souvenirs. As a consequence of their lack of utility, their dimensions may be exaggerated either up or down.

The question is nuanced in Chigmecatitlán, however, where crafts were always aimed at outside markets rather than internal use. To use a coals-to-Newcastle analogy, people in Chigmecatitlán do not use palm crafts because they weary of them. "They are tired of them, they can't stand them. It's like clay in Acatlán." (The last comment alludes to Acatlán in southern Puebla.)

Like the proverbial shoemaker whose children go barefoot, artisans may refer to their handiwork as "*juguetitos,*" little toys, but their children rarely play with the toys.[8] Jacinto Flores was not allowed to play with miniatures as a boy in the 1970s. "Miniatures were something fantastic, untouchable" (cf. Rubín de la Borbolla 1963:19). One woman whose parents sold crafts, however, remembered playing with palm dolls when she was a girl in the 1960s. Another artisan created a medium-sized bull rider expressly for her seven-year-old son, but after the fashion of toys, it was left out in the rain and disintegrated.

I asked Doña Vicenta Chávez if people ever placed miniature implements ceremonially in babies' hands at baptism to symbolize their future occupations according to gender. This practice, which Sahagún documents among the Aztecs in the *Florentine Codex,* remains customary among some Mayan Indian groups. Putting her own spin on the question, she said people in Chigmecatitlán were too poor to put toys in babies' hands.

January 6 is Epiphany, when the Three Kings leave presents in children's shoes. A few days after Epiphany, I asked the shy girls who used to descend on my house in their white Monday school uniforms asking for a drink of water and poking desultorily at things, what the Three Kings brought them. "Nothing," they said. Embarrassed, I passed out some packs of Wrigley's gum. I had temporarily forgotten how different Chigmecatitlán was from the image of Mexico in my mind.

I found no idiosyncrasy in the character of the town that would have explained why people produce miniatures, some parallel with another aspect of their lives or even some "pattern of culture" à la Ruth Benedict (1934). I did not find anything linking miniatures to their particular situation in life: not a direct tie to antiquity, not playfulness, not a personal affinity for the diminutive. The townspeople were overwhelmingly non-collectors, people with sparse material culture except the meaningful geography of the local landscape, a "sense of place" (Feld and Basso 1996).

My research in Chigmecatitlán failed to support the hypothesis of a pre-Hispanic legacy for the small objects its inhabitants produce. Instead, the recent influence of middlemen has been crucial to the process of miniaturization. They—not the Mixtec palm weavers—are responsible for ever-decreasing scale. As a local vendor succinctly put it, "It's gotten smaller because people look for small."

Sabino Vázquez, the villain of José Flores's narrative, selects only miniatures from Don José's assortment of sizes. I conclude that miniatures have been literally "selected for" historically from a range of sizes being made. Since the 1960s, pressure from middlemen has resulted in the near disappearance of large and medium sizes and an intensification of small size. These middlemen may be outsiders (*ñu kó*) like Sabino Vázquez, the first lady, and the governor; insiders (*ni'i viñu*) like Jacinto Flores; or "people of Catarina" (*ñu*) whom the artisans constantly invoke. "We just can't make them any smaller!" is the plaintive response of the weavers. That *all* of the impetus for shrinking crafts is coming from dealers contradicts the longstanding, generic portrayal of Mexican Indian artisans as miniaturists par excellence. One must conclude that, at least in Chigmecatitlán, the Mexican "delight in minuteness" (Castro Leal 1940:17) is on the part of the middlemen and consumers, not the artisans.

CHAPTER 5

The Priest: Ritual Contexts of the Miniature

Ihe rigorous exercise of Catholic ritual provides a framework for life in Santa María Chigmecatitlán, and devoutness is a hallmark of the town as seen by the local people themselves. Catholic practice runs parallel to the production of miniatures, but occasionally religion and crafts intersect. How does local Catholicism impinge on the production of palm toys? Victor Turner and Edith Turner (1982:215) have theorized a link between Catholicism and iconophilia—a historic attachment to art—as opposed to the word-centeredness of Protestantism. Guided by the knowledge of the abiding native Mexican religious practices of antiquity, one might expect to find locally made objects employed as ritual paraphernalia. This chapter examines the religious context of craft making in Chigmecatitlán and, ultimately, the complexity of these issues.

> Sir: The priest of Santa Maria Chicmecatitlan, for two years going on three, has been suffering patiently the disobedience, scorn, insults and surreptitious accusations of his parishioners, whom he has tried at the cost of suffering to keep in peace and repose, as well as to reduce to the subordination so necessary for every community and Kingdom, for the common tranquility of superiors and subordinates; far from achieving the desired object, they continue with their wild ideas to the point that it has entered their heads to banish him *(AGN-Criminal, 334, 7, f. 261)*.

With these anguished words, the parish priest of Chigmecatitlán, Mariano Paz y Sánchez, begins a testimonial in self-defense to the Royal Prosecutor-Protector of Indians.[1] It is 1811, the last decade of three centuries of Spanish colonial rule. The parishioners of Chigmecatitlán have accused him of misdeeds before the viceroy and archbishop of Mexico. Their complaints have resulted in his superiors chastising him in a decree and ordering him to conform to the established tariffs for the sacraments, to treat the Indians well, and not to demand their unpaid personal service (AGN-Criminal, 334, 7, 261v). The priest retaliates by accusing the parishioners of insubordination and charging an outside teacher from Tepexi named Bernabé Pablo Ojeda as the ringleader who has corrupted the villagers.

The priest's testimony, at times self-righteous, at times condescending, at times paranoid, unfolds in a cathartic unveiling of loneliness and pain so eloquent that it is difficult not to sympathize with him in part. His letter reveals the extreme depth of misunderstanding, rooted in cultural difference and a contest for power, between the priest and the Mixtec Indian villagers of Chigmecatitlán. This conflict parallels the relations between the priest, other outsiders, and the townspeople in the ten months I lived in Chigmecatitlán.

A struggle for religious hegemony has been waged off and on in the stark desert of Chigmecatitlán since the Spanish political conquest of southern Puebla in 1520 and 1521. Chigmecatitlán belonged to the parish of Tepexi de la Seda (now Tepexi de Rodríguez) until it was raised to its own parish in 1768 (AGN-Indios 62, 41, 58–59; Jäcklein 1978:112). That Chigmecatitlán was marginal to the sphere of influence of the Tepexi clergy, and thus had the opportunity to develop its own systems of worship, is suggested by Dr. Rubio's report in 1653 on his visit to the Dominicans of Tepexi. Rubio writes that there was only one religious who spoke "Chochona" [Popoloca; Jäcklein 1974:21], who had to minister to all thirty-two towns in the parish of Tepexi.[2]

In the nineteenth century, as now, the conflict was between the normative efforts of an outsider priest and the ingrained customs of the townspeople. The geographical setting of the town has not changed much over the centuries, and it is tempting to project an eternal, stable identity onto the Indian villagers and priest of then and now—which would be a mistake. But it is compelling how, over the centuries, the town has received outsiders with more or less altruistic or selfish purposes, and how the two motives intertwine, making it almost meaningless which is which. The landscape of the town is like a bare stage set on which people play the characters of good and evil, like angels and devils in the Pastorela they perform every year on December 28.

This chapter is about conflict and dissonance: conflict between townspeople and outsiders; dissonance between the pleasant charm that the colorful miniature crafts project, even now, and the often men-

FIGURE 5.1 Angels march onto the stage in the Pastorela or Shepherds' Play, Chigmecatitlán. December 28, 1995.

acing circumstances of life in the town as I experienced it. My objectives in this chapter are twofold. First, to show how miniatures and other crafts are incorporated into Catholic ritual life in the town. Second, to highlight the contrast, from my perspective, between the happiness and playfulness the palm figurines portray and the harshness and hostility of the environment in which they are produced. The narrative action that ties these themes together is the arrival of a new Catholic priest in town and his clash with a born-again evangelist doctor already residing there, culminating in the banishment of the doctor. In this volatile climate of rumor, violence, and distrust, there was suspicion that I might be a missionary as well.

This chapter also attempts, through a narrative of "engaged subjectivity," to uncover the awkward circumstances of fieldwork. I intersperse the modern ethnographic account with transcripts from the 1811 criminal case between an accused Chigmecatitlán priest, Mariano Paz y Sánchez, and his parishioners to suggest historical echoes between that conflict and the current conflicts over the proper observance of religious ceremonies and the presence of outsiders in the contested space of the town.

Late at night in July 1997, the priest, the kindergarten teacher, the clinic resident, and I are rattling along in the cab of the priest's dilapidated white pickup truck on the lonely dirt road from the highway turnoff at La Monera toward Chigmecatitlán. The headlights pick out shadows of looming cacti and rocks. I have returned after a year away and am now rooming at the medical clinic with the two other women. This afternoon we have driven to Puebla for them to vote and to fill up the water bottles, which are rolling around in the back of the truck.

For the third time since my arrival two weeks ago, the priest is obsessively picking at the scab of events leading to the ousting of the evangelist doctor by a mob last November, when I was already home in Austin.

"He must have been like some kind of Lucifer!" the kindergarten teacher commiserates.

Until now I have held my tongue out of fear: of meddling in an internal dispute, of being ostracized for disagreeing with the priest, of being labeled an evangelist, of being run out of town myself. But I can't stand it any longer.

"He was not a Lucifer. He was a good person! You didn't know him," I snap at the teacher.

When I first came to Chigmecatitlán to do research on the miniature in October 1995, I was persona non grata to some of the people, half of whom ignored me when I greeted them in passing (*adiós* or *kuani*). "People from Chigmecatitlán don't talk," a man from across the river in Huatlatlauca agreed. Their coldness was disconcerting. The doctor, in contrast, was friendly from the start. He reassured me that he, too, had been lonely with no one but the scorpions when he first arrived from Puebla two years earlier. He set out to renovate the abandoned stone house he rented down the street and brought his young family to live there on a five-year plan.

He was a medical doctor and his wife ran a pharmacy, but an incident in November 1995 made it obvious to me that they were also born-again evangelical missionaries. While carrying a heavy bucket of water in the dark, I stumbled into an uncovered trench that the plumber had dug for the sewer pipe. Surrounded by the rubble and mud of my half-ruined house that night, I realized for the first time how isolated I was. By midnight I was dragging myself down the street to the doctor's house, witnessed impassively by the street dogs and a drunk recumbent on the pavers. The doctor came back with me in his bathrobe. Instead of a pain pill, he pulled out a Spanish-language paperback Bible and asked me to read the twenty-fifth Psalm of David out loud, which I awkwardly did. Evidently he thought my psychic pain greater than the pain in my foot.

> *PSALM 25 (Prayer for Guidance and Deliverance)*
> *To you, O Lord, I lift up my soul,*
> *O my God, in you I trust;*
> *do not let me be put to shame;*
> *do not let my enemies exult over me.*
> *Do not let those who wait for you*
> *be put to shame.*

Reading the psalm about "my enemies," I now realize he thought we had a common enemy: the people of Chigmecatitlán.

> My parishioners, who belong to the district headed by Tepexic de las Sedas, have the ill luck of bringing to this Town of yours a plebeian Indian from there, whose name is Bernabé Pablo Ojeda, with the pretext that he would teach the children, and look how he has managed his affairs. He has turned them from bad to worse with his complaints: which is why at my request a case has been brought against him for seduction in the aforementioned Tepexic, as the case file found in the tribunal will convince you *(AGN-Criminal, 334, 7, f. 261)*.

The doctor and his wife were well regarded at first. His likeness stares out of snapshots of the school committee, proof that he was a *"principal,"* an eminent person worthy of respect. He was the sole physician in town. The latest clinic resident, a Panamanian fulfilling her social service at the state-run clinic, had allegedly pleaded sexual harassment as an excuse to flee her post. Tipsy patients pounding on the clinic door in the middle of the night unnerved her, someone stole her clothes off the clothesline, and the municipal president reprimanded her for charging ten pesos per consultation instead of the approved three pesos. The last straw was an argument with the proprietor of the town's only telephone over the cost of a long-distance call home. The clinic resident escaped in tears on the 2:30 bus to Puebla and sent her boyfriend to collect her boxes.

After her departure, the evangelist doctor and his wife were the only local source of antibiotics, condoms, and scorpion antivenin. They provided other valuable services: in addition to volunteering at the schools their children attended, the doctor's wife, for a fee, would bake birthday cakes, sew dresses for town dances, and make costumes for school pageants.

The charismatic doctor helped advance my fieldwork by introducing me to artisans, recording and typing up a Mixtec practice dialogue, lending me books, and inviting me to lunch with his family. We traded ideas for fixing our rented houses; when I installed screens on my windows to keep the mosquitoes out, he followed suit. He lectured me on my errors of propriety: If a woman drinks beer in public, it means she's looking for a man. Don't look into the cantina when you walk by. Don't say anything negative or blasphemous, because everyone has some good in him. But don't trust anyone except God.

My impression is that the doctor's missionary activities caused barely a ripple. I heard he was reviewing the Lord's Prayer in Mixtec with the "brothers" in town, who numbered only two families, as far as I knew. He handed out New Testaments and invited friends to drink coffee and watch a video in Mixtec on the life of Christ. Fortuny (1989), in her study of Protestant conversion in southeastern Mexico, notes that many converts first attend meetings for entertainment, embracing Protestantism as religious experience only later as needed to solve concrete personal problems. As for me, I felt impatient but not threatened by the doctor's persistent religious references. For example: One morning he kept me company while I was scrubbing laundry in my yard. As we listened to the odd rhythm of bells at the parish church, he remarked that someone died and he had attended at the death. I prodded him for details on the code of the bells, but instead he suddenly asked, "Are *you* prepared to die?"

> On the last day of October of last year before noon I ordered the volley bells readied so that, when the hour struck, they would ring with the solemnity the day demanded. On the stroke of twelve a continuous chiming began, knowing the spirit in which they did it, I dissembled without speaking the slightest word. The ringleader *fiscal*[3] came in very drunk and said, "Mister, the Townspeople are complaining, because last year they did not ring very much on this day. Now I have come to tell you that even though the bells might break, the Town will pay for them to ring all day and all night."

. . . I suspended the ringing and he countered by ordering that it continue, I was thus obliged to go out and get the Sacristans down, so the ringing would cease. Afterward it continued just as wild until midnight without ceasing an iota. I leave Your Excellency to wonder how my spirit felt such a keen provocation as this? *(AGN-Criminal, 334, 7, f. 263v).*

In the triangular interactions between the doctor, the townspeople, and me, the personal intersected with differences in class and ethnicity. I sometimes sensed that as outsiders, the doctor and I were subtly competing for influence over the local people. A mutual friend was working on both my house and the doctor's house. I remarked to the friend that the presence of caliche soil in Chigmecatitlán meant the land was covered by an underwater coral reef millions of years ago. The doctor countered by telling him I was mistaken; the fish fossils at the nearby Pie de Vaca museum were formed when it rained for forty days and forty nights.

My general aversion to evangelism, nevertheless, was hypocritically sublimated until my turf was threatened. I envied the doctor's privileged access to artisans' homes, which I lacked. Like many outsiders, the doctor could not resist the business opportunity to buy miniatures to sell outside the town. He began to commission miniature mariachis for a colleague to sell at a shop in Ciudad Juárez on the Texas border. I resented what I saw as a conflict of interest; as a doctor he made house calls, I fumed, then he used the opportunity to buy crafts and try to convert people. I saw it as exploitation, uncomfortably aware that, in a sense, all of us outsiders were exploiting the people of the town, who, in most cases, had not bid us to come.

My friendship with the doctor inevitably backfired. I learned much later that an old man we visited died believing our long interview about the town's history was only a cover for my supposed goal of converting him. I began to subtly distance myself from the doctor and his family, partly out of worry that our friendship was tarring me with the same brush, and partly because I made other friends in the town and relied less on their generosity.

"THEY ARE VERY CATHOLIC HERE . . ."

Suffice it to say to Your Excellency that there is not a day of my life that they do not give me cause for displeasure. Every day at four in the morning, if not earlier, the flock of mayordomos for the saints enters the church to burn candles and incense giving me a rude awakening with the clamor, and it is not just that, but that since my arrival all my effort has been [to see that] women not enter the church at that hour, and I have not succeeded, despite having repeatedly arisen at that hour to remove them, leaving the men *(AGN-Criminal, 334, 7, f. 264)*.

Muffled footsteps outside my window before dawn; black-hooded women wearing the large scapulars of their sodalities; the soft, high-pitched singing of "Las Mañanitas"; the stately, slow band revving up; the deep, booming drum coming in half a beat later: these murmurs of processions in the dark added to my feeling of fear, alienation, strangeness, and being out of place. Nighttime, when many religious ceremonies were held, was tinged with horror. I was already uneasy from the scorpions and other creatures that would scurry out from under anything I picked up.[4] I could not get used to the sudden explosions of cannons and the *buscapiés*[5] that men and boys were snapping in the plaza for the entire month of December and well into January. The drunks who unintelligibly harangued me put me on edge. The priest said later he saw me as a misfit, *un bicho raro*. Women who met me for the first time would cluck, "*Sola? Está SOLITA? No tiene miedo?*" It finally occurred to me to ask what I was supposed to be afraid of, but they were silent. At New Year's, when young men dress up as women or as rustic old men in serapes and go from house to house begging for alms to buy more fireworks, there was a loud pounding on my door that I didn't answer since I was already in bed. Next day the telephone lady said I did well not to open the door.

I was looking forward to my first *posada,* the party held from December 16 to Christmas Eve that is a staple of Mexican folklore (Pettit and Pettit 1978). Two families a night hosted posadas for each of the nine days until Christmas Eve. On the first night of Las Posadas, I joined a procession of revelers who were singing and carrying a statue of the archangel Gabriel, Mary on a donkey, and Joseph to the house of the hosts (*ve chun, 'casa fiesta'*). Unfortunately, the customary piñata had been supplanted by teenagers on the roof showering the crowd below with sweets. The manna turned aggressive as the teenagers hurled the treats at the crowd now cowering against the wall. A hard projectile hit me in the eye, but no one offered aid. After that, my attitude toward the town was increasingly hostile.

An overriding sense of religious obligation, which to my eyes verged on the fanatical, ruled Chigmecatitlán. Catholic ritual permeated everyday life. Others concur with this assessment (Manrique 1964:203). Ochoa (1993:53) describes Chigmecatitlán as a "small town that lives its faith at all hours." Even the priest considered Chigmecatitlán exceptionally devout, remarking, "There are people who do research, like you; people who work; and people dedicated to the cult. Chigmecatitlán is dedicated to the cult." The townspeople habitually tempered their statements with "*si Dios quiere*" (God willing) and "*Gracias a Dios*" (thank God). The women spoke approvingly of a new clinic resident because she stuck religious cards in the window frame at the clinic. The children wore brown cloth scapulars of the Virgen del Carmen to protect them from evil.

If a strong sense of religious obligation defines the townspeople's relationship to the town, the mass and the procession are its main public manifestations. One might ask, "will there be fireworks?" I was told, but never, "will there be a mass?" All festivals, including children's birthdays and graduations, were commemorated with a mass. There were people so devout they attended mass two or three times a day. The parish church of the Immaculate Conception of Mary could seat about 250 people, and they went early to "*ganar banco*" (get a seat) at major masses. Late arrivals and mothers with young children stood or knelt quietly outside the portal in the glaring sun. Chigmecatitlán was unusual because almost as many men as women attended. They sat divided by gender, the women looking ominous from behind, their heads draped with black rebozos.[6]

At first I went to mass out of obligation. Not being religious, I felt out of place. I wanted to faint from the continual kneeling and standing, the old women squeezing against me, and the stench of dirt and sweat.

> Often, after the Sabbath chores of the annex [Santa Catarina], it is necessary for me to go personally with the Alcaldes through the greater part of Town, getting people of both sexes out of their houses so they will go to mass. I have found in the houses pairs of yoked oxen, I have found them heading for the fields, I have found donkeys saddled up with loads on their backs, about to take a journey, while the church bells call to mass; I have brought the oxen up to the plaza, the donkeys to the rectory and the men to the church, whom after mass I have sent on their way in peace. I have met others on the road whom I have turned back to hear mass and

many have gone in one door and out the other. I would wear Your Excellency out if I continued to relate all that these children of God do, and I would still leave much unsaid *(AGN-Criminal, 334, 7, fs. 264–264v).*

Besides the mass, the other *sine qua non* of Chigmecatitlán ritual life is the procession.[7] A procession minimally consists of the priest, people singing and carrying a holy image, and one of the three bands in town (Los Fuentes, Los Rangel, or Los Sandoval). Processions leave the church; move counterclockwise around the four corners of the town, which are marked by blue crosses; and file back into the church.

Space is periodically reinscribed through the procession in the same way as Dorst (1989:4, after MacCannell 1979) notes that tourists reinscribe the important cultural sites by driving on the roads. The procession can be interpreted both as sanctifying the town with the presence of the saint and as "showing" the town to the saint. Social identity is performed and confirmed via participation in the procession. I was told it was poor etiquette to merely watch a procession. One should join in. The evangelist doctor and his wife were conspicuous for their absence when processions passed their doorway.

DEATH OF THE OLD PRIEST

They brought him to the convent to be buried, where the Indians of the district, with weeping and lamentations that accompanied the grief of the religious and citizens, together celebrated his funeral rites and buried him in the chancel of the high altar.
—Fray Francisco de Burgoa, 1674

The longtime parish priest, Abraham Barragán, died suddenly in March.[8] An ambulance brought his body from the Puebla hospital back to Chigmecatitlán to be buried under the altar. Most of the town turned out to receive him at the wayside shrine on the edge of town, and the archbishop of Puebla came for the funeral. Padre Abraham, a native of Chigmecatitlán, had been the priest for thirty-six years.

I was away when the old priest died and had just driven up when a young woman came to tell me the news. I remember her telling me pointedly *"son muy católicos"* here and that they do not tolerate evangelists. She said Padre Abraham had been very strict about Catholicism, that the townspeople don't like it when someone is "of another religion" (Catholicism was always framed in opposition to all other, unspecified religions), and that missionaries who had come to town in the past had been pressured to leave. "They are capable of running them out, and if they won't leave, they are capable of *killing* them," she had said, in what I took as an oddly misfired threat toward me.

MINIATURES HUNG ON THE SAINTS AS VOTIVE OBJECTS

I had given up on finding any ritual use of the miniature in Chigmeca-titlán when I stumbled across it by accident. It was March 1996 and I had given some friends a ride up the hill to the retreat house that Padre Abraham had built behind the Guadalupe chapel. An earlier priest, Luis B. Palacios, had built the chapel up on a wild hill to replicate the sacred shrine of Guadalupe on the hill of Tepeyac in Mexico City. A group of "*muchachas*" was going to break their four-day religious retreat, and their relatives were waiting to receive them with bouquets of carnations and gladioli.[9]

While the girls were clapping, singing, and swaying in performance, I wandered into the back room and my heart froze. There on a table stood a statue of Christ riding on a donkey, and from the donkey's reins dangled miniatures. Palm stars hung from the bridle; palm ndo'o baskets, a palm bicycle, and a raffia baby rattle hung from the reins. Awaiting the procession of Palm Sunday, the statue was known as "Ramonato" or "Ramoncito," alluding to Domingo de Ramos, or Palm Sunday.[10]

My companions said the crafts were hung on the figure of Christ, carried on a litter in procession, to ask for good sales and, occasionally, to learn to weave. Other artisans I asked consistently confirmed these meanings. A third, perhaps complementary, interpretation is that miniatures are placed on the figures as alms or tithing; the miniatures are later gathered and the proceeds given to the church. People hang artesanías on virtually all the holy images, such as San Antonio, San José, and the Virgen de Guadalupe, "*para que venda y para que aprenda*" (to sell and to learn). Don Benigno Rosas said people hung offerings on saints when he was young and that he had done it himself, "to give thanks for having learned, so the labor will turn out well." León Pérez, a longtime supporter of leftist opposition parties, confirmed the general meaning while personally repudiating the custom; he had never put anything on a saint because his figures, which are relatively large and rough, "wouldn't look right," and besides, "the blessing ought to be for everyone."

I had never noticed, while hearing mass in the dim parish church of the Immaculate Conception, that the statue of San Pedro had a small palm ika basket suspended from the rosary around his neck and a raffia giraffe and ika basket on the support bracket holding up his shelf.[11] Nearby, two palm baskets along with several metal milagros accompanied San Martín de Porres in his glass case. A figure of San Antonio in a niche in the barrio church of San Antonio had miniatures fastened to its case: palm and raffia animals and ika baskets with pineapples. Woven crafts were similarly hung on the saints' statues in Santa Catarina, which is ministered to by the same priest as Chigmecatitlán.

The ex-voto or votive art tradition in Mexico and elsewhere in the Catholic world expresses a spiritual quid pro quo. Symbolic objects are attached to the image of a saint to repay a divine favor. Unlike other forms of tribute such as alms or candles, Medina San Román (1997:109) points out, "the votive offering has a representational character that differentiates it from . . . other types." In Charles Peirce's terms (1931–35, 1958, cited in Firth 1973), this representation may be iconic (a school

TABLE 5.1 Inventory of Crafts as Votive Objects. Church of Santa Catarina Tlaltempan, July 15, 1997

1) In front of a lithograph of the Sacred Heart of Jesus: a three-dimensional woven raffia rectangular block with white and black raffia turkeys and a woven inscription:

Sr. Has Que Nuestro	Lord Make Our
Hogar Sea Un Sitio	Home A Place
De Amor Porque	Of Love Because
Tu Estás Con Nosotros	You Are With Us

2) San Pedro: a little raffia *nda'cho* wallet on a string hanging from his hand.

3) San Isidro Labrador: a raffia *ika* basket of flowers hanging from his finger.

4) San Martín de Porres: a raffia flower tucked into his forearm and a raffia *nda'cho* wallet hanging from his hand, like the one on San Pedro.

5) Virgen de la Asunción: a small red-and-white raffia vase with flowers, set on the floor of her glass case.

graduation photo, little metal animals) or indexical (the umbilical cord from a successful birth, the cast-off crutches of a patient who has been healed).

An icon resembles what it signifies. An index is directly related to, or evidence of, what it signifies. For example, smoke is an index of fire. Most milagros are iconic; a metal milagro of a mule might represent the desire to obtain a real mule. In Chigmecatitlán, on the other hand, a woven palm mule represents palm weaving; thus miniatures used as milagros here are indexical. Miniatures are used as ex-votos within tight parameters reflecting their role as commodities: to petition for better sales or to improve the palm weaver's technique.[12]

An analogous example of the use of miniatures to appeal for divine intercession in mastering a craft is found in the Maya highlands, where "minuscule weavings" are made as offerings to saints and the Virgin as petitions to instruct girls and perfect women's weaving (Oettinger, in Egan 1991:viii; Turok 1988a:82–83). Turok (1988a) locates this votive practice in the syncretism between offerings to Catholic divinities and to the pre-Hispanic patron goddess of weaving. The appeal to the supernatural for weaving skill demonstrates that this ability is not taken for granted, in contrast with the myth of Indian artisans' innate talent as miniaturists.

A precedent also exists for offering miniatures to appeal for improved sales. Starr (1899:117) lists votive offerings of a mercantile character in Guanajuato. "Miscellaneous Votives: Small hat of straw: taken from the shrine of our Lady of Lourdes at León. Was given by a hatmaker to gain success in his trade."

Contrary to what one might expect, decorative palms for Palm Sunday are not locally made, but purchased in Tepeaca or elsewhere.[13] Nor are they plaited, twisted, or woven, just minimally decorated with carnations, oleander, plumeria, or rosemary. In fact, my neighbor asked me to buy some of her woven palm wallets so she could buy a "*palmita*" for Palm Sunday. A man known as El Flaco, who kept a lunch stand in the market, brought royal palm fronds to sell on the eve of Palm Sunday. On Palm Sunday at 7:00 a.m., a procession of people carried palms into church to be blessed by the priest, later to tack over their doorways or prop against the immense tables they used as home altars. If anyone died during the year, their relatives tied the palm into crosses and stuck them in the burial mound.

The absence of palm weaving on Palm Sunday is surprising because this seasonal Catholic craft appears to be closely related to the style of palm weaving in Chigmecatitlán. Pettit and Pettit (1978:117) identify palm flowers (probably from next-door Huatlatlauca or Santa Catarina) as decorations for Palm Sunday. The current absence of weaving for Palm Sunday in Chigmecatitlán confirms that palm objects are construed exclusively as external commodities to be exchanged for cash, not as objects for internal ritual use in the community. Ordinary, everyday crafts temporarily constitute the material trappings of faith when they are attached to the statues of divinities.

THE OUTSIDERS

What is most notable is that they don't want anyone to serve who is from out of Town, for as many *mozos* as I have had, they have tried to retract with bad advice, threats and whatever their ill-disposed heart dictates, extending to the *fiscales* not doing their jobs *(AGN-Criminal, 334, 7, f. 262)*.

The structural enmity between the local townspeople and the resident outsiders—anthropologists, doctors, evangelists, priests, schoolteachers—became apparent in the summer of 1997 when I was living with other outsiders at the clinic. Many people of Chigmecatitlán were openly hostile and suspicious of strangers. "People here are very distrusting," a woman told me. There were hints that the townspeople (*ni'i viñu*) viewed outsiders (*ñu kó*) as interchangeable members of a class.

Ochoa (1993) suggests that the discomfort and even insults to which he and his team were subjected on their field stays in Chigmecatitlán were payback for years of being mined for information without benefit to the town.[14] Outsiders had to deal with austere living conditions. The male teachers assigned to the town lived in a depressing row of rooms on the edge of the road into town. The female kindergarten teacher slept on top of the pupils' desks shoved together in an unused classroom. Ochoa (1993:19) and his fellow anthropology students from the Escuela Nacional de Antropología e Historia sheltered beneath the town bandstand. The clinic residents fared better; they had a stove, refrigerator, and hot shower at the clinic.

Many outsiders stationed in Chigmecatitlán found it undesirable because it was so insular, an hour's drive from the paved highway. It was said that priests in the nearby small towns—Huatlatlauca, Molcaxac, Zacapala—were assigned there as punishment. The clinic residents said they were assigned to Chigmecatitlán because of low test scores. First-year teachers with no seniority were assigned to Chigmecatitlán; at least two of the teachers in 1995 had requested a transfer after their first year.

The clinic residents and rural teachers were not used to living away from home without relatives to look after them. I heard that the teachers from all three schools (kindergarten, primaria, and telesecundaria) and the clinic resident had formed a "family" to share one another's homesickness and for logistical and emotional support. During the day, the shortwave radio gasping and blaring in the next room kept the clinic residents company: Chigmecatitlán, Chigmecatitlán, *report.* Chigmecatitlán, Chigmecatitlán, *respond.* At night, a pair of medical students stationed at separate clinics conducted lovers' quarrels on the airwaves against a background of crickets and cicadas while lonely residents at other clinics listened idly through the night.

"SI DE DIOS HABLAN! DE MÍ QUÉ NO DIRÁN?" (IF THEY COMMENT ABOUT GOD, IMAGINE WHAT THEY SAY ABOUT ME!) ——MOTTO SEEN ON A TRUCK

Anyone who enters the rectory is spoken ill of, insulted, he is a tale-bearer, whoever talks with the priest has sold out, a traitor, they even say that one or two old women who attend the sacraments are my friends, gossips who whisper in my ear *(AGN-Criminal, 334, 7, f. 264v).*

Gossip reputedly rules any small Mexican town, and Chigmecatitlán was no exception. Rumors and innuendoes constituted an important form of communication, I was told: "Here we have newspapers, magazines, stories, soap operas, jokes, historians—they exist but in a different form," that is, as gossip.

One day the daughter of a friend came over to collect some money. She confided that two women had warned her not to associate with me because I was supposedly "of another religion." She said I had been observed walking around town carrying a great big Bible and meeting with a group of people at my house late at night to pray. I was chagrined by this story, though the accusations were grotesque in their invention. I was several months into my fieldwork and people still didn't know who

I was? Though by now I realize it is commonplace for anthropologists to be mistaken for missionaries, at the time I felt I had gone wrong somewhere. Hadn't they seen me at mass, in the processions?

"THIS TOWN IS FULL OF SIN . . ."

Your Excellency. I am a man like any other, I have many defects; but the origin of the ill-will of my Indians towards me is only because I do not neglect to tell the truth from the pulpit, because I restrain licentiousness, because I want them to learn the catechism and for them to confess and take communion at the time ordered by the Holy Church, because I have not entrusted another to hear their prayers, because I do not let them confess by simply repeating things they don't understand, but rather, as far as they are capable of understanding the mysteries necessary for their salvation, because I didn't let one of them marry when he wanted without showing adequate proof of the death of the husband of the widow he wanted for a wife, because I took away their favorite numen [Bernabé Pablo] Ojeda, because they are idiots, ignoramuses, and above all deluded, arrogant ingrates, who when a favor is done for them judge themselves deserving of more and finally because I don't let myself be governed by them *(AGN-Criminal, 334, 7, f. 265)*.

Into this situation came a restless young priest from Puebla, assigned by his superiors on a three-month basis to conduct the major masses of Holy Week. I first heard the new priest in the charged atmosphere of dread on Maundy Thursday. The saints were shrouded in purple cloths symbolizing the Passion. In his sermon, the priest said there was a lot of sin in the town, but that people loved God. In contrast with the big cities, here people do not repeat a rote formula in confession, and some do not know how to confess, but when they confess, they cry. He said we should pray for a priest who would love the town and who would teach, because there was so much to learn.

The birds were nesting in the church chandelier, chirping and swooping in and out.

"*Señor, ten piedad de nosotros. Piedad de nosotros ten Señor*" (Lord, have mercy on us), the congregants sang.

In that first sermon, the priest condemned Protestants, who he claimed wanted to destroy the Catholic Church by getting rid of the Eucharist, which is the basis of baptism, marriage, and the priesthood.

"*Protestante*" in Spanish sounds like *protest,* a feature the priest used to full effect to suggest that Protestants were dissenters and trouble-makers. For him, Martin Luther was still an adversary worth attacking. What century is he living in, I wondered, the sixteenth?

Little did the priest know, when he told the townspeople to pray for a priest who would love and teach the town, that they would write a letter to the archbishop of Puebla asking that he be kept on indefinitely. Someone wove him a gigantic *misterio,* an abbreviated rosary, with ten yellow beads made of raffia that could be seen from the back of the church as he led the counting of the rosary.

> The Indians not only opposed the full payment of [my] fees but they also went on to usurp and take over the economic administration, which is my responsibility alone, wanting to do processions with just the singers, a function prohibited to them by the third Mexican council. One day, having said that I would do the procession with good grace after I returned from saying mass in the annex [Santa Catarina], so as not to trample on the wise prohibition of said council, when I eagerly arrived to carry it out they had already gone ahead, I complained with the harshness I thought due, their revenge was that in two or three days, without my permission they went up onto the dome of the church at midnight, on the eve of Santa Cruz, and played as many old and out-of-tune instruments as they could lay their hands on, the small bells and even the organ, with the pretext of rejoicing for the day, they gave me to understand that I did not command them *(AGN-Criminal, 334, 7, f. 263)*.

The priest attempted to adjust the townspeople's practice of Catholicism to contemporary church doctrine. The townspeople, meanwhile, resisted his modifications and began "teaching him what we do here." The old priest, Padre Abraham, had insisted that everything be done a certain way. The superior who sent the new priest told him "*trátemelos con cariño*" (treat them with affection), i.e., don't weaken the strength of their faith. Still, there were some things the new priest balked at, like holding three vespers on the same day for three different groups of merchants. He ended up holding just one mass, paid for by one group, with the others attending. The priest also suggested fewer *novenarios.* People were used to celebrating a saint's day every day for nine or even twelve days before the actual commemoration.

The conflict between folk practices and official dogma is an old one. Ingham (1986:35) informs us that "part of the religious heritage of Catholicism was an ongoing struggle between the particular and the universal, the laity and the clergy, about proper practice." Christian's (1981) work further demonstrates that Catholicism was by no means monolithic even within sixteenth-century Spain.

The impassioned young priest cajoled his audiences by conducting the sacraments and sermons as compelling performances. Church was the most entertaining place in town to be. It was pleasant being read to. After lecturing to an adult study circle one evening from the *Nican Mompohua*—a bilingual account in Náhuatl and Spanish of the apparition of the Virgin of Guadalupe to Juan Diego—the priest launched into details of ritual practice he wanted to correct: People carrying statues in processions should be paired by height so it does not look like the statues are "doing the mambo"; duplication of the same saint in any one area of the church should be avoided (e.g., the Virgen Inmaculada should be curtained when the Virgen del Carmen is present); the only candles in the church should be three on either side of the altar for fiestas, seven for major solemnities. Later the priest ruefully pointed out the alms from the collection plate that evening: only 1½ pesos.

Some of the priest's intended corrections attack syncretic practices of Mexican folk Catholicism observed since the sixteenth century. For example, the distinct personalities ascribed to various guises of the same saint recall the pantheon of gods and goddesses of ancient Central Mexico (Giffords 1991) as well as the popularity of regional apparitions of saints in Spain. It is striking that the priest was advocating modernizing trends that were influenced by the very Protestantism he condemned. The streamlining of Catholic spirituality since Vatican II—turning the emphasis away from material culture such as icons, milagros, and candles—was ironically a move to emulate the Protestant churches that were drawing Catholics away (cf. Fortuny 1989:43).

CRAFTS ON THE ALTARS OF CORPUS CHRISTI

On Saturday afternoon, June 8, 1996, my neighbor and other men in the Hermandad del Santísimo had started digging postholes with steel digging sticks on the street corner outside my house to hold the supports for a temporary altar known as *tsia'va* or "*sombra*."[15] There would be five altars in all; one at each of the four corners of the town and a fifth outside the church.[16]

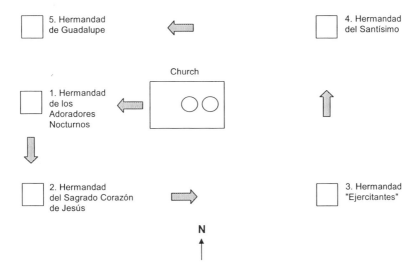

5. Hermandad de Guadalupe

4. Hermandad del Santísimo

Church

1. Hermandad de los Adoradores Nocturnos

2. Hermandad del Sagrado Corazón de Jesús

3. Hermandad "Ejercitantes"

N

FIGURE 5.2 Diagram of Corpus Christi procession altars.

The Corpus Christi mass was held Sunday morning at 11:00, followed by the procession at 11:30. The procession moved counterclockwise through the five altars of the hermandades of the Adoradores Nocturnos, the Sagrado Corazón de Jesús, the Ejercitantes, the Santísimo, and Guadalupe. The procession included twelve or thirteen people carrying the satin banners of their *hermandades,* the priest walking under a canopy and holding up a sunburst monstrance that contained the consecrated Host, and, at the rear, a brass band. Women walked on the priest's left, men on his right. At each altar the priest knelt and prayed, censed the monstrance, and elevated the Host to the four directions with outstretched arms as a bell struck.

The hermandades had barely managed to finish decorating the altars ahead of the procession. The posts were wrapped in laurel boughs. Suspended from the bamboo rafters were showy, locally made crafts: baskets, rattles, purses, flower vases, clowns, and mulitas with pineapples. Large raffia figures were evidently preferred because miniatures would be invisible from a distance.

One of the Corpus Christi altars in Chigmecatitlán included live woodpeckers for decoration, a practice not found in the ethnographic sources. The old priest had banned the custom because "people are paying more attention to the woodpeckers than to the Blessed Sacrament." I speculate that with the death of the former priest, the townspeople felt free to resuscitate an old practice. The red-headed woodpeckers, known

FIGURE 5.3 Members of the Hermandad "Ejercitantes" in front of their
Corpus Christi altar, June 1996.

as *chiquitos* or "little ones," were bound by their legs "like chickens" in
clusters of rattles and *ita tsiní,* yellow flowers with an aroma like freesias
that came from a shrub that grew in the ravine (*Thevetia thevetioides*).
The woodpeckers spread their wings and hung upside down heart-
breakingly, but they were released from the altar about twenty minutes
later to fly away after the procession passed through.

Chigmecatitlán and neighboring Santa Catarina are the only towns
I have heard of that decorate Corpus Christi altars with palm and raffia
crafts. The origin of this custom is unknown. It is everywhere part of the
Catholic liturgy to build ephemeral shelters through which the priest
carries the eucharistic Host (i.e., Christ in the form of bread) in procession (Weiser 1958). Curcio-Nagy (1994:3, 5), who considers Corpus
Christi the most significant festival in colonial Mexico City, writes that
the Indians built large canopies of thatch over the streets, and that some
confraternities built altars along the procession route, but unfortunately,
no descriptions exist. Altars identical to those of Corpus Christi are also
set up for a feast known as the Santo Jubileo, celebrated both in Chigmecatitlán (January 25, 1996) and Santa Catarina (March 26, 1996).[17]

The decoration of altars with crafts and woodpeckers in Chigmecatitlán dates back at least three quarters of a century, because old people

remember it from their childhood. When Dolores Escamilla, an octogenarian, was a girl, they celebrated the Santo Jubileo with sombras from which they hung cylindrical baskets, rectangular baskets, giraffes, small mules, bail baskets, and live chiquito woodpeckers. Marta Cabrera (age 76) remembered procession altars or "sombrita" at both Corpus Christi and Santo Jubileo. "For decoration" they had cylindrical or rectangular baskets, fans, mats with designs, and purses. They had the yellow flower ita tsiní, but the woodpeckers (three or four per altar) were not tied in flowers, but by themselves.

Rolando Romero's eyes brightened when he remembered from his boyhood how they would trap the woodpeckers in their nests burrowed in the columnar cacti and tie them by their legs, and how the birds would sing on the procession altars of Corpus. The yellow flowers were the same as now. The altars also had bail baskets, rattles, cane baskets, cylindrical or rectangular baskets, and small fans.

Santa Catarina has a similar custom of decorating procession altars with crafts. The idiom of decoration differs in the two towns, as people from Chigmecatitlán indicated when I showed them photographs of the Santa Catarina altars. In Santa Catarina, the tsia'va or "sombra" canopies were of willow branches and other greenery brought up to the mesa from the creek near Zacapala. In Chigmecatitlán, the river is inaccessible by truck so most "sombra" canopies are muslin or plastic sheeting. In Santa Catarina the altar decorations were more exotic and commercial, comprising plain and painted gourds, real and plastic fruit, fold-out paper party centerpieces, plastic blow-up toys (e.g., a rabbit), and electric lights. The two towns coincided in the use of ndo'o baskets, chains of raffia bead necklaces looped together, clowns, bail baskets, and *ollita* jugs. Instead of chiquitos tied by their legs, one of the altars in Santa Catarina included mockingbirds in cages. "They sing to God," was the owner's explanation.

The beautiful and ephemeral Corpus Christi and Santo Jubileo altars are one of the few sites where crafts are publicly displayed within the town's borders. Significantly, though, like the votive use of miniatures, this use of crafts in Catholic ritual is ultimately commercial. The crafts thus displayed are considered especially valuable as commodities because they have been sanctified through their proximity to the Host and their having been censed by the priest. Some people keep the crafts from the altars in their cardboard box of merchandise because "If they mix them with the merchandise they are going to sell, they sell more; it is blessed."

The contagious power of the sanctified crafts strongly resembles a practice Serna ([1892]1987:283), writing in 1656, describes in his handbook of suspected pagan activity the missionaries aimed to eradicate by punishing its practitioners under the Spanish Inquisition in Mexico: "putting amid their corn and merchandise, some little idol or its equivalent or representation, in the belief that it will increase and conserve those things into which it is put." It is therefore possible that the Corpus Christi altars in Chigmecatitlán syncretically meld European and Indian ritual genres. Durán (1971:426), in fact, explicitly compares the colonial pageantry of Corpus Christi to the fifth Aztec month of Toxcatl.

BANISHMENT OF THE EVANGELIST DOCTOR

Your Excellency can imagine, once the people of that Town [Santa Catarina] were thus influenced, how they would become, they became insolent to such a degree that it was worse than the parish seat [Chigmecatitlán]. Now it not only had to do with fees, but with viewing the priest as Lucifer. I suffered and suffered more *(AGN-Criminal, 334, 7, f. 262v)*.

It is the summer of 1997 and "Love Is Blue" plays on the loudspeaker while the graduating sixth-grade couples perform a carefully practiced dance on the basketball court. My status has changed since I first arrived in Chigmecatitlán; amazingly, I am seated at the head table and handing out diplomas along with the municipal president, priest, clinic resident, librarian, and council members. Nevertheless, though I have made many allies, all is not harmony. "We don't want the ideas of outsiders," the municipal president remarked sternly in his speech to the graduating class, and I couldn't help wondering if it was directed at me. More likely he was remembering the evangelist doctor. My relations with the townspeople improved markedly by the end of my field stay, partly because of persistence and partly because the new priest intervened on my behalf. His public endorsement of my project repaired my reputation.

I had returned to town after a year's absence to learn that my friend the evangelist doctor and his family had been forced out of town by a mob who surrounded their house at night. The banishment was preceded by two public showdowns between the evangelist doctor and the priest, in which each tried to demonstrate his superior mastery of scripture. Witnesses said the doctor was smiling Jesus-like, which only made the priest apoplectic. The doctor wanted to preach in the temple, the priest explained later, demonstrating with a high karate kick what he would like to have done to the doctor. The priest ordered anti-Protestant messages, in which Catholic dogma and flag-waving patriotism were conflated, to be lettered on the wall of the cantina and another building facing the doctor's house, one attacking the Jehovah's Witnesses and one attacking the Baptists, since the doctor's exact denomination was never ascertained.

> Moreover, with the whole town intoxicated, for thus they celebrate all the fiestas, I foresaw them mutinying and committing an attempt against me and my family, and in the end the burden of blame would be on me *(AGN-Criminal, 334, 7, f. 264)*.

The forcible ousting occurred at 8 p.m. in November 1996; a crowd massed outside the house where the doctor, his wife, and their small children lived; they acceded to leaving town the next morning. Someone snapped a photograph of the family's metal kitchen chairs out on the sidewalk, chairs we had sat on when they invited me to lunch. One of the townspeople videotaped the event as if it were a religious spectacle like the Pastorela. The detail that affected me the most in the recounting was that the new window screens that the doctor had put in to imitate mine had been slashed. The destruction of a symbol of "outside ideas" chilled me.

It was said that the priest had incited the banishment of the doctor because he could not tolerate "another religion" in town. The priest, the municipal president, and my landlady were considered the instigators. The doctor retaliated by suing all three in court for violation of his civil rights. The priest, municipal president, and town council were called to testify before a tribunal. The townspeople were mortified because a Puebla newspaper carried the story.

In the aftermath of the expulsion of the evangelist doctor, many of the townspeople were loath to talk about it. The outsiders seemed uneasy, conscious now that the town was capable of violence. It could happen to us. A Mexican film records an infamous incident in 1968 in San Miguel Canoa, a Nahua town in Puebla, in which a mob of villagers lynched some visiting university employees who were using the town as a base camp to scale the Malinche volcano. An autocratic priest who claimed the university employees were Communists inflamed the villagers' violence and distrust: "It was said [over the town loudspeakers] that some Communist students had arrived who were going to raise the red and black flag in the town church" (Pérez Turrent 1984:11).

Catholic missionizing in colonial Mexico had overtones of the struggle between God and the devil (Ingham 1986). The same can be said now of Protestant evangelism. In Indian towns, the devil is often associated with non-Indians (Ingham 1986). In this light, the schoolteacher's remark at the beginning of this chapter, comparing the doctor to Lucifer, is not surprising.

Protestants are unencumbered by observations to the saints, Ingham (1986) points out. This suggests one reason why Protestant evangelism threatens Chigmecatitlán: from a functional point of view, Catholic ritual is the glue that keeps the town together; it gives the emigrants a reason to keep coming back. As long as there is no adequate source of income in the town (craft weaving, candy making, and farming are inadequate for subsistence), the population cannot live in town full-time. Minority Protestant sects such as the Jehovah's Witnesses are considered marginal to mainstream religions in the United States, but they have made deep inroads in Mexico. They may be perceived as a threat because they mean fewer people to carry out rituals to Christ, Mary, and the saints, which are important for maintaining emigrants as members of the town.[18]

Banishment, though rare, has been in use since the colonial period. Burgoa ([1674]1934:366), the Dominican priest in Oaxaca who worked in several towns in the Mixteca, reports on banishment as punishment for alleged witchcraft. Mariano Paz y Sánchez, the troubled priest of nineteenth-century Chigmecatitlán, worried that the town was on the verge of banishing him.

When I asked Don Jacinto about the expulsion of the doctor, he said he had pointed out to the townspeople that they do not inquire if the person buying crafts from them is "of another religion." He inferred that what they really object to is evangelism. "Thank God I'm an atheist," he concluded wryly.

I am not the first to have suffered at their hands, since our founder seven have governed, the first impeached,[19] Vera could not stand them, Andrade was lost, got sick and died only to have one of the Indians raise the troops to harm him, Quiroz spoken ill of, Calderón defamed, Polanco afflicted and I defamed. Can it be possible that the Indians are innocent and the Priests perverse. Judge me, Your Excellency, the worst person in the world, but it is not credible that my six predecessors have all been bad *(AGN-Criminal, 334, 7, f. 265v)*.

The theme of this chapter is the unraveling of a romantic version of Mexico one might construct based on assumptions about life in a small town full of creative artisans who make toys and miniatures. My bitter experience, presented from a baldly subjective viewpoint that does not approximate the "native point of view," clashes with the playfulness of the colorful woven palm couple dancing the *jarabe tapatío* or the band playing in the *kiosko*. But in some contradictory sense, perhaps I am nonetheless furthering a sense of romantic "otherness" by reproducing other familiar tropes of Mexican exoticism: incomprehensible faith as an organizer of daily life, the isolated town as the subject, ethnocentric "us" versus xenophobic "them." Despite my intention to deconstruct tradition by focusing on how particular, individual characters enact the goals of institutions, the ethnohistoric quotations I have included ironically tug the analysis toward the romance of timeless continuity. In conclusion, I have attempted to portray ambivalent experience.

This chapter locates the crafts of Chigmecatitlán within the context of religions—Catholic and Protestant—which are themselves dynamic and in gradual flux. I have depicted the town as a scenario for competing ideologies driven by the tension between the villagers' need to engage outsiders for their expertise and services, and their desire to control and manage those outsiders. Catholicism was a stabilizing force through which social identity was confirmed and beauty created. On the other hand, its rigid intolerance for heterodoxy erupted into a witch hunt of malicious accusations and the physical suppression of disruptive faith. The relationship between the priest and the townspeople was not one of simple domination, however, but a complex negotiation of power. Standing in the mob in the darkness outside the evangelist doctor's house, someone leaned across to the priest and whispered in his ear: "Either you run him out, or we'll run you out."

I have highlighted the places where religious practices—inarguably syncretic, but predominantly Catholic—impinge on the miniature. If crafts are a mediating form between the town and the outside world, this chapter analyzes how crafts are involved "backstage" (Goffman 1959) in ritual within the town's borders, where tourists rarely go. I found that crafts are used as ex-votos and as decorations on procession altars for

FIGURE 5.4 Santa Claus, angel, and devil. Each approximately one inch tall.

Corpus Christi and Santo Jubileo. Regarding scale, miniatures are mainly used as ex-votos, while larger figures are used as decorations on the procession altars. Size is constrained by visibility and appropriateness, not portability or any other factor.

In both cases, crafts are found where the crosscurrents of religion and commerce intersect. Those who seek the authenticity of indigenous practice uncontaminated by outsiders may find the conjunction of ritual with the commercial unexpected. In the case of the Corpus Christi and Santo Jubileo altars, objects are fleetingly redefined as ceremonial, then revert to being secular commodities. The figures are recycled, utilized in two stages: first as adornment and second as merchandise. It is a cost-free means of decorating altars and meeting religious obligations.

Similarly, crafts used as ex-votos, attached to the saints, are not expressly created as religious symbols, but are run-of-the-mill woven crafts. In both cases, the ritual value of crafts is not inherent in their conception or design, but emergent in their use.

PLATE 1 Indians and Columbus, miniatures from Chigmecatitlán.

PLATE 2 Couple with *china* and *charro* dolls they make.

PLATE 3 Pink plastic thread at a store in Chigmecatitlán.

PLATE 4 Miniature nativity from Chigmecatitlán. Height of Virgin Mary
one inch. 1996.

PLATE 5 Statue of Christ ("Ramoncito") riding on a donkey with miniature palm *nda'cho*, palm bicycle, and raffia rattles hanging from the reins, awaiting the procession of Palm Sunday. Retreat house, Guadalupe chapel, Chigmecatitlán.

PLATE 6 Woodpecker and *ita tsiní* flowers suspended from the Corpus Christi altar of the Hermandad de Guadalupe.

PL. 78

XIXᵉ Siécle

COSTUMES MEXICAINS.

Extraction du Pulque du Maguey(Aloes) au moyen d'une langue (altruiste avs.
laquelle en l'aspire

PLATE 7A *Tlachiquero*. Lithograph by Claudio Linati. 1828.

PLATE 7B *Tlachiquero*, probably from the 1960s. INAH, Collecciones
Mestizas, Box 17, No. 31743(63).

PLATE 8 Palm and plastic baskets (*ika*) to hold candy for Las Posadas at the Mercado de Jamaica, Mexico City, December 1995.

CHAPTER 6

Learning and Forgetting: The Art of Weaving Palm

Three times I heard the story of the kui-kui, a dun-gray bird with a curved-down beak that pecked at the ground and could only say its name: kui.

> *El kui-kui estuvo en la escuela por varios años pero nomás aprendió a decir "kui." El cenzontle nomás pasó afuera de la escuela, escuchó la lección, y se aprendió todo.*

> The kui-kui went to school for several years but all he learned to say was "kui." The mockingbird just passed by the schoolhouse, overheard the lesson, and learned it all.

Palm weaving is often dismissed as the simplest of crafts. In the United States, "basket weaving" is synonymous with self-indulgent college courses—a supposedly dilettantish waste of time. The predominance of women in palm weaving, its minimal technology, and its ephemerality have contributed to its being seen as a lightweight of the material culture world (Rubín de la Borbolla 1974:170; Snoddy Cuéllar 1993:259; Turok 1988a:82). Having tried to take weaving lessons from the woman next door in Chigmecatitlán, I can affirm that palm weaving is not as easy as it looks. My neighbor attempted to demonstrate a basic *petaca* or wallet. I had trouble with the "start," which required anchoring the palm strips with a row of twined palm basting, and with the staggered over-one, under-two motion. As the kui-kui story implies, exposure to weaving does not yield uniform proficiency in all artisans.

This chapter delves into matters that seem obvious: how people learn to weave alone and together. It also explores how they individually and collectively forget how to make figures they once mastered; how innovation replaces the status quo. This inquiry focuses on the circulation of weaving methods and designs between individuals. My aim is to penetrate the laconic mystique of phrases like "traditional designs" and

FIGURE 6.1 Artisan demonstrates how to weave a palm *petaca* or wallet.

"Indians are inspired by their natural surroundings," so often stated in the folk art literature.

How artisans learn to weave is not a neutral topic in Chigmecati-tlán; rather, it is laden with emotional meaning. To ask people how they obtained their weaving skills is to bring up poignant memories of the parents who taught them to weave as children or died before teaching them, of the suffering and hunger that obliged them to learn to weave, of their jealousy of rival artisans who stole their ideas.

Contrary to what is commonly assumed, palm weavers do not necessarily acquire weaving techniques and designs unconsciously and naturally from infancy. The transfer of knowledge is more likely to be expressed as "stealing" than as "sharing." Individuals often consider themselves self-taught artisans who have struggled to learn. This situation complicates the idea of a continuous chain of weaving ability inherited from pre-Hispanic Mixtec ancestors.

Forgetting in the chapter title refers to discarded techniques and designs people once wove but no longer know how. Richard N. Adams (personal communication, 1991), who has worked with models for the dynamics of culture, said—regarding the loss of the ways of the past— to imagine if all the conversations in a room were still present; it would be cacophony. The new must displace the old.

LEARNING TO WEAVE PALM

The traditionality of folk art lies in its inheritance from generation to generation, as Marion Oettinger (1990:197–98) elegantly describes: "Mexican folk artists learn their art and skills from a variety of sources. In more traditional communities, folk art skills are passed on from mother to daughter, father to son. Children begin to learn the crafts of their parents early, sometimes making practice pieces as soon as they can manipulate the medium." There are many nuances to childhood instruction, however. At its most benign, children learn to weave, generally around age eight, by imitating their parents as a kind of game. A Santa Catarina artisan, for example, describes seeing her friends weave and wanting to emulate them.

> *"No one taught me . . . one learns as a little girl . . . I would go over to my girlfriends' houses and see them . . . instead of playing, I wove. "Mamá," I said, "dye palm for me." My mother made petates and chiquihuites. But I didn't really weave until I was grown up."*

A less idyllic example is Doña Valentina Ibáñez, who began to weave around age ten, staying home with her mother making tortillas and weaving large and small nda'cho wallets. Her father, who worked in the fields, would take a burro loaded with nda'cho to Puebla and return with "*vestido, pan, chilito*" (clothes, bread, chiles).

One shade of difference between these two examples is that in the first, weaving was voluntary, while in the second, the child's weaving contributed directly to purchasing household staples. Many artisans said they were forced to weave as children of poverty (e.g., Pastor Flores, Chapter 2). One of the reasons some children drop out of school is to help their parents weave (Ochoa 1993:37). Parents may send a child to apprentice with a skilled artisan, like Catalina Escalante, who at age ten, as the eldest girl, went to her aunt's to become proficient as a weaver because her mother had trouble supporting the family (cf. José Flores in the workshop of Don Refugio Bello, Chapter 2). Another artisan said she nags her sixteen-year-old son to weave a basket or two when he is resting from working on the road so they will mount up to a dozen or a gross. At the worst extreme are cases where parents punish or even beat their children until they learn to weave (e.g., Benigno Rosas, Chapter 4).

Children begin with elementary components such as the mule's feet (*ka'a pe'e*), base (*nukatsi*), ball (*kitsindú*), or market basket (*ika*). As one artisan put it, "Knowing how to make a little market basket and the mule's little feet, one can make any figure." Carmen (age ten) and Ana (age twelve) told me they start weaving little market baskets at ten o'clock in the morning. They work quickly, winding the palm thread around the spokes of the base, conversing or watching television as they work. Their mother strips the palm into threads for them. The hardest part is fixing the wide base strips in place. They use manicure scissors to snip the palm.

THE REVOLUTIONARY NEIGHBOR

The first time I visited artisan Don Agustín Vidales in 1996, I showed him a miniature hunter with an animal on his back that I had bought nearly ten years earlier on Corpus Christi Sunday in the Mexico City Zócalo. The delicate plaiting of the figurine, with eight strips instead of the usual six, revealed Don Agustín to be the maker. "My great-grandfather was a hunter like that," he mused. His memories of learning to weave revolve around his next-door neighbor Bernardo Mendizábal, a soldier in the Mexican Revolution (1910–ca. 1917) who deserted from the army after narrowly escaping a bullet. Mendizábal was carrying a bedroll on his back suspended from his forehead with a tumpline at the time and later found a tuft of cotton indicating that the bullet had just missed the nape of his neck. He fled back home at about the age of forty to become one of the most inventive palm weavers ever to work in Chigmecatitlán. As a boy, Agustín was always over at his house.

> *Buyers came from far, far away. They wanted a surprise. He wove an airplane with its windshield and pilot [indicates a wingspan of about fifteen inches]. He also made an eagle on a cactus. Later they asked for others.*
>
> *You know how stupid children are. They don't appreciate things. He was very fond of me. My mother made me learn to weave those dolls with him.*

Don Agustín's mother, a campesina who only wove small petates, petacas, and tenates, obliged him to learn to weave tlachiqueros under the tutelage of Bernardo Mendizábal, because "we were very poor."

Not all children are enculturated into palm weaving in infancy, however. Some parents stigmatize weaving and consider it a poor way to earn a living; they prefer their children not take up palm weaving since they have other ambitions for them. I met one girl whose parents, though poor, forbade her to weave baskets like her girlfriends. There were also cases of stubborn children who refused to learn to weave.

I encountered several artisans whose inheritance of the Chigmecatitlán legacy was even more haphazard and who did not learn to weave until adulthood. For them, peers were more important than parents as weaving instructors. It took Teresa, El Flaco's daughter from Veracruz, five months to learn from a friend to make a raffia baby rattle.

One of the local schoolteachers had just mastered weaving a little yellow raffia basket, inspired by her cousin Juana Barragán, one of the few people in town who could walk and weave at the same time. The schoolteacher said she had felt idle in comparison.

Former municipal president Fernando Vidales resolved to train himself to weave by emulating one of his council members in a moment of leisure after hiking down to the river to see if the soil was suitable for repairing the road. He showed off his invention, a small white raffia dove in a blue basket, as well as a plain palm basket in which he had allowed the palm to get too saturated, causing it to crack. He said he now knows to keep the palm damp on the ground. This example shows that not everyone is privy to a common body of technical knowledge. The need for individuals to constantly reinvent techniques on their own is evidence of the jealousy with which many artisans guard their procedures, a situation contrary to the idea that artisans are able to absorb traditional methods from the mere fact of living in the milieu.

When they get married, many adults actively start weaving. This is logical since the new couple is now responsible for its own household income, and married couples tend to work on crafts as a unit. Either spouse may teach the other to weave. Like other Mixtec communities, the residence pattern tends to be virilocal (Ravicz and Romney 1969); brides traditionally go to live with the groom's family and join their palm-weaving unit. A married woman may return to her mother's house if her mother is widowed, leading to the situation of married couples de facto living apart in their respective mother's houses. Exogamy is permitted with people in other towns; non-Mixtec outsiders who move into town often take up weaving or selling palm crafts. Usually each member of a family specializes in a different element, complementing rather than competing with each other in their choice of design.

Dr. Atl, a pioneer in the literature of Mexican folk art, makes constant reference to Mexicans' supposed innate artistic capacity, which he sees as residing in their hands: *"conciencia digital,"* as he terms it (Atl [1922]1980:39). Chigmecatitlán artisans similarly may conceive of weaving as embodied knowledge, in the sense that their fingers work mechanically while their mind is elsewhere, watching television or listening to the radio. Ex-municipal president Fernando Vidales poetically evoked weaving "last night sitting in the doorway, in darkness, with my fingers studying the path of the strands." One weaver remarked that she did not need to count rows because "my fingers already know." Another said, "One's hands already have the measurements—they guide one." A third said that while weaving, "I'll be watching soap operas. My hands are working and my eyes are on something else." She scolds her daughters when a television show attracts their attention and they stop weaving; their hands have not yet incorporated the physical, kinetic memory of weaving.

"YO INVENTÉ"

Artisans in Chigmecatitlán do not pursue individual name recognition, as is the impulse with the discovery and canonization of folk artists in the Western art world (Briggs 1980:140–41; Oettinger 1990:27–28). In short, they do not sign their work. However, their lack of concern with name recognition does not indicate a lack of proprietary interest. For all the artisans who acquired their techniques from parents, friends, and spouses, an equal number claimed to be self-taught. A common perception about their enculturation as artisans was that no one had taught them to weave; they taught themselves and they "invented" whatever they made. Their narrative typically followed this progression:

Buscaba, buscaba yo la forma.	I searched and searched for the form.
Yo inventé.	I invented it.
Ellos me copiaron.	They copied me.

"*Buscaba, buscaba yo la forma*" is an unusual verbal construction in Spanish, both in its reduplication and also in the word *buscar,* in the sense of coming up with a design, which is evidently a borrowing from Mixtec (*nanduku yu = buscar yo* [*crear una artesanía*]). The perception of having independently "invented" techniques could be a result of so many people learning through observation rather than through formal weaving instruction. It also reflects the jealousy with which the secrets of weaving are guarded. To teach someone else to weave may be socially sanctioned. Several people criticized one artisan for coaching her young neighbor on how to improve her miniature clowns and musicians. An artisan and vendor from Santa Catarina suggested that the people of Chigmecatitlán had not taught *me* to weave because "they're jealous."

Don Jacinto offered two explanations for this proprietary interest: creative pride (i.e., the desire to be recognized for an innovation) and economic interest (i.e., the fear that if someone copies your designs, you will lose business). For example, about fifteen years ago, José Flores and Catalina Escalante went to sell on the Day of Guadalupe (December 12) at the church of the Virgen de Guadalupe in Oaxaca. Doña Catalina sensed that people were scrutinizing the pieces or buying just one in order to copy it. Because, according to Don José, if you can weave, you can examine a piece and figure out how it is made, or, if not, dismantle it. According to a study of craft makers in Ghana, "An artisan who introduces a new product or style that is attractive to consumers enjoys the advantage of a brief monopoly, until the change is adopted by other artisans" (McDade 1998:209).

From my point of view, these fears did not seem realistic in the big picture. I saw the repertoire of designs in the community as relatively static and people's "inventions" as glosses of existing models. Nevertheless, this individual attachment to particular innovations is significant because it poses an alternative interpretation to the seamless appearance of commonality, shared tradition, and continuity that a collection of pieces from Chigmecatitlán presents to the outside observer.

THE MYSTERIOUS STRANGER

The painful, fitful, sometimes haphazard process of innovation can be glimpsed in two separate conversations with Patricia Flores and León Pérez, a couple who have run the battery-powered public address system from their house on the town square for twenty-five years. They weave bandstands and nativities with a distinctive rough look (see illustrations in Martínez Peñaloza 1982:41; Pettit and Pettit 1978:22, top; Winn 1977:57). The pair have made nativities since 1955 or 1960. Don León dyes the palm and weaves the stable, manger, decorations, costumes, and crown; Doña Patricia weaves the base (*petatillo*) and the bodies of the Holy Family (*santitos*). They modeled the stable (*jacalito* or *portalito*) after Herod's Palace in the town square. This section is based on separate conversations with Patricia Flores on June 8, 1996, and her husband, León Pérez, on June 28, 1997.

The couple's recollections center on their struggle to engender new figures on their own and with the participation of a mysterious stranger turned client after a chance meeting.[1] Doña Patricia and Don León attempted to conform to their client's desires by working out the construction of the requested figures. The prospective customer became a catalyst for change, though ultimately the creative efforts he spurred were abortive. As Patricia Flores points out, most people don't want change.

> León Pérez [smoking an Alas cigarette]: I left here at age nine. The "cacique" here [in the 1940s] was really a pain. He fined my family for not sending me to school, and he wanted everyone to do rounds at night. It still makes me mad.
>
> Patricia Flores: I was born in Jalapa [Veracruz]; I lived all my life in Mexico City. My mother was ill. People want to come back to be with their family when they die. I was six when she brought me here and died. I was raised by my aunt in Mexico City, where I went to primary school.
>
> León Pérez: I'm from the Barrio [San Antonio]. There were seven

children, my mother and father. We went to live in Candelario de los Patos, north of La Merced [in Mexico City]. At nine years old I looked around for something to do. I was the eldest. A man paid me fifty centavos to watch a newsstand. It was enough to buy coffee with milk and bread for my whole family.

I taught myself to read there. "La Prensa," someone would say. I didn't know which it was until I could make out the P. El Universal, La Prensa, El Pepín, El Chamaco *were the magazines there were.*

Later on I delivered newspapers in Mexico City: Excelsior, Novedades. *Once I got both bike wheels caught in the track with the streetcar coming and I got the wheels out just in time.*

I met my wife when I was delivering La Prensa. *I knocked on the door and she answered.*

Patricia Flores: *I met my husband in Mexico City. He was a newspaper delivery boy. At age eighteen I met him; he worked at* Novedades *delivering newspapers on a bicycle. He was also from Chigmecatitlán.*

León Pérez: *My wife was born in Jalapa. She made baskets [ika] for Las Posadas. I told my wife, "We're never going to get ahead like this." I was already making bands of musicians in Mexico City. My father played treble clarinet in the band. He played with the Herreras; he wasn't from here. My mother wove little wallets. When I had time I liked to weave in the afternoons, at night. My father would find me weaving at two in the morning, but I couldn't sleep until I figured out how to do something.*

The bandstand was the last thing I invented. I didn't like the first one I made. It was shapeless. After awhile I started to figure it out. It took me a month to figure out how to do the roof. The bandstand is very mystifying. I'm proud I didn't copy it from anyone. Now other people copy the design.

Patricia Flores: *When we got married there was no such thing as a bandstand, mariachi, band, or nativity. We came back here to live in a reed house. I quit my job; we didn't pay rent here. There were wallets, little ika baskets, tenate baskets. Little mules, little dolls, little petates, bracelets were already being made here. We bought palm and started to work. We made some little ika baskets but they sold very cheaply. We got together ten gross of ika baskets made with six strips, which sold for two pesos the gross. We went to Mexico City to look for an order.*

My husband knew his way around all of Mexico City. We went to one market—nobody bought anything. We went as far as Toluca—nobody was buying. A man in a big car stopped. He was looking, looking for palm crafts. He was from El Salvador or maybe the United States; he also sold silver and woven blankets. He drew for us on a piece of cardboard in his car for about three hours. He sketched about eighty figures:

Indian with firewood
Woman making tortillas
Mariachi
Bullfight
Bandstand with a band
Mule with pineapples
Little hats
Little skeleton with candles, flowers,
 little coffin, and incense burner

FIGURE 6.2 Bandstand (*kiosko*) contains eight musicians and bandleader. Retail price at El Parián market, Puebla, 110 pesos (eight pesos = $1 U.S.). July 1997. Height 5½ inches.

"And anything else you can make up out of your own heads. I buy by the thousand. Give me your address so I can pick up the merchandise."
Were there hotels, was there a restaurant?

He paid us twenty pesos for our time.

In a week we made one gross. We suffered because we hadn't made the things he wanted: "It's missing this, that, and the other." But he paid for everything, though at a lower price.

He came back about three times. We were able to make twenty or thirty pieces. Nobody could make the things he wanted. The man sadly said goodbye, sad because he could not help us.

CONFIGURATIONS OF NATIONALISM

Chigmecatitlán artisans are generally reluctant to attempt new designs, which are difficult to develop. Creativity often consists of reassembling existing elements into hybrids: combining a snake with a basket to make a cobra, or clowns with a band to make clown musicians. Blanca Gómez told me, "Whatever people learn is what they make. They just copy. People are not creative. It takes effort to start weaving a figure. Since they already sell what they make, they don't change it."

I asked José Flores and Catalina Escalante, the couple credited with inventing the miniature in the 1960s, whom they considered creative. They could barely think of anyone. One artisan they mentioned "used to be more *curioso*. He made raffia monkeys, herons, turkeys, peacocks. Now he drinks a lot." When I visited the artisan in question, he said the buyer will say, "Make me one of these" and he says, "How should I make it?" With the exception of rare innovators like the ex-revolutionary soldier Bernardo Mendizábal in the 1930s, miniaturists José Flores and Catalina Escalante in the 1960s, and entrepreneur Jacinto Flores in the 1990s, the artisans of Chigmecatitlán literally copy existing designs.

The inventory of motifs in Chigmecatitlán is primarily composed of national, not local, symbols. Most of the designs that the mysterious man on the roadside outside Toluca sketched in his car were familiar archetypes well established in Mexican popular imagery by the middle of the nineteenth century. The china poblana, charro, horseback rider, tlachiquero, firewood carrier, hunter, and Apache Indian are national icons reproduced in dozens of craft media throughout Mexico. These designs in the form of wax figurines were familiar to travelers to Mexico

FIGURE 6.3 *El ranchero* and *La china* by Hesiquio Iriarte, in *Los mexicanos pintados por sí mismos* [1854–55].

in the 1850s. Samuel Ramos (1962:102–103) in *Profile of Man and Culture in Mexico* writes:

> "Nationalism" was founded on the belief that Mexico was already complete in itself. Such a belief is supported by an inclination to the picturesque—mountain scenes, dotted with Indian figures in their typical white cotton suits and with cactus plants. Recent art has undertaken an amplification—as in a resounding box—of the "picturesque" dimensions that have found wide acceptance, especially among Yankee tourists. But this Mexico of the charro (Mexican horseman) and the Mexico of the china poblana (colorful style of women's regional dress), as well as the Mexico of the legendary savage constitute a Mexico for export which is just as false as the romantic Spain of the tambourine.

In Esparza Liberal's (1994:76, 78) assessment, "The popular types embody . . . the desire to magnify the national essence, in frank accordance with the romantic spirit of the era. Furthermore, this work benefited from the prestige of the exotic and the attraction Mexico wielded over foreigners." Don Jacinto had reserved for a client in Italy a plastic bag full of miniatures of Zapatista leader Subcomandante Marcos holding the Mexican flag. Rather than reflecting pan-indigenous solidarity, in this context Marcos is the contemporary equivalent of nineteenth-century national icons like the china and charro for the tourist trade.

One of the early coiners of this nationalist iconography was Italian illustrator Claudio Linati (1790–1832), who imprinted lithographs of picturesque native characters based on watercolors he sketched in Mexico from 1825 to 1829 (Esparza Liberal 1994). Other popularizers of these archetypes were the book *Viaje pintoresco* by German illustrator Carl Nebel ([1836]1963), who traveled in Mexico from 1829 to 1834, and Mexican *costumbrista* writing such as *Los mexicanos pintados por sí mismos* ([1854–55]1974; Esparza Liberal 1994:76, 78). American photographer C. B. Waite further disseminated this cast of characters in his prolific photographs of Mexican people, which he distributed as postcards at train depots in the early twentieth century (Montellano 1994). Fine artists such as Diego Rivera and Jean Charlot, engaged in building a national culture in the 1920s through 1940s, incorporated stylized versions of these "native types" into their own art. The images have been recycled back into the design of palm figures from Chigmecatitlán. In the ultimate example of design coming full circle, a new figure has appeared recently in Chigmecatitlán: a flower vendor inspired by Diego Rivera's paintings.

The intertextuality between the palm nativity and other regional nativities of plain and painted pottery, wheat straw, and tin illustrates the inspiration that strikes in the crafts store. The crossover between craft media continues to have an impact on contemporary palm weavers in Chigmecatitlán searching for new designs. The proliferation of chess sets in various materials throughout the country, including palm in Chigmecatitlán, is evidence of design for the market. Starr includes in his *Catalogue of a Collection of Objects Illustrating the Folk-lore of Mexico* (1899:23) two chess sets with nationalist themes: "Spaniards and Cubans" and "Republican and Imperialist Parties" (i.e., during the French Intervention of Maximilian and Carlota). Both were made in Puebla. Jacinto Flores won first place in 1992 for his Aztec chess set in Guanajuato in a competition under the auspices of FONART and MNAIP.

State crafts competitions build identification with familiar motifs by rewarding designs that reproduce conventional canons. Some artisans in Chigmecatitlán have entered government-sponsored competitions, a risky but potentially lucrative strategy. Carmen González was planning to enter a contest in 1997 with a miniature symphony orchestra she was developing guided by an orchestra diagram purchased at a stationer's in

Puebla. The contest, held by the Secretaría de Desarrollo Social (SEDE-SOL), FONART, and Pulsar Internacional, offered a first prize of 11,000 pesos ($1,375 U.S.). Carmen was inspired by a neighbor who had won a nativity competition in Mexico City in 1996 and earned a cash prize and a diploma signed by Esther Echeverría, director of FONART.

OUTSIDE INFLUENCE AND NATIONAL DESIGNS

The intervention of outsiders who determine motifs is an old story. American author Katherine Anne Porter, who wrote the catalogue for one of the earliest exhibitions of Mexican folk art (Porter [1922]1993), lived in Mexico City sporadically between 1920 and 1931 (Porter 1970). In a letter, she expresses her impatience with other Americans imposing their commercial ideas on the crafts scene.

> *The main streets are now lousy with Art Shoppes where you pay a peso for a blue goblet that you once bought in the market for ten centavos from the Indian who made it. The Indian still gets his ten centavos from the Art Shoppe owner. Various American art-lovers have scattered out to the old pueblas [sic] to teach the Indian how to 'refine' his product and make it more acceptable to the market (Porter to Kenneth Burke, October 6, 1930, in Porter 1990:25).*

Fernández Ledesma added his prophetic voice to the subject of tourist influence and national motifs in 1930: "Intelligent people will quickly fathom and determine the good and worthwhile, discard and eliminate that ersatz Mexicanness manufactured for tourists. Here lies the threat and imminent danger: the small producer, poor and besieged by taxes, doesn't think twice about earning a bit more when the wholesalers and criminal traffickers commission a 'more national' product which they themselves invent, of course, with brazen ignorance" (Fernández Ledesma 1930:51).

Recently in Chigmecatitlán, the evangelist doctor asked Carmen González to make mariachis, which he hoped would sell well at a friend's store on the U.S. border. He brought her a miniature nine-piece mariachi made by Clemente Flores but requested that she give the musical instruments bulk instead of weaving them flat. The doctor told her that mariachis wear tight pants with a decoration up the sides and that they wear ties. At the time, my own reaction was annoyance that the doctor, an outsider, was "meddling" with local inspiration. Realistically, it is natural for artisans to accept outside commissions and to attempt to make what sells. Don Jacinto once remarked, "every design I make is to sell."

Another example of externally inspired design are palm bracelets and rings. Doña Vicenta Chávez has been weaving them since the 1930s in hues of magenta, green, red, and sulphur yellow. They resemble horsehair and human-hair rings from eighteenth-century England with names woven in. Doña Vicenta recalled that she started making this jewelry after a local man brought silk prototypes from Mexico City for Chigmecatitlán artisans to copy, also supplying the silk floss, but the artisans substituted palm strands.

Television has also given artisans creative fodder. Catalina Escalante wove characters from the television show *Las Burbujas*—Ecoloco, Mafafa Musguito, Memelovsky, Mimoso Ratón, Patas Verdes, and Pistachón—around 1980. I asked one artisan who watches television while weaving if anything on television had inspired her. She mentioned that she would like to weave the singer Pedro Fernández or maybe maria-chis in white suits (she clarified that she thought they were white, but she had a black-and-white TV set so they might have been another light color). Artisans use any visual medium at hand as a guide. A plastic cookie bag, for example, lent the design for a miniature clown.

The use of pre-Hispanic symbolism is limited. Don Jacinto said he would like to make Maya, Nahua, and Huichol Indians. My sugges-tion that artisans weave Mixtec characters from the *Codex Nuttall* was greeted with tremendous skepticism. When pre-Hispanic cultures are depicted, they are selectively reduced to Aztec, not Mixtec, in keeping with the primary mythology of Mexico (cf. Errington 1998:176–79).

FORGETTING

"Pobrecita, ya no pinta y teje igual" (Poor thing, she doesn't dye and weave the same)—that was how a group of women reacted when I showed them a ndo'o basket I had bought from an aged acquaintance. They did not consider her basket *"bonito"* or pretty. Many regard old age as a time when weaving skill diminishes, sometimes because people's eyesight "gets tired." One artisan told me she had saved a small, plain palm ndo'o as a memento of her grandmother who died four years ear-lier; her grandmother used to make large baskets but in old age could only make small ones.

Just as frequent, however, is the notion that old people are the bearers of special expertise that will disappear from the community when they die. The written version of Don Abraham Cortés's foundation narrative expresses this concern:

> *Nowadays people keep searching, they weave miniature curiosities of palm and raffia; they keep searching so as not to lose the tradition and fame of crafts in Chigmecatitlán. Some time ago they asked the state government to set up a craft workshop so the few artisans still living who know how to weave the finest objects could earn a salary to teach us and our children because the crafts of Chigmecatitlán form part of the popular art of Mexico (Abraham Cortés, Datos Importantes Fundacíon y Vida y Desarrollo de Santa María Chigmecatitlán del Estado de Puebla. Pue., n.d.).*

The passage demonstrates the fear that weaving is a vanishing tradition that should be salvaged, adding the larger frame that this skill constitutes part of the national patrimony. Although it is rare for people to keep sentimental or antique pieces from the past, one seller, Luis Zamora, had reproductions made of a pair of dolls holding pineapples, inherited from his parents, like one a girl gives comic actor Clavillazo (Antonio Espino) in a vintage 1950s Mexican movie. Reviving old models such as this is uncommon, however. Few, if any, artisans now make pe-tates with names woven in; wrapped, twined, embroidery thread baskets; double-weave miniature hats; child-size fire fans; finger traps; thimbles; palm ollitas; bird rattles; flowering plants on a base with a dove on a stem; *otate* baskets (made of solid cane); or *capisayo* rain capes. As one man observed, "It used to be everyone wove. But there is no economic return, and people have either died or emigrated."

To judge by old people's recollections of their parents' and grandparents' work, many people in Chigmecatitlán once specialized in the nearly lost art of fine petate weaving. Pánfilo Pérez's mother-in-law could incorporate any design the client requested into her petates. Another woman used to weave petates fine enough to put on a bed. Several people knew how to weave letters, names, and mottoes into their work. Perhaps these were like the petates formerly made in San Felipe Otlaltepec, a Popoloca town in the district of Tepexi: "Formerly, complicated motifs were woven in, especially animals and abstract geometric and square shapes" (Jäcklein 1974:157).

A melancholy notion exists in the community that children today are not learning to weave, due to emigration. García and Hernández (1986:7) write that children are no longer becoming adept at weaving because they have other job possibilities outside the community. The nostalgia was evident in a conversation with a man living in Cárdenas, Campeche, who shuttles constantly back and forth between Mexico City and Campeche buying and selling *"cositas."* He had brought along his son, who did not speak Mixtec, to stay with the boy's grandparents for two weeks and experience small-town life. The man said "crafts are being lost," and that it used to be every child could make a mulita or a muñequito but now all they can make is canastas. I think, however, this fear is exaggerated, because many children who live in town are learning to weave one way or another.

Jäcklein (1974) gives an account of an entire Popoloca community in southern Puebla, San Felipe Otlaltepec, in which the skill of palm weaving has been forgotten.

> *The women of San Felipe have long since unlearned pottery and weaving. Of their ancient textile skills, only the manufacture of mats has actively continued, while they have abandoned the production of woven market baskets, cylindrical baskets, sacks, tumplines, sandals, toys, decorative objects, birdcages, and cradles. The men also used to make some of the objects mentioned. The people of San Felipe are ashamed of the fact that nowadays they are no longer able to manufacture these useful articles as the need arises. When a woman makes a palm basket, which rarely occurs, she prefers to do it in private, out of embarrassment about the defective manner and lack of skill in its elaboration. Some old people of San Felipe still know how to manufacture little palm toys; for example, stars, animals, and fruit (Jäcklein 1974:140–41).*

The passage conveys the sadness of the Felipeños about the atrophy of a formerly varied production. The pattern that emerges is an understanding that the relationship between pre-Hispanic and modern weaving is nonlinear, discontinuous, and precarious; an entire locale can revive the art of weaving palm or just as easily forget it.

CHAPTER 7

Petty Commodities: Selling the Miniature

A middle-aged Mixtec woman sat on the flagstones of the Mexico City Zócalo in the summer of 1997, perfectly at ease because she had been coming there to sell palm crafts with her mother since she was only six years old. Facing her was the gaping pit where the Templo Mayor, the Great Temple of the Aztecs, once rose. To her right, behind the Government Palace, was the obscure apartment where she scrubbed clothes on weekends for her son who was studying to be a doctor. Beneath the pavement on which she sat, the Metro Zócalo station teemed with passengers, and below that, the swampy ground of the former Lake Texcoco slowly settled in anticipation of another earthquake. But this was not Tenochtitlan; this was Mexico City. A pair of legs in shorts and sandals appeared in her field of view. A friendly voice asked, "*Cuánto cuesta?*" She negotiated prices, straightening her tiny figurines, animals, and baskets, planting them firmly upright. In the back of her mind, she hoped the city officials would not come by that day and order her to move.

Selling crafts to outsiders, whether Mexican or foreign, is the culmination of the system of weaving miniatures. Cook de Leonard (1953:429) mentions "the Mixtec traders from [Chigmecatitlán], who reach far away with their little baskets and curiosities of fine palm dyed in various colors." The ancient Mixtecs also had a reputation as consummate traveling merchants: "Commerce occupied an important place in Mixtec life, and it is possible that merchants may have enjoyed a superior status to that of the farmers" (Spores 1967:9). This chapter follows artisans from Chigmecatitlán and Santa Catarina to the provincial marketplaces and metropolitan boutiques where they ply their woven palm and raffia merchandise. Such dislocation, temporary or permanent, is a necessary facet of many artisans' lives. Virtually no tourism occurs in Chigmecatitlán; one rarely sees a sales booth within the town borders.[1]

In this chapter, I compare two sales environments: a popular market that Novelo (1993:69) describes as "production by the poor for the poor" and an elite market aimed at "tourists and middle- and upper-income urbanites" (Cook 1993:60). The two spheres are complementary, since the existence of the popular market gives elite consumers reason to believe they are participating in something age-old and typical and endows the palm commodities with transcendent cultural meaning.

PERILS OF THE ROAD

Ravicz and Romney (1969:386) write of the Mixtecs that travel, "and roads are sources of potential danger, in indigenous thought. This attitude tends to restrict movement and migration, as well as to affect outlook on those, especially strangers, who travel. Many stories, tales, and news items of dire happenings connected with trips support this."

There are people in Chigmecatitlán who have never traveled beyond the familiar neighboring towns, not even to visit the city of Puebla, a three-hour bus trip away. Most of the populace, however, is accustomed to the discomfort and possible dangers of riding the dusty Líneas del Sureste bus back and forth on selling trips to the outside world.

Before leaving town, sellers appeal to the Immaculate Conception of Mary, patroness of Chigmecatitlán, "May we come back safe, may it go

FIGURE 7.1 Bus from Puebla, headed for Santa Catarina Tlaltempan.

well." According to Jesusa Zamora, Chigmecatitlán vendors do not have their own saint, but San Martín Caballero is the patron saint of vendors in general.[2] On arrival in another community, they cross themselves before the patron saint of the local town or fair before they begin selling.

One legendary hazard to travelers is the character known as the *tentzo*.[3] A friend told me the tentzo are short, malevolent beings that people sometimes run into in the countryside. They have feet like a duck, ask for money but cannot spend it, and sometimes transform into women. Not everyone believes in the tentzo. When I asked Don Abraham Cortés (1907–97), he responded tersely, "I've walked around at night. I've never seen or heard one."

Bands of robbers are another rumored hazard to travelers. Cook de Leonard (1953:423), who in 1951 briefly visited the Popoloca area of Puebla in the vicinity of Chigmecatitlán, writes: "The isolation of the territory, practically without means of communication, and the rumors of assaults on travelers, have been an obstacle to visitors." One artisan with a reputation for hard drinking blamed his alcohol addiction on his chagrin at being robbed. About thirty years ago he went out to sell candy in Minatitlán, Veracruz, and on the way back he was robbed of two thousand "*varos*" (pesos). "*Me chingaron*" (They screwed me). He was so angry he took to drinking *ndudi* (*aguardiente,* cane rum) for three years. Former municipal president Fernando Vidales was on a bus around 1973 when it was robbed on the way into town. The Pan Bimbo van was also robbed, which is why it ceased coming to Chigmecatitlán. During the administration of Municipal President Aristeo Cabrera Armijo (1987–90) "they assaulted everyone: taxi drivers, passenger buses, trucks, Sabritas, beer distributors. There were one or more gangs." The driver of a beer delivery truck was murdered on the dirt road to town in the late 1980s or early 1990s. The itinerant dye seller did not venture to Chigmecatitlán until around 1993 because people in the town advised him that it was too dangerous. While I was staying in the town in June 1997, the clinic resident and her mother fell victim to a holdup on the bus around 9:30 at night on the road from Puebla to Chigmecatitlán.

I asked one artisan if she was afraid to travel to fairs, and she said no, because a group of people goes. She has sold through traders but enjoys the experience of going out herself and selling. The hardest part is finding a place to sleep: at El Parián, a market in Puebla, they took their own blankets, bought petates to sleep on, and camped out under the tiled porticoes where the next day they awaited customers.

The colonial city of Puebla boasts countless miniature crafts among its stores and museums. Miniatures for the tourist trade are dense among the window displays concentrated around El Parián and 6 Oriente Street off the former La Victoria market.

El Parián is an open-air collection of crafts booths under tiled archways. The Venezuelan shopkeeper at one of the booths was showing my friend Margarita and me seven carved stone elephants in graduated sizes small enough to store in a single pill capsule. They were discussing how the elephants were for good luck when the tiniest one spilled out of Margarita's hand onto the floor; we never found it again on the speckled terrazzo tile.

SELLING IN THE PAST

Palm weavers from the state of Puebla have sought out markets in Mexico City since at least the mid-nineteenth century. A period travel account remarks: "The makers of mats or *petates* of Puebla appear to have no other market than Mexico to dispose of them: thus they all scatter themselves through the streets and cry out in a uniform manner: *Petates de la Pueeeebla! . . . jabón de la Pueeeebla*: (Mats of Puebla . . . soap of Puebla)" (*Manual del viajero en Méjico*, pp. 131–33. Paris: Marcos Arróniz, 1858. Cited and translated by Starr 1899:16).

Trains of packmules and burros were the major mode of transport for large embarcations of palm goods through the early twentieth century. Even as late as 1956, there was no regular bus transit; one had to walk carrying large burlap sacks of merchandise on burros.

"When I was a boy [in the 1930s] I'd sell to those from here and those from Catarina," Pastor Flores remembered. "Those from here were Agapito Escamilla from the Barrio, and Antonio Espinosa. Sr. Agapito would go to Mexico City to sell. He would go on foot to Molcaxac, where he would catch a bus. Or he would go with a burro as far as the Mila train depot near Santa Cruz [Huitziltepec]. From there he would take the train to Puebla and then to Mexico City."

"NO HACEN BULTO"

One advantage of miniatures, according to some Chigmecatitlán artisans, is that they do not take up space in transit compared with the bulky palm goods of the past. In the 1950s Tomás Zamora and Luz María

Guajardo were local *mayoristas,* or wholesale dealers, who bought large-sized merchandise from artisans in both Chigmecatitlán and Santa Catarina. Tomás Zamora distributed crafts to a house of artesanías in Toluca, State of Mexico, run by Sr. Manuel Solís. Their daughter Imelda Zamora remembers her father filling gunny sacks with oversized palm necklaces, which were all that the residents of Santa Catarina knew how to weave at the time; necklaces were piled waist-high on the floor of the house. Her father would hoist the crafts on burros and hike through the cactus desert to the highway at La Monera, where a car would transport them to the nearest train station—Mila—at Santa Cruz Huitziltepec, then to Puebla (*Tensio*) or Mexico City (*Ñu Koyo*).

By contrast, Doña Imelda's younger sister Clara Zamora, who sells three times a year at fairs, can fit her entire stock of miniature palm merchandise neatly in two plastic jars and a cookie tin. Doña Clara estimated the value of the miniatures in the tin at 500 to 1,000 pesos. Miniatures are advantageous, she told me, because *"no hacen bulto"* (they aren't bulky). With mules no longer common as beasts of burden, people have to carry the merchandise themselves, making large loads less feasible.

THE SOCIAL STRUCTURE OF MARKETING

There are approximately fifty sellers in Chigmecatitlán at different levels, most of whom are also artisans (Table 7.1). For purposes of analysis, sellers can be divided into two spheres: popular and elite (Novelo 1993). As Novelo (1993:48–49) explains: "We can point to basically two spheres in which craft products circulate. One, the low sphere directed toward popular consumption. By contrast, the craft products aimed at the tourist market, both interior and exterior, circulate in the high sphere directed

TABLE 7.1 Mixtec Terms for Traders

nde xe ña'a	*'gente que vende'*	intermediaries, sellers, vendors
xe ña'a te	*'usted compra, él compra'*	buyer
diko ña ko	*'vender cosas ella'*	she is a trader
diko ña te	*'vender cosas él'*	he is a trader
diko ña ve	*'vender cosas él o ella (de cariño)'*	he or she (affectionately) is a trader
diko ña x	*'vender cosas él o ella (despectivo)'*	he or she (derogatory) is a trader

TABLE 7.2 Social Structure of Marketing Crafts from Chigmecatitlán

	Popular Sphere	Elite Sphere
Time of year	seasonal; vendors sell three times a year	year-round
Place	regional fairs, markets in towns and cities	tourist markets, shops, government stores in cities
Craft Size	large, medium, small, miniature	miniature
Material	palm, raffia	palm
Customers	poor and middle-class Mexicans (children and adults)	middle- and upper-class Mexicans, tourists (adults)

toward affluent consumers." The popular market consists of *poquiteros,* casual vendors who typically sell directly to the public three times a year at regional fairs. The elite market consists of professional vendors who sell year-round to select shops in Puebla and Mexico City. These are ideal types; most vendors combine aspects of both spheres. The social structure of marketing palm crafts is summarized above (Table 7.2). A schism exists between the popular and elite markets regarding craft size and materials; the popular market favors large or medium-size crafts made of plastic, and the elite market favors miniature crafts made of palm.

Four vendors from Chigmecatitlán had set up their wares outside the bustling main market in Tepeaca on Palm Sunday of 1996. Their stock of medium-sized raffia figures was appropriate for their intended clientele of mainly children of the poor. One artisan, who sells once a year on All Saints' Day in Ciudad Mendoza, Veracruz, where she has kin, emphasized that she cannot sell miniatures there: "They won't buy [miniatures] there. They buy large things there: large baskets, large clowns."

According to Pierre Bourdieu (1984:468), the classification of consumer items commonly follows pairs of oppositions, hence "distinction," or the ability to distinguish between high- and low-class markers. For Bourdieu (1984:367), the working class "rejects specifically aesthetic intentions as aberrations," seeking out things that are functional and practical. The artisans' own preference for the ease of weaving with plastic raffia has also contributed to the current situation that about half of the town's production is plastic and half palm.

The elite market, whether Mexican or international, shuns plastic; most Americans find it hard to reconcile hand work with artificial materials. Novelo (1993:46) believes that for elite consumers, natural materials, preferably the same ones pre-Hispanic groups used, are integral to the overall package: "Aesthetic evaluation, attending to the qualities of originality and hand labor, is also linked to the raw materials utilized, privileging those that existed prior to industrial civilization."

THE POPULAR SPHERE

Artisans in the popular sphere go out to sell about three times a year, often to towns where other emigrant relatives live (García and Hernández 1986:8). Because no single artisan can weave a sufficient inventory, a vendor accumulates pieces from various relatives and distributes them through networks based on kinship. For example, Casimiro Méndez markets his china and charro dolls through his brother in Oaxaca. Basilio Herrera, who also makes china and charro dolls, said he was thinking of taking advantage of his children's residence in Tapachula, Chiapas, to sell to American visitors. Fernanda Pineda sells her nda'cho baskets via her children in Minatitlán, Veracruz.

These artisans usually leave town to sell just before national holidays, which the Mexican public traditionally associates with certain toys and miniatures such as the mule and the palm bead necklace (Pettit and Pettit 1978; see also Table 0.1).

The Mule

The mule with saddlebags, sold during Lent, Corpus Christi, and All Saints' Day, has been made since the 1950s or earlier and is one of the most recognizable Chigmecatitlán objects nationwide. According to Fernández Ledesma (1930:38), "They are purchased to be given as 'mascots' to wish people an abundance of material wealth in the course of the year." Eduardo Noguera (1939:24) explains that "the toy mules and the costumes that the children wear on this day represent the paying of tithes to the church by the natives, after the conquest of Mexico. Since the Indians were not in a position to pay with money, it was permissible for them to bring products from the different regions of Mexico in lieu of money." A similar custom is observed on December 12, Day of Guadalupe. In addition to the mules, palm toys from Chigmecatitlán including baskets, mats, and pineapples may be attached to the *huacales* or crates the costumed children carry into church.

The Necklace

The palm bead necklace, made since the 1950s or earlier, is a traditional accessory used nationwide in Mexican celebrations. Schoolchildren of both sexes wore red, white, and green necklaces in folk dances or *bailables* on September 16 and the spring festival. Palm beads adorned cars in parades along with the emblem of the PRI. The beads were originally twice as large as the ones made today. In the 1950s, necklaces contained half a gross of beads and sold for one peso. In 1955 and 1956 the Germans bought a lot of them (Inocencio Rodríguez). "The gringas would wear several in different colors" (José Flores). Necklaces sold better when one vendor had the idea of mixing ten colors of beads in a necklace. He had already shortened them since mothers said they were too long for their little girls.

Important selling days in the popular sphere include:

Candlemas (La Candelaria)	February 2
Lent	(Moveable feast)
Holy Week	(Moveable feast)
Day of the Child (Día del Niño)	April 30
Corpus Christi	(Moveable feast)
Mexican Independence (Fiestas Patrias)	September 15–16
All Saints' (Todos Santos)	November 1–2
Las Posadas	December 16–24
Christmas	December 25

Artisans in the popular sphere also sell on regional feast days commemorating the titular saints of small towns. Below are some of the provincial fairs that annually attract sizeable contingents of Chigmecatitlán artisans.

Amecameca, State of México (Señor del Sacromonte)	First Friday of Lent; lasts two weeks
Tepexi de Rodríguez, Puebla	First Friday of Lent
Tepalcingo, Morelos (Señor de Tepalcingo)	Third Friday of Lent
Tepeyahualco, Puebla (Cristo de Nazarén)	Fifth Friday of Lent

Tejalpa, Puebla	Fifth Friday of Lent
San Pablo Anicano, Puebla (Nuestro Señor de la Paz)	First Tuesday after Holy Week
Tepeaca, Puebla	April 30, Día del Niño
Tlacotepec, Puebla (Señor del Calvario)	First Sunday in July
Orizaba, Veracruz	All Saints' Day

Other traditional regional venues for Chigmecatitlán crafts are Huajuapan de León, Juxtlahuaca, and Tezoatlán (Oaxaca); Acatlán, Atlixco, Matamoros, Puebla, and Tehuacán (Puebla); and Córdoba (Veracruz) (Jacinto Flores; Ochoa 1993:45).

A provincial fair in honor of Nuestro Señor de la Paz was held in the small town of San Pablo Anicano outside Acatlán, Puebla, on April 9, 1996. Fifteen sellers from Chigmecatitlán had arrived by bus on the *víspera* or eve of the feast and stayed three nights. They were dispersed throughout the fair, their merchandise arrayed on plastic sheets on the ground. Ifigenia Pineda, selling raffia mules carrying pineapples, said it was her first time and she was having trouble with her spot since the adjacent vendor had reserved an eight-meter section of sidewalk. Only Jesusa Zamora and her brother Luis Zamora had collapsible booths, which they had transported in the cargo hold of the bus. No one seemed to be selling much; they were competing with each other and with artisans from Olinalá, Guerrero, who were offering painted red gourds and wooden toys.

All sellers know their market, according to Don Jacinto. Run-of-the mill, inexperienced sellers compete among themselves and drive prices down. They may not have enough money to wait or hold out for higher prices. The most experienced sellers do not compete, but get up and leave so prices won't drop. Those who know the milieu well are never at the same place at the same time, and everyone sells what the others don't. They either put away duplicated merchandise or hold the price firm.

Sales trips might be expected to have overtones of religious pilgrimage, given their inherent link with the Catholic festival calendar. The long-distance trade routes of Aztec and Mayan merchants were thought to be congruent with pilgrimage routes to visit oracles (Linda Schele, personal communication). The same was true of Spain, where Catholic

FIGURE 7.2 Selling Chigmecatitlán crafts at the festival of Nuestro Señor de la Paz, San Pablo Anicano, Puebla.

group pilgrimages (*romerías*) were occasions for fairs. I investigated the connection between sales trips and pilgrimage in regard to Chigmecatitlán but found little intersection. Townspeople undertake a difficult annual pilgrimage to the Basilica of Guadalupe in Mexico City, a five-day trek on foot, departing February 7. Others bicycle (leaving February

10) or board a chartered bus (leaving February 11), all delegations converging on the Basilica on February 12, when the archbishop of Puebla delivers a mass for pilgrims from the state of Puebla. But people do not normally carry crafts to sell on their journey to the Basilica, either as devotional objects or to sell.

THE ELITE SPHERE

Vendors in the elite sphere, rather than selling directly to the public, act as intermediaries between artisans and retail stores. They supply crafts to urban bazaars (Bazar Sábado, La Carreta, La Ciudadela, Feria de Puebla, El Parián) and shops (Miniaturas Felguérez, Regalos Hansen, Sanborns) that cater to relatively affluent Mexicans and foreigners. Upscale venues also include state outlets for crafts such as DIF-Puebla, the FONART chain, Museo Nacional de Artes e Industrias Populares (MNAIP), and the Museum of Anthropology gift shop.

These vendors either collect merchandise weekly at artisans' homes or wait for artisans to deliver to them. Jacinto Flores and his wife, for example, navigate their bicycles through the rocky lanes of Chigmecatitlán to pick up merchandise at artisans' houses on Saturday through Monday. They *"reparten,"* or distribute merchandise wholesale, on Thursday and Friday, the days when Mexican shopkeepers are most likely to have cash on hand and time to attend to them.

Other artisans drop goods off at the mom-and-pop store of Don Genaro Arizpe, who buys everything. *"El lo agarra: canastas, muñecos, collares"* (He grabs it up: baskets, dolls, necklaces). One artisan commented that there is nothing to eat until the corn ripens, so she takes her crafts to Don Genaro, who sells them in Mexico City "or somewhere." It did not concern her if a buyer turned around and sold her crafts for a profit. I was struck by many artisans' apparent lack of curiosity about the fate of their crafts; most people I asked said they did not know what sellers or customers did with the merchandise.

The usual markup is 100 percent each time the product changes hands, i.e., a retail price of 400 percent of the artisan's price:

Artisan	Intermediary	Store
1	x 2	x 2
	(maximum)	(normal; it can be higher or lower)

For example, if the artisan receives three pesos, the intermediary receives six pesos and the store receives twelve pesos. Sellers observe points of etiquette such as not earning a profit when selling in the confines of the town and giving pieces gratis to visitors rather than charging them on the first visit. Artisans set one price for local buyers and a higher price for Santa Catarina buyers.

Those who deal with an international clientele say they discern differences in buying habits by nationality, though their observations vary. Doña Imelda Zamora, for instance, said that Mexicans appreciated the work more than foreign clients. A clerk at the Regalos Hansen gift shop remarked that Mexicans tended to buy miniatures for their own collections, while foreigners (e.g., from Spain or Cuba) bought them as presents. Don Inocencio Rodríguez said the Japanese and French bought a lot from him, but Mexicans hardly bought anything. One of the proprietors of Miniaturas Felguérez told me Americans, Germans, Mexicans, and Spaniards all bought different "lines" of miniatures. The traveling dye seller from Puebla, who handles Chigmecatitlán crafts as a sideline for tourist outlets in Acapulco, Cancún, Mérida, and the coast of Tabasco, said "gringos" bought the most miniatures. "They want what is different. Mexicans aren't as interested in crafts. Gringos seek out the handmade object as an example of Mexican culture and tradition."

The gift shop Regalos Hansen in Coyoacán, Mexico City, is typical of the elite market. Jacinto Flores furnishes the shop with miniature figurines such as clowns and musicians. Pieces there retailed for thirteen pesos each in February 1996, the expected markup of about 400 percent over the artisan's income of three pesos. An eighteen-piece nativity was priced at two hundred pesos, also the predicted 400 percent markup.

The rows of tiny palm figurines in the glass case at Regalos Hansen confirmed Don Jacinto's strategy of varying the designs so customers would buy several as a collection. When his aunt solicited his advice about weaving miniature clowns (*payasitos*), Don Jacinto suggested tactics to encourage customers to buy more than one: various color combinations; different hats—a straw hat, a newsboy's cap, a baseball cap—and various objects in their hands—dumbbells, a parasol, a beachball. Designs such as the baseball team, chess set, nativity, mariachi, and marching band are automatically conducive to multiple sales because they come in sets of eight, a dozen, or more figurines.

The shop clerk said patrons ask who makes the figures, how they make them, and where they are from. "Who makes them, just one per-

FIGURES 7.3-7.4 Miniature clowns. Clown holding balloons shows finer weave than the rest.

son or more than one?" "What beautiful work," they say. She relays Don Jacinto's response that his relatives make them, that they are woven like friendship bracelets, and that they are from Puebla. Customers request something "typical," she said.

The slim narrative she supplies makes the pieces more meaningful to the consumer (Causey 1997, Graburn 1976, Stewart 1993). June Nash (1993:10) sums up well the tacit assumptions and desires of the customer buying a handmade object: "The intrinsic value of crafts to the sophisticated traveller or catalogue customer is precisely the human labor embodied in the product and what it tells about a whole way of life." Just as a souvenir of the Eiffel tower paraphrases the real tower, miniature crafts are epigrammatic of full-sized crafts. As souvenirs, they may also represent, implicitly, the travels of the owner, the lifeways of the maker, and the mythology of Mexico.

Another participant in the elite sphere of marketing is Don Inocencio

Rodríguez, an artisan and vendor from Santa Catarina Tlaltempan who sells palm toys on the sidewalk at the Universidad Nacional Autónoma de México (UNAM) in Mexico City. Because he sells year-round and occasionally supplies government crafts stores such as FONART, he falls nominally into the elite category. On weekends he also sells at the Jardín Centenario in front of the main church in Coyoacán, a colonial neighborhood of Mexico City.

Disguised behind a baseball cap and tinted shades, Don Inocencio crouched on a two-gallon can padded with a scrap of cardboard on the covered walkway outside the Facultad de Filosofía y Letras at UNAM. He drank a large bottle of beer while he talked with world-weary savvy about the past. While conversing, he sold two small nda'cho wallets and a small bird for four or five pesos each to a young international student. He and his wife, who still lives in Santa Catarina, collaborate on weaving palm animals. I offered to help him arrange his merchandise, and he readily asked me to untangle the Otomí bead (*chaquira*) bracelets and necklaces from San Pablito, Puebla, which he also sells, that had been jumbled together after the weekend in Coyoacán. Adjacent vendors displayed their modest wares aimed at university students: books, poetry journals, fashion magazines, T-shirts, sweaters, and earrings.

Don Inocencio Rodríguez worked stints as a part-time migrant laborer harvesting pineapples in Loma Bonita, Veracruz, in May and June of 1945; Texas cotton in 1957, and Baja California lettuce in 1961. He interacted occasionally with government agencies such as FONART, whose 1994–95 identification card he still carried; though he no longer actively sold crafts through that agency, they continued to supply him credit. He also benefited from low-interest loans from BANFOCO, the predecessor of FONART.[4] He formerly supplied palm merchandise to the Mercado San Juan and Mercado de la Merced, historic markets deeply entrenched in the cultural life of the capital.

His trajectory echoes Ravicz and Romney's (1969:391) description of the Mixteca: "young men emigrate seasonally or permanently. Some go to the sugarmills of Puebla, others to pick cane or crops in Veracruz. Many have worked as braceros in the United States; those who return bring new ideas, new material elements, money. Some move to Mexico City in search of work."

In 1956 and 1957, when not picking cotton, Don Inocencio Rodríguez distributed palm crafts to Casa Cervantes, a now-defunct establishment on Avenida Juárez in Mexico City that had sold popular art to tourists since 1923. He wove tiny blue fire fans for Casa Cervantes to attach to their advertising cards.

Don Inocencio Rodríguez's biographical sketch suggests the instability of artisans' interactions with government craft agencies and private businesses. Above all, it illustrates the resourcefulness required to make a living by making and selling crafts.

CASA CERVANTES, S.A.
Arte Popular Mexicano
Mayoreo y Menudeo
Av. Juárez 18
Establecido en 1923
México 1, D.F.
Tels.　　*13-12-84*
　　　　35-47-46

Sucursal Oaxaca
Porfirio Díaz 5
Oaxaca, Oax.
　　—From Casa Cervantes letterhead, 1957

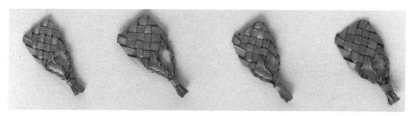

León Pérez, the weaver of rustic nativities and bandstands in Chigmecatitlán, worked with Casa Cervantes in the same era. About 1952, he began delivering to Casa Cervantes every two weeks. The first thing he made was a band of musicians; he earned fifteen centavos per figure. Sr. Cervantes also requested little pine trees [*pinitos*] about three centimeters tall and little doves to stick on Christmas cards, which required Don León to start weaving doves flat to fit in an envelope; before that, they were three-dimensional.

Casa Cervantes ordered a palm nativity from León Pérez around 1955 or 1960 ("People were always asking me to make one") and displayed one of his medium-size nativities in their window. When he arrived he saw people with their noses pressed against the glass discussing what it was made of, unaware that the artisan was present. They were saying it was "petate," which to him is something you sleep on. León Pérez added ruefully that customers did not believe he made the figures himself; they thought he just bought them.

PROJECTING AUTHENTICITY

Tourists in the elite sphere attempt to forge an authentic experience in purchasing an object; there is "collusion between native sellers and buyers in constructing authenticity" (Joel Sherzer, personal communication, October 1996). Chigmecatitlán artisans oblige by emphasizing the conventions of Indianness, "dressing the part" in representing themselves to highly educated buyers for whom specific Indian identity matters.[5] "We have been kept out of expositions because we don't dress like Indians," Don Jacinto said. "The anthropologist, the government demands it."

Jacinto purposely wears a woven shirt and trousers when he leaves town on selling trips. "I own a jogging suit; I own a T-shirt that says 'Made in Japan'" (i.e., urban, mestizo, transnational clothing). He avoids those when he goes out to sell or buyers will not believe he is an Indian. It is a mutual fantasy, he says; at exhibitions people want the experience of buying crafts from someone who looks like an Indian. He is acquainted with people who wear braids and bead necklaces when they go to market, then change into European dress when they get home. "In FONART, too, if the Huichols don't dress as Indians they don't buy from them. They are asking to be fooled."

GENERIC CRAFTS

When selling in the popular sphere, however, townspeople *deemphasize* their identity as Mixtec speakers and as people of Chigmecatitlán unless pressed, instead assuming the role of anonymous purveyors of the typical. Women seem to "let their hair down," removing their ubiquitous rebozos from their heads when selling outside of town. Doña Imelda Zamora said when customers ask where the crafts are from, she gen-

FIGURE 7.5 Shopper, Bazar Sábado, San Ángel, Mexico City. February 1996.

eralizes "from the state of Puebla." People ask things like "aren't you from Michoacán?" The long-distance mobility of small-time vendors to other states on selling trips undoubtedly also has caused mistaken identity. The handmade object has undergone "a transmutation from being a local product which expresses the social and economic conditions in which it was created, to a product which embodies the multiple subjectivities of the national spirit, a specific symbol of Mexicanness" (Medina 1975:9). Ironically, first- and second-graders in 1995 were greeted with photographs of Chigmecatitlán's familiar musician and clown miniatures as illustrations in their own national textbooks.[6] This exemplifies what Néstor García Canclini (1993:65) terms the "reduction of the ethnic to the typical."

The Bazar Sábado in San Angel, Mexico City, is a privately owned crafts market where attribution is vague and aesthetics are paramount. Open since 1960, it receives ten thousand Mexicans and tourists each Saturday (Romero 1993:100, 102). Inside the building and in two flanking plazas sit fee-paying vendors whom the management has approved, while uninvited squatters hover on the periphery. In 1996 I counted forty-five booths at the Bazar Sábado selling Mexican miniatures, including familiar palm mules and baskets from Chigmecatitlán. Amid this unlabeled profusion, the geographic origin of the crafts was practically indecipherable.

A few blocks away, a similar phenomenon, which García Canclini (1993:65, see also 77, 78) terms the "dissolution of the ethnic into the national," occurs at La Carreta, an ample crafts store in the San Angel neighborhood where various retail booths cluster under one roof. I located miniature clowns, bands, a mariachi, and strings of palm baskets and beads from Chigmecatitlán in March 1996. Consistent with its upper-middle-class Mexican clientele, the crafts were exclusively palm. A clerk I asked insisted the figures came from the State of Mexico. Most salespeople are reticent about giving the source of goods even if they know it. The clerk may simply have been uninformed, but government-sponsored stores such as FONART make a practice of shielding the provenience of crafts from customers by using coded tags on merchandise.

At the cultural center in downtown Puebla (Arte Popular-DIF Puebla) I asked if certain miniatures were from Chigmecatitlán and was told by the shop women there that I would have to ask the manager for that information. A mystique of origin is cultivated; provenience is treated as sensitive information so customers will not go there to buy directly from artisans. "Like all curiosities, . . . souvenirs function to generate narrative," writes Stewart (1993:147). If a narrative attaches to the souvenir bought under these conditions, it is a narrative of the "typically Mexican" or perhaps "Indian" but not from any specific ethnicity or town.

MINIATURAS FELGUEREZ
"Reminiscencias Miniaturas"
Hamburgo 150-1A
Plaza del Angel
México, DF
CP 06600
Tel. 5 14 14 05
    —Receipt from Miniaturas Felguérez

A tiny store in the Zona Rosa known as Miniaturas Felguérez has been a mainstay of the miniatures trade in Mexico City since 1981. The store with its trademark chrome-yellow shelves was, until its recent closing, single-handedly responsible for much of the dissemination of Mexican miniatures to travelers and locals who flock to this fashionable shopping district. The original store was a fixture for fourteen years on

Hamburgo Street at the corner of Niza. The small space was "barely able to contain four customers at a time, while others often wait on the sidewalk" (Masuoka 1990), and a second outlet across the street in Plaza del Ángel opened circa 1994.

The owners, Luis and Alicia Felguérez, originally went into the miniatures business because their regular crafts workshops kept going broke due to anti-artesanías laws and taxes. Miniatures, which could be made at home outside the workshops, were the only profitable crafts. Sr. Felguérez specializes in humorous "two-inch skeleton figures" or *calaveras* acting out wry commentary on the news of the day; he follows in the footsteps of the political satire of the Mexican master engraver José Guadalupe Posada (1852–1913) (Masuoka 1990). When I visited Sr. Felgúerez, he was already selling a miniature of "El Chupacabras," a sinister character from the front page at the time. In addition to his caricature figurines, the shop sold legions of dollhouse-size items including some from Chigmecatitlán. A palm rock band with amplifiers and microphones was displayed in the window of the second store; it was made by Honoria Flores from Chigmecatitlán.

RESTRICTIONS ON SELLING

Among the obstacles Chigmecatitlán sellers face in their business transactions are the restrictions that authorities have imposed on outdoor selling. Federal District policies prohibit artisans from selling on the streets and plazas of Mexico City. Laws to regulate vendors and relocate them outside the city in concrete-block venues such as the Central de Abastos are a constant thorn in the side of artisans.

Artisans in Chigmecatitlán in 1997 were complaining that it was hard to find a place to sell on the city streets. "One used to be free to sell on the public highway in Mexico City and Puebla," an artisan commented. The Mexico City Cathedral was formerly the biggest market, especially Thursday and Friday of Holy Week, Thursday and Sunday of Corpus Christi, and September 15 and 16. "There weren't any problems with asking permission to sell," another said. Mexico City is difficult now because of city ordinances against sidewalk vendors.

"*No tengo plaza,*" Doña Clara Zamora began, worrying that she had no marketplace. She said it was getting harder to sell: "We hardly have a marketplace. One doesn't earn much. They used to permit selling in

Mexico City. Sales used to be very good on September 15 in the Zó-calo." Now artisans are not allowed to sell in Mexico City before 2:00 p.m. Her sister Doña Imelda Zamora, who until 1996 sold miniatures on weekends at the Zócalo across from the Templo Mayor, had to relo-cate to a site outside the Museo de Arte Contemporáneo in Chapultepec Park. Agents from the Departamento del Distrito Federal forced the artisans to move on, "the ones with the white vans. They take the mer-chandise."

Things were no better in Puebla. I received a note from a friend whom I had asked to call on José Flores and Catalina Escalante, inno-vators of miniature figurines. "I didn't get to see your friend. All of the 'ambulantes' had been run off by the police; squads, platoons, battalions of them in full riot gear, defending the city against the vicious sidewalk salespeople" (Stephen Bray, September 17, 1998).

The campaigns of the past decade against sidewalk vendors may be a reaction to the overpopulation of the cities, economic hard times, and an influx of cheap imported merchandise for sale on the streets, but handmade crafts are an innocuous minority among the commodities for sale.

Jacinto Flores maintained that support for retailers is ultimately beneficial to artisans. He believed retail craft stores ought to be eligible for the same government loans as artisans, and that retailers should be allowed to sell on consignment if they wish. He wanted the town to in-vest in its own display racks like the ones in which huge conglomerates like Pan Bimbo and Sabritas display snack foods, and he had engaged a carpenter to build a display case for one client. He envisioned a "modern system of sales" in which "there will be a vendor in every city or town; we're no longer interested in selling only in Mexico City or Puebla."

In a study of Irish arts-and-crafts makers who became "instant inter-nationals," McAuley (1999:67) finds that the small size of a company is not a barrier to exporting and that trade fairs and networks are impor-tant in setting up contacts to export and reach distant markets. The dis-tinguishing feature of artisans who successfully internationalized was "that the entrepreneurs view themselves as businesspeople rather than craftspeople." According to McAuley's analysis, Don Jacinto, as a micro-entrepreneur, and others like him who define themselves as business-people are the most likely to be able to penetrate the global market.

CONCLUSIONS

The marketing of palm miniatures caps the cycle of craft production in Chigmecatitlán. Artisan-sellers have historically traveled far afield, confronting occasional risks in pursuit of a market but often enjoying the experience of leaving town. The market is split in two complementary, overlapping spheres: popular and elite. Distribution in both markets is still accomplished by individuals personally transporting merchandise to market, though crafts tend to be smaller than they were nearly a century ago.

The popular market relies on family networks from whom casual sellers amass merchandise to supplement the crafts they make themselves. Casual sellers interact face to face with their clientele, often middle-class or working-class Mexicans, at fairs around three times a year. Their merchandise is likely to concentrate on medium-size articles made from raffia. Such sales are inextricably embedded in seasonal observances of familiar Mexican holidays. However, the popular market has been dampened in the past few years by officials clamping down on selling in public plazas.

In the elite market, full-time sellers also rely on kinship networks to supply them with merchandise, but they distribute to stores outside Chigmecatitlán with whom they have an impersonal relationship. Merchandise in the elite market is likely to consist of miniature articles made of palm. The maintenance of tradition tacitly encourages sellers who deal with an upscale market to "dress the part" to enhance their transactions. Nevertheless, the identity they portray, and that which ultimately attends pieces from Chigmecatitlán in an urban shop, is of generic "Indianness" or of Mexican folk art rather than specifically Mixtec or from Chigmecatitlán.

Private Town, Public Longing

The small town of Chigmecatitlán on the northern edge of the Mixteca region of Puebla has a dwindling population but one claim to distinction: the charming miniature palm crafts it produces. The Mixtec-speaking inhabitants, who take up palm weaving as an economic recourse when they are in town and stop weaving when away, view the "little toys" they make strictly as commodities. Yet to the country at large—and the tourists who visit Mexico—the miniature crafts project nostalgic qualities of picturesque rurality, romanticism, and nationalism—qualities reinforced both by the crafts' subject matter and their diminutive scale. The imputed atavistic dexterity, ingenuity, and patience of the artisans, as well as the presumed activities of their daily life, are present in miniature simulacra displayed for sale. Susan Stewart (1993) uses the word *longing* to describe the yearning desire of Western tourists, travelers, and collectors for the miniature. This town guards its own privacy and anonymity while producing crafts that fulfill the public's longing for tradition.

During the Porfirio Díaz dictatorship of more than thirty years, "native art was socially outcast" (Covarrubias 1940:138). After the Mexican Revolution of 1910, the Mexican government and others fostered an artistic renaissance (Covarrubias 1940). Mexican fine artists participated in the consolidation of popular cultural forms into an expression of Mexico as a place of splendor. Mexico's massive archaeological monuments had been since the nineteenth century motives for national pride suitable for international display (Morales-Moreno 1994:175). The sensibility of artists and intellectuals who admired the aesthetic qualities of popular crafts and recognized the inherent nobility of their makers—primarily mestizo and indigenous campesinos—brought the abundant richness of crafts into the national limelight. The growth of tourism from the north provided a large market as Americans, too, enthusiastically bought Mexican crafts and "curios."

The elite collections of popular art of the 1920s and 1930s embraced large-size palm figures from Chigmecatitlán. These toys of palm fronds tinted bright red, yellow, green, purple, and fuchsia were the epitome of guileless amusement. The Roberto Montenegro collection from 1934 still retains a palm trombone player on a wooden base and a horseback rider with several pineapples in deep baskets.[1] The Nelson Rockefeller collection includes figures from Chigmecatitlán from the 1930s (Oettinger 1990:167). In the same decade, Fernández Ledesma (1930:after p. 36) illustrated a *"venadito"* (deer) from Chigmecatitlán in his *Juguetes mexicanos*.

The situation of small-scale crafts in Chigmecatitlán modulates many of the notions inscribed in the literature of Mexican folk art, chief among them a belief in the ancient heritage of miniature objects. Researchers and aficionados of Mexican crafts have inferred an unbroken legacy between the ancient Mixtecs' reputed prowess as miniaturist artists and the modern Mixtec weaving of tiny animals and human figurines in dyed palm. Five hundred years of history are seemingly collapsed in these sprightly miniature crafts, which have become quintessential symbols of Mexican national identity.

But my interviews with artisans in Chigmecatitlán as well as a comparison of modern pieces with those in museum collections confirm that crafts were once *larger* and are getting *smaller* under the influence of outsiders, from commercial middlemen to politicians, who have visited the town. Writers have been seduced by the idea that Mexican Indian artisans are traditionally inclined to make tiny things. In Chigmecatitlán, the townspeople's relationship to the miniature is artificial, imposed from the outside; intermediaries have urged palm weavers to increase their market by decreasing the scale of their crafts. Since the 1960s, pressure from middlemen in pursuit of "the typical" has resulted in the near disappearance of large- and medium-size crafts and an intensification of small size.

Postmodern researchers look at historical legacies as having many gaps, and traditions as constructs that are constantly being reinvented. Accordingly, people in Mexico make miniatures not just because they are a pre-Hispanic tradition but because consumers *believe* they are a pre-Hispanic tradition and have promoted them as a coveted national legacy.

In the early twentieth century, weavers in Chigmecatitlán were producing a range of sizes of nominally utilitarian articles such as wallets and baskets as well as anthropomorphic and zoomorphic figures. Most were defined, even then, as toys for exterior trade. These factors weaken the classic transformation of crafts, said to hold sway in Mexico, from functional to decorative and from internal to external markets. Palm weaving in Chigmecatitlán has been aimed at external markets since its inception.

In contrast with the standard portrayal of Mexican crafts, most raw materials for basketry are not native to the town: palm fronds, plastic raffia, and bottle caps originate in other states; the brilliant dyes are manufactured in Germany. The crafts circulate in a "global" economy both in the materials they incorporate and in their commercialization (cf. Tice 1995:77 on the international origin of *mola* materials).

The emergence of plastic raffia has fed the anxiety of folk art consumers who mourn the loss of tradition in the countryside. Ironically, raffia figures are aimed at the regional, popular market for use as children's toys, thereby enhancing the legitimacy and authenticity of palm products for urban, affluent consumers. Handmade objects will continue to coexist with factory-made products in regional markets and plazas as long as their prices remain low (Turok 1988a:27).

Although I have emphasized the recent genesis of the miniature, intriguing hints of ancient practices have cropped up: woven rattles containing pebbles gathered by red ants or coyulli beans, live woodpeckers suspended among bunches of Thevetia flowers, the similarity between a knot used in weaving and one in the *Codex Nuttall,* the probable dating of the twilled nda'cho basket to the Preclassic (800–150 BC at Coxcatlán Cave), and archival evidence of the town's existence in 1520.

However, popular Catholicism, rather than ancient Indian religion, is the more direct inspiration for diminutive art in Mexico. Chigmecatitlán artisans put an unusual commercial spin on votive miniatures, placing them in contact with holy statues in the hope of attaining better skill and sales.

The designs as well as the emphasis on miniature scale are based on national stereotypes rather than local experience. Artisans derive their notions of what constitutes appropriate subject matter from other folk art media. The same characters that foreign travelers promoted in the nineteenth century have ended up populating the universe of palm miniatures in Chigmecatitlán. The artisans are indigenous Mixtecs, but their crafts express nonspecific "folk" origins.

I view miniatures as a codification of stereotyped understandings of ethnicity and nationality, in which artisans are more or less willing participants. The town of Chigmecatitlán has cultivated its autonomy against outsiders and has resisted external rule, persistently attempting nevertheless to extract needed cash and other support from the greater state that surrounds it. Artisans' economic success depends partly on their ability to produce symbols that consumers in the boutiques and bazaar stalls of the remote metropolis can easily "decode." Artisans *need* consumers to believe in a romantic version of the history and significance of miniatures.

Palm crafts mediate between townspeople and outsiders. As a form of communication, however, crafts are ultimately mute or at least equivocal signifiers. Most artisans profess indifference to the destination of their crafts or what the consumers do with them; they do not share the positive response many consumers feel toward miniature crafts. For the artisans, each figure is a reminder of the history of the invention and execution of that particular design. The artisan might have struggled to learn to weave, buy the palm or raffia, complete a quota of a dozen or a gross, and elicit divine intervention to acquire more skill and better sales. These discourses do not accompany the crafts to market.

I have downplayed the rational logic of the miniature—cheapness, portability, and efficient use of material—because I think the practical benefits of compactness obscure an understanding of the miniature's appeal for its enthusiasts, which is based more on historical, aesthetic, and emotional impulses. To quote Lévi-Strauss (1966:22), a miniature is "a material object which is also an object of knowledge." Collecting miniatures, like collecting in general, is a particularly Western form of knowledge.

Ethnographic writing itself stems partly from the Western impulse to collect (Clifford 1988). This book is the result of conflicting tendencies: on one hand, the positivist urge to know, to interpret through scholarly inquiry. On the other hand, occasional contradictions, ambiguous statements from my informants, and fragments I have not "unpacked" threaten to overflow the neat boundaries of this narrative.

As Albers (1970, preface, n.p.) sagely points out, "all art is an act of condensation." This book emphasizes the centrality of the miniature to people's lives in Chigmecatitlán and, in so doing, necessarily compresses and flattens the vastness of real life in the town. It is an aide-mémoire, a tiny world cribbed within pages.

In this brief portrait of a town and some of the people who pass in and out of it, the objects they collectively conjure out of plain palm fronds or extruded plastic strips, and the complex life that surrounds these objects, tremendous emotion adheres to tiny things. As Jacinto Flores said, reckoning that miniatures could command higher prices with a potency other crafts could not, *"La miniatura es algo especial"*: The miniature is something special. Even now, after years of subjecting the data to objective analysis, as I gaze down on the minutiae I have collected from Chigmecatitlán, the rapture of the miniature short-circuits analytical skepticism and I still share Edward Weston's (1973:157) view of toys as "an inexhaustible source of pleasure." For the artisans, whether the recourse to the plenitude of smallness is a greater boon or affliction remains in doubt.

Imagining the Future of a Mexican Craft

What is the future of Chigmecati-tlán crafts in the twenty-first century as the small town, the traditional locus of popular folk art in Mexico, is vacated by mass departure from the countryside and peasant artisans become post-peasant artisans? This is more than a practical question; it is also a symbolic question, because the deservedly exalted reputation of Mexican folk crafts has since the 1920s provided Mexico with a valuable source of cultural identity. "Crafts have become a symbol of Mexicanness," Novelo (1993:7) states. Along with other instantly recognizable aspects of Mexican life, crafts are something that "defines Mexican culture" (Novelo 1993:8). "The artisans engaged in traditional modes of production have become the producers of 'ethnicity' and the keepers of traditions around which the nation gathers and gains a sense of local, regional, and national identity," Kaplan (1993:120) writes.

Medina (1975:9) points out the disparity between the people who make crafts barely to survive as paupers, and those who "exalt and disseminate" popular art. Novelo (1993:73–74) likewise asks, "Is it reasonable that crafts should come from a production that is insufficient to give most artisans food to eat, while they are granted a privileged place in the construction of a national identity?" This is an important question. Novelo (1993:74) sees the self-organization of artisans as the answer, but she also urges: "something can be done in the meantime if the intellectual admiration for crafts also becomes preoccupation and reflection on the overall conditions in which [crafts] are produced" (Novelo 1993:77).

Crafts have historically been an adjunct pursuit of campesinos who farm small family plots for auto-subsistence, the classic peasant mode of life. In the 1970s, when socialist models of progress informed higher education in Mexico, some intellectuals concluded that Mexican crafts were a "sign of underdevelopment" (Novelo 1976:7) in a society that was attempting to modernize and industrialize. There was guilt on the part of the intelligentsia that folk art, so crucial to the construction of a Mexican national identity, was produced by campesinos with a miserable standard of living, and it was assumed that if their financial circumstances improved, they would stop making crafts. In the 1970s Medina squarely and succinctly posed the contradiction that was discomfiting intellectuals: "popular art is produced by campesinos." Yet—"this widely known statement ignores the dramatic meaning implicit in it at the present moment of the country's development, which has inexorably condemned the campesino to disappear" (Medina 1975:10).

As Michael Kearney has shown in his book *Reconceptualizing the Peasantry* (1996), both right-wing and left-wing development planners in the 1960s and 1970s expected the peasant worldwide to disappear—the right wing through agricultural "greening" programs that would make small farms obsolete, the left wing through the Leninist model that the campesino would eventually be integrated into an urban proletariat. As Kearney points out, development projects have failed and the Mexican campesino has not disappeared but has been transformed into what Kearney calls the "post-peasant"—no longer permanently residing in a rural village, but engaged in complex economic webs that defy containment in traditional anthropological categories. Post-campesinos in Mexico are migrant and transnational, and they are engaging in various types of enterprises: wage-labor, petty commerce—selling crafts (possibly made by some other ethnic group)—at the beach or in a parking lot; and occasionally returning to the rural village to farm their family plot.

Government programs have attempted to halt emigration and maintain campesinos in place on the land by bolstering artisanal production (García Canclini 1993:39; Novelo 1976:27, 1993:68). A policy statement for crafts under President Carlos Salinas de Gortari, for example, explicitly advocates craft making as a means to create jobs and retain people in their place of origin (SECOFI [1991]:11). There is indeed some evidence that crafts may provide an alternative to emigration, for example, in the state of Michoacán (García Canclini 1993:39). Journalist Martha García (personal communication, June 1997) similarly attributes Chigmecatitlán's lack of migration to the United States to the palm weaving industry.

The efficacy of palm weaving as an economic strategy is open to question. Cervantes (1963), Medina (1975:11), and Zaldívar Guerra (1975:73) warn that dependence on crafts is a recipe for misery. García and Hernández (1986:8) cite the townspeople as complaining that "*la artesanía ya no deja*," i.e., crafts are no longer bringing in enough money and therefore people are continuing to migrate out.

Erdman Gormsen (1977:26), who studied the effect of crafts on economic development, including palm weaving in the Mixteca, is more optimistic. He notes "a certain economic progress" in Chigmecatitlán and its neighbor Santa Catarina, gauging by the house construction and remodeling going on, which he attributes to their specialty of fine palm weaving, in contrast with nearby communities in the Mixteca that weave only common, poorly remunerated petate mats. He notes, however, that some of the income is coming not from palm weaving but from the itinerant sales of candy (Gormsen 1977:26; Ochoa 1993:45). Gormsen (1977:26) also points out the relative disparity within Chigmecatitlán—judging by the comfort of their houses—of intermediaries versus artisans. In Chigmecatitlán, intermediaries are better off than people who only make crafts, yet they are not as well off as the comerciantes who sell smuggled goods, candy, and other merchandise and live beyond the borders of town most of the time. It appears that the wealthiest (relatively speaking), such as the local "*ricachón*" or "rich guy," have made money not from selling crafts, but from selling other manufactured goods, black market or otherwise.

The current administration of Mexican president Vicente Fox seems to be embracing migration in a very pragmatic way and attempting to redefine migration to the United States not as an economic failure but as an economic opportunity. In Chigmecatitlán, it might be argued that crafts could not exist in the current agricultural crisis without emigrants to subsidize them. The influx of money from emigrants who reside semipermanently outside the town, but still consider it their homeland in spirit, allows those who remain in situ to continue to produce crafts. The Mexican government is thus in the ironic position of encouraging the merger of Mexico and the United States into a borderless territory economically speaking, while attempting to maintain the "authentic" value of Mexican crafts as symbols of a traditional campesino identity that no longer fully exists. Chigmecatitlán artisans will doubtless continue to find a niche for their miniature crafts as a legacy that stabilizes the notion of a Mexican national culture in an age of disruption caused by accelerated economic change.

Notes

INTRODUCTION The Lilliputization of Mexico

1. Oles (2002) gives a comprehensive review of early displays of Mexican popular art.

2. Quote is from Martínez Peñaloza 1972:14. Elsewhere he writes, "I have not been able to find out the destination of these objects," but notes that those given to Brazil were displayed in 1922 (Martínez Peñaloza 1972:80, note 1). See also Oles 2002:20, 177, note 24.

3. Publications that contain a section on Mexican miniature crafts or are wholly devoted to them include: Atl [1922]1980; Beltrán 1979, 1985*; Charpenel 1970*; Coronel Rivera 1996; Dörner 1962; Espejel 1972, 1978; Evans 1952; Fernández Ledesma 1930*; González y González et al. 1993; Harnoncourt 1928; Hernández 1981; León 1984*, 1996*; *Lo efímero y lo eterno del arte popular mexicano*, 1971*; López Domínguez 1983; Marín de Paalen 1976; Martínez Peñaloza 1981, 1982; Oettinger 1990*; Pettit and Pettit 1978*; Rubín de la Borbolla 1963*, 1974; Sánchez Santa Ana 1991*, 1992*; Sayer 1990*; Scheffler 1982*; Starr 1899; Tarazona Zermeño and Tommasi de Magrelli 1987*; and Toor 1939, [1947]1985 (* = mentions Chigmecatitlán crafts).

4. The Preclassic figurines are almost always broken. They begin in 1600 BC on the Pacific coast of Guatemala and Chiapas. Until 300 BC they are solid clay (Michael Coe, personal communication, 1998).

5. Examples, both from the Classic period, are clay dolls from Teotihuacán (Matos Moctezuma 1993:16, 17, 20) and a clay dog on wheels from Tres Zapotes, Veracruz (Matos Moctezuma 1993:19–21).

6. The Mixtec codices include Zouche-Nuttall, Colombino-Becker I, Becker II, Bodley, Selden, Vindobonensis, and Egerton. The Borgia Group codices include Borgia, Cospi, Fejérváry-Mayer, Laud, and Vaticanus B (Byland 1993:xiv–xv).

CHAPTER 1 Chigmecatitlán from a Distance

1. San Pedro y San Pablo Tequixtepec (= Tequecistepec; Gerhard 1986) in the district of Huajuapan de León, Oaxaca, not to be confused with San Miguel Tequixtepec in the district of Teposcolula, Oaxaca.

2. No place glyph for Chigmecatitlán has been identified. An artist created the current glyph showing a dog between two bundles of reeds for a 1946 book on Puebla place names (Franco 1946:401). The editor commissioned the artist to design glyphs for all the towns that lacked them, based on the local derivation of their names.

3. *Pancololote*: *Matelea (Gonolobus)* sp., Asclepiadaceae (milkweed family).

4. Santa María Mixtecos and Santa Catalina Mixtecos appear on a list of thirty-one towns that donated money for the new bells of the parish church of Tepexi (AGN-Indios 58, 3, 5v; Jäcklein 1978: 110, footnote).

5. The Pastorela or Shepherds' Play, known locally as the *"comedia,"* is a dramatic spectacle descended from the medieval "mystery play." Community actors perform the roles of angels, devils, shepherds, Herod, and the Holy Family.

CHAPTER 2   Palm Weaving as a Microindustry

1. *Sideroxylon (Mastichodendron) capiri* (A.D.C.) Pittier *"tempisque."*

2. *Cemitas*: bread rolls with sesame seeds, popular in the city of Puebla, or sandwiches made from the rolls.

3. The Plaza de San Franciso is a well-known plaza in the city of Puebla. The Feria de Puebla is an annual exposition that runs from mid-April to mid-May at the Cerro Loreto.

4. For a list of government and private organizations offering credit and other support to Mexican artisans, see Novelo 1976, appendix; Stephen 1991.

CHAPTER 3   Brittle Memories: A History of Weaving Palm

1. Secretaría de Gobernación y Gobierno del Estado de Puebla 1988:302.

2. Foundation narratives for Chigmecatitlán include: Franco 1946; Bonifacio Peregrina, as told to Fidela Hernández Nava de Calixto, 1961; Abraham Cortés, "Datos Importantes Fundación y Vida y Desarrollo de Santa María Chigmecatitlán del Estado de Puebla. Pue." n.d.; Plaque on the auxiliary town hall, Santo Domingo Tonahuixtla, Puebla, 1992; Paisanos de Tequixtepec, "Hipótesis sobre la fundación de Santa Ma. Chigmecatitlán," *Tequix* 1994 (4):4–5; Consejo Municipal de Participación Social, Chigmecatitlán, "Antecedentes históricos: Visión general de la situación educativa de Chigmecatitlán, Puebla," n.d.

3. Parish records note the marriage of Eligio de Jesus Fernandes and Maria Tomasa on 17 July 1895 (Church of Latter-day Saints, Family History Center, Microfilm 1106682. Mexico, Puebla, Chigmecatitlán: Church Records: Matrimonios).

4. (*Codex Vaticanus 3773* or B, 1993:18; Seler 1963) from the Borgia group of codices, considered to be from the Puebla-Tlaxcala region.

5. Jäcklein (1978:5) believes the archaeological site of Tepexi El Viejo was the center of an area intermediate between the Mixteca and the Aztecs before the conquest. The Popoloca probably moved away after a defeat by the Aztecs and founded a new settlement of Tepexi (later de la Seda, now de Rodríguez) either in 1503 (Cook de Leonard 1961:91, cited in Jäcklein 1978:20) or after 1520 (Gorenstein 1971, cited in Jäcklein 1978:20).

Gordon Brotherston (1995:105, 210) reproduces the place glyph for Tepexic (Tepexi; 'ravine') from several pre- and post-conquest pictorials. Tepexi is still known in Chigmecatitlán as *Ñu Kavá* 'town of the ravine.' However, not all scholars agree with Brotherston that the Tepexic glyph (a split hill with or without a superimposed checkerboard) refers to the place now known as Tepexi de Rodríguez; some believe there were many local Tepexics in the Mixteca (John Pohl, personal communication, 1998).

6. The lost Relaciones Geográficas for Tepexi are Census #215 (Cline 1972:195, 218, 366) and Census #313 (dated 1608; Cline 1972:229, 369; Cook de Leonard 1961:106).

7. "Descripción de Quatlatlauca, por su Corregidor Antonio de Vargas. 2 de

setiembre de 1579." Benson Latin American Collection, JGI-XXIV-16, University of Texas, Austin.

8. "Descripción de Quatlatlauca, por su Corregidor Antonio de Vargas. 2 de setiembre de 1579." Benson Latin American Collection, JGI-XXIV-16, University of Texas, Austin; see also Rosquillas 1986:44.

9. *Codex Mendoza,* folio 42, in Berdan and Anawalt 1997:88–89; Historia Tolteca-Chichimeca, cited in Jäcklein 1978:13, 123.

10. "Oval, wickerwork, willow market baskets with handles may very well be European" (Foster 1967:123). "Twilled . . . work presumably is native American" (Foster 1967:123).

11. The same knot also appears on a flat stamp from Texcoco (Enciso [1947]1980:139v).

12. "Descripción de Quatlatlauca, por su Corregidor Antonio de Vargas. 2 de setiembre de 1579." Benson Latin American Collection, JGI-XXIV-16, University of Texas, Austin.

CHAPTER 4 Shrinking Crafts

1. José Flores played with Los Sandoval for thirty-one years starting at the age of seven. He now plays saxophone with Los Fuentes when in town for religious holidays.

2. "*Mis pulmones ya no aguantan.*" According to José Flores, his lungs (i.e., back) would ache from weaving as if he had been swinging a pickax or mattock. Damaged vision is another health hazard artisans blame on working in small scale (Ochoa 1993:35); José Flores and Catalina Escalante's son said they no longer weave miniatures because "it destroys the eyesight."

3. Abraham Cortés, "Datos Importantes Fundacíon y Vida y Desarrollo de Santa María Chigmecatitlán del Estado de Puebla. Pue.," n.d.

4. This size range is common to many Mexican crafts, for example, in the pottery of the Barrio de la Luz, Puebla (Kaplan 1994a:1).

5. Don Benigno was fifty-four years old at the time of our interview in July 1997 (i.e., he was born in 1942 or 1943). He started making tlachiqueros smaller at age twenty-four (in 1966 or 1967). This chronology roughly matches José Flores's recollection that he and his wife started making miniatures around 1965.

6. INAH, Colecciones Mestizas, Box 17, No. 31720(63), 31722(63), 31723(63). Height of figures 22 cm–24.3 cm (8 $\frac{3}{4}$"–9 $\frac{3}{4}$"). Unfortunately, the INAH catalogue cards simply list "Puebla" as place of production and "*grupos mestizos*" as the makers, but people from Chigmecatitlán identified the figures from photos as being locally made. Curator María Eugenia Sánchez Santa Ana said they were catalogued in 1963 when the museum moved from La Moneda to its current building. The collections were sorted out at that time and could be from the 1940s, 1950s, or 1960s.

7. The first lady is ex-oficio head of the DIF (Sistema Nacional para el Desarrollo Integral de la Familia), a social services agency.

8. *Yuchin* 'juguetitos'; *yuchin ñú* 'artesanías'.

CHAPTER 5 The Priest: Ritual Contexts of the Miniature

1. The ten-page testimony of the parish priest, Mariano Paz y Sánchez, is addressed to the Señor Fiscal Protector de Naturales under Fernando VII, Mexico, June 6, 1811 (Archivo General de la Nación, Grupo Documental Criminal, Vol. 334, Exp. 7, fs. 261–265v). The villagers of Chigmecatitlán had accused the priest before

Viceroy Francisco Xavier Venegas and Archbishop of Mexico Francisco Xavier de Lizana (see Gerhard 1986:414).

2. Calderón Quijano 1945:794–96, cited in Jäcklein 1978:237–38. Tepexi was originally a Franciscan mission (Jäcklein 1978:41). Dominicans replaced the Franciscans in Tepexi in 1567, the same year that the Franciscans left seven other places, though Jäcklein notes that the first documentation of Dominicans in Tepexi was in 1574 (Vetancurt 1697:IV:29, cited in Jäcklein 1978:42).

3. *Fiscal:* in Indian towns, one of the Indians in charge of making the others fulfill their religious obligations.

How and when to ring the church bells was a source of friction in Chigmecatitlán. Ingham (1986:48) similarly notes that a priest in Tlayacapan, Morelos, kept a large dog "to prevent the mayordomos from climbing the roof of the church to ring the bells during fiestas." In modern Chigmecatitlán the bells are rung every fifteen minutes on All Saints' Day and All Souls' Day, November 1 and 2.

4. A succession of frightening insects, scorpions, and spiders is prominent in the accounts of visitors to Chigmecatitlán (Manrique 1964:199; Ochoa 1993:31).

5. "those crackling little explosives that skitter about underfoot, *buscapies,* or 'foot-searchers'" (Pettit and Pettit 1978:145).

6. In the past, the graveyard was across the street from the church where the basketball court is now. Men were buried on the left (north), women on the right (south), in the same arrangement as they currently sit in church.

7. Ochoa (1993:242) considers the brass band to be the essential cultural form in Chigmecatitlán, perhaps because his thesis focuses on bands. He adduces the townspeople as support: "On numerous occasions we asked the Mixtecs what they thought was the most outstanding element in their culture, and they always responded emphatically, bands!" For my part, however, I see the band as just one component of the procession.

8. Burgoa ([1674]1934:314) is describing the funeral of the Dominican Fray Diego del Río, who was born in Burgos, Castilla la Vieja, and died in Mixtepeque, Oaxaca; the convent he refers to is that of Tlaxiaco in the Mixteca.

9. The "Santos Ejercicios" were religious retreats that catechists from Puebla offered to groups graded by age and gender: *señoras, señores, muchachas, muchachos, niños,* and *niñas,* successively. The retreats have been held since about 1980 and have been influenced since about 1990 by a trend within the Catholic Church known as "Renovación Cristiana," which borrows from some of the popularizing tendencies of Protestant churches.

10. Cf. Turok (1988a:184): "In the aforementioned Ocumicho they have invented a new saint, 'San Ramos,' who, according to the interpretation of this P'ure pecha community, corresponds to the figure of Jesus Christ entering Jerusalem mounted on a burro on Palm Sunday."

11. The people of Santo Domingo Tonahuixtla, a sister town in the municipality of Xayacatlán, district of Acatlán, Puebla, gave the San Pedro statue recently as a gift and received a statue of Chigmecatitlán's patron saint, the Immaculate Conception of Mary, in reciprocation. This exchange of sacred images is mentioned in the foundation narrative engraved on a plaque on the auxiliary municipal president's office in Tonahuixtla, Puebla.

12. It is unclear whether a particular figure represents just one kind of figure or palm crafts in general.

13. Starr (1899:124) remarks: "On Palm Sunday, palms are brought from the *tierra caliente* to all the great cities of Mexico. In the market-place the sellers sit and

plait these into simple or complex designs, some of which are very pretty." He writes that on Viernes de Dolores, the Friday before Palm Sunday, "at street-corners are squatted busy workers who have brought in great bunches of cycas-fronds and of palms. The cycas-fronds are sold in their natural condition, but the palms are split into long strips and woven into fancy forms—stars, wreaths, etc. Of the basal scales quaint artificial flowers are woven. All of these are sold for small prices and are put up in churches or homes" (Starr 1899:79).

14. Ochoa (1993:19) writes: "On one of our first visits to the community, we wanted to interview a *curandero* but before we could pose a question, he interrupted, saying: '. . . I know, I know, you are from the indigenist center. Do you not understand that we are fed up? You always come asking us things: how we live, how we work, what we eat. Then you promise to help us, you leave and never do anything. Then others come and others, but everything stays the same.'"

15. Corpus Christi is traditionally celebrated on Thursday, sixty days after Easter, but has been officially moved to the following Sunday.

16. Responsibility for the sombras and the altars they contain is rotated each year through hermandades or confraternities, sometimes congruent with merchant groups. Guilds have historically participated in Corpus Christi processions; Torquemada mentions that artisans participated in the sixteenth-century Mexican processions of Corpus Christi: "And then the trades go by, each with its device on its float" (Fray Juan de Torquemada, *Monarquía Indiana,* cited in Novelo 1996:98).

17. Santo Jubileo, or Holy Jubilee, is held in Santa Catarina the Tuesday after the fifth Friday (counting from Ash Wednesday), i.e., the Tuesday before Palm Sunday.

18. CIESAS (1989) has published a seven-volume ethnographic study of Protestant conversion in southeastern Mexico by various authors, of which Vol. 5 by Patricia Fortuny Loret de Mola is especially lucid.

19. The founding priest of the parish of Chigmecatitlán was Joseph Bustamante y Robles, who served from 1766 to 1793.

CHAPTER 6 Learning and Forgetting: The Art of Weaving Palm

1. The theme of the stranger as a catalyst for innovation in popular art parallels an experience in Santa Apolonia Teacalco, Tlaxcala: "Nobody knows for certain the origin of basketry in the town, but the old people say that baskets were not made there until 'a man came from far away, a man who wasn't from here,' who was the first to weave baskets in the town" (Zaldívar Guerra 1975:61).

CHAPTER 7 Petty Commodities: Selling the Miniature

1. Luis Zamora set up a booth during the Pastorela in December 1995, but he said it was the first time he had done so. Ochoa (1993:218) mentions craft sales during the Barrio San Antonio fiesta (June 13) attended by returning emigrants and people from neighboring towns.

2. During the colonial period, the patron of merchants was Ecce Homo (Manuel Carrera Estampa, *Los gremios mexicanos,* cited in Novelo 1996:109).

3. The end of the shadowy Tentzo range, visible from Chigmecatitlán, is painted as a bearded man in profile (*tentzo* = Náhuatl 'beard') on a map that accompanies the Relación de Huatlatlauca ("Descripción de Quatlatlauca, por su Corregidor Antonio de Vargas. 2 de setiembre de 1579." Benson Latin American Collection, JGI-XXIV-16, University of Texas, Austin). The tentzo is popularly known in central Puebla as the

hill where one goes to make a pact with the devil (Mendoza and Mendoza 1991:41; Gabriel Moedano, personal communication, 1996). García and Hernández (1986:32) collected the following story in Chigmecatitlán: "The Tentzo is the devil; he is polyform, scary, there is a hill by that name, it looks like a man lying face up resting on his elbows; on that hill there is an underground city, that is where people whom the devil carries away end up; when a fiery streak is seen in the sky, it is said the Tentzo has risen. Once when they were building the road from Chigmecatitlán to the Tepexi highway, a man appeared dressed as a charro all in black with gold buttons, who approached the project engineer; no one knows what they said to each other; two weeks later the engineer died."

4. BANFOCO, Banco Nacional de Fomento Cooperativo, was founded in 1961, FONART in 1974 (Echeverría Zuno 1993:68).

5. Novelo (1993:51, 81–82) cites a 1981 survey carried out by Anne-Lise Pietri in conjunction with FONART, which showed that 33 percent of FONART customers were college students or professors and 26 percent were professionals.

6. Miniature musicians on a framed flag illustrating the Himno Nacional Mexicano, in SEP, *Libro integrado primer grado* (1 ed. rev. 1994), 174–76. Miniature clowns in SEP, *Libro integrado segundo grado recortable* (1994, 1 ed. rev. 1995).

CONCLUSION Private Town, Public Longing

1. Museo Nacional de Arte, Tacuba St., Mexico City. Colección Roberto Montenegro, Arte Popular, #14 - Musician (trombone player) on a wooden base and #15 - Horseback rider with several pineapples in deep baskets. Both are listed as "Palma tejida. Estado de Mexico."

Glossary of Mixtec and Spanish Terms

Following the Mixtec transcription system adopted by the Summer Institute of Linguistics, a final "n" nasalizes the vowel, as in French "*vin*" or "*pain*."

alcade	Town official
ambulante	Sidewalk vendor
artesanía	Craft
beisbolista	Baseball player
cacicazgo	Chiefdom
campesino	Peasant
canasta	Basket with bail handle; *ika*
carrizo	Reed
charro	National costume, a fancy-dress horseman. A *charro* and *china poblana* dance the *jarabe tapatío* at the opening of a rodeo
china poblana	National costume based on nineteenth-century *mestiza* dress
chiquihuite	Basket
chiquito	Little, also type of woodpecker
colación	Candy given to guests during Las Posadas, Christmas Eve, or New Year's
comedia	Pastorela, Shepherds' Play
comerciante	Merchant, trader, seller
compadre	Relationship formed between parent and godparent
Corregidor	Chief magistrate
cosita	Small thing
criollo	Of local origin
curandero	Folk healer
curva del diablo	Devil's curve
de temporal	Non-irrigated
diputado	Congressional representative
Domingo de Ramos	Palm Sunday
ejido	Communal land grant
fayuca	Black market goods, often electronic equipment
fiscal	In colonial Indian towns, one of the Indians in charge of making the others fulfill their religious obligations
guamúchil	Acacia with spiral fruit; palm ornament in the shape of a ball with a spiral tail

huarachito	Little sandal
Huasteca	Region comprising part of San Luis Potosí, Hidalgo, Veracruz, and other states
huauchinango	Type of chile
huipil	Indigenous women's garment
ika	European-type market basket with a bail handle; *canasta*
ika estambre	Basket made with twined technique using yarn
indito	Little Indian
itacate	Take-home portion, portable meal
jagüey	Shallow pond
jarabe tapatío	Mexican hat dance
jarana	Plucked guitar-like instrument
jarciería	Establishment that sells cleaning supplies: brooms, mops, brushes, rope, raffia, cables, gunny sacks, thread, cords, rags, squeegees, etc., originally of agave fiber but now also of plastic
jinete	Horseback or muleback rider
juguete	Toy
juguetero	Toy maker
kiosko	Bandstand
mano and metate	Grinding stones
mayordomo	Sponsor of a religious feast
mestiza, mestizo	Mixture of Spanish and Indian
Mexicanidad	Mexico City ethnic revival movement with Aztec components
milagro	Metal charms representing body parts, animals, or other things, attached to images of the saints
monte	Wild land, hills, countryside
mozo	Manservant
mulita	Little mule
muñequito	Little doll
nda'cho	Rectangular basket or wallet, often in two parts that fit together; *tenate*; *tompiate*. Often called *petaca* (tobacco pouch or cigar case); also *cartero* or *monedero* (wallet)
ndo'o	Basket with a round base and lip; *tenate*; *tompiate*
Niño Dios	Christ Child
ofrenda	Offering
ollita	Little jug
otate	Solid cane
paisanos	Fellow countrymen, compatriots
Pastorela	Shepherds' play performed at Christmastime, held on December 28 in Chigmecatitlán
pescanovia	Finger trap
petaca	Wallet; *nda'cho*
petate	Woven mat
picante	Chile peppers
piñera, piñero	Dolls holding pineapples
poblano	From Puebla
Porfiriato	Regime of Porfirio Díaz, 1876–1910

pueblo	Town, people
puesto	Market stall
pulque	Fermented beverage made from sap of agave
rebozo	Shawl
sacabocado	Hollow punch
sombra	Shade; Corpus Christi altar
telesecundaria	Secondary school with classes beamed by satellite
tenate	Basket; *nda'cho* or *ndo'o*
tierra blanca	White earth used for cement and scrubbing
tlachiquero	Pulque harvester
tlapalería	Hardware store (from Náhuatl *tlapa* 'paint')
trastero	Hutch
tsiduma	Scorpion
viejito	Little old person
zócalo	Town square, especially the central plaza of Mexico City, site of the Metropolitan Cathedral, Government Palace, and Templo Mayor museum

Bibliography

Adovasio, J. M. 1977. *Basketry Technology: A Guide to Identification and Analysis*. Chicago: Aldine.

Albers, Anni. 1970. *Pre-Columbian Mexican Miniatures: The Josef and Anni Albers Collection*. New York: Praeger.

American Federation of Arts. 1930. *Mexican Arts: Catalogue of an Exhibition Organized for and Circulated by the American Federation of Arts*. Introduction by René d'Harnoncourt. [Portland, Maine]: Southwood Press.

Andrews, E. Wyllys. 1961. *Dzibilchaltun Program. Preliminary Report on the 1959–60 Field Season*. New Orleans: Middle American Research Institute, Tulane University.

Anguiano, Marina. 1982. *Artesanía ritual tradicional*. México: FONART.

"Arte popular." 1954. *Boletín del Buró Interamericano de Arte* 3 (March 1954): 55.

Atl, Dr. [Gerardo Murillo]. [1922]1980. *Las artes populares en México*. México: Instituto Nacional Indigenista.

Babcock, Barbara A., Guy Monthan, and Doris Monthan. 1986. *The Pueblo Storyteller: Development of a Figurative Ceramic Tradition*. Tucson: University of Arizona Press.

Bachelard, Gaston. 1994. *The Poetics of Space*. Translated by Maria Jolas. First published 1958 as *La poétique de l'espace*. Boston: Beacon Press.

Barbash, Shepard. 1993. *Oaxacan Woodcarving: The Magic in the Trees*. San Francisco: Chronicle Books.

Baudrillard, Jean. [1968]1996. *The System of Objects*. Translated by James Benedict. London and New York: Verso.

Beezley, William H., Cheryl English Martin, and William E. French, eds. 1994. *Rituals of Rule, Rituals of Resistance: Public Celebrations and Popular Culture in Mexico*. Wilmington, Del.: Scholarly Resources.

Bellasi, Pietro. 1983. "L'iconographie de la vie quotidienne. Lilliput et Brobdingnag." *Cahiers Internationaux de Sociologie* (Paris) 74 (1983): 47–56.

———. 1985. "Lilliput et Brobdingnag: Métaphores de l'imaginaire miniaturisant et mégalisant." Translated from the Italian by Jean-Dominique Goffette. *Communications* (Paris) 42:229–44.

Beltrán, Alberto. 1979. *El juguete y las miniaturas como una herencia cultural*. Cuadernos de Trabajo, Museo Nacional de Artes e Industrias Populares del INI. México: Instituto Nacional Indigenista.

———. 1985. "El juguete indígena." *México Indígena* 1, no. 3 (Mar.-Apr. 1985): 32–35.

Benedict, Ruth. 1934. *Patterns of Culture.* Boston: Houghton Mifflin.

Berdan, Frances F., and Patricia Rieff Anawalt. 1997. *The Essential Codex Mendoza.* Berkeley: University of California Press.

Bonfil Batalla, Guillermo. 1996. *México profundo: Reclaiming a Civilization.* Translated by Philip A. Dennis. Austin: University of Texas Press.

Bourdieu, Pierre. 1984. *Distinction: A Social Critique of the Judgment of Taste.* Translated by Richard Nice. Cambridge, Mass.: Harvard University Press.

Briggs, Charles L. 1980. *The Wood Carvers of Córdova, New Mexico: Social Dimensions of an Artistic "Revival."* Knoxville: University of Tennessee Press.

Brotherston, Gordon. 1995. *Painted Books from Mexico: Codices in UK Collections and the World They Represent.* London: British Museum Press.

Burgoa, Fray Francisco de. [1674]1934. *Geográfica descripción.* Tomo 1. Publicaciones del Archivo General de la Nación 25. México: Talleres Gráficos de la Nación.

Byland, Bruce E. 1993. Introduction to *The Codex Borgia,* edited by Gisele Díaz and Alan Rodgers, xiii-xxxii. New York: Dover.

Calderón de la Barca, Fanny. 1940. *Life in Mexico During a Residence of Two Years in That Country.* Reprint of 1931 ed. New York: E. P. Dutton and Co.

Caso, Alfonso. 1932. *Las exploraciones en Monte Albán. Temporada 1931–32.* Publicaciones del Instituto Panamericano de Geografía e Historia (Mexico) 7.

———. 1940. "Pre-Spanish Art." In *Twenty Centuries of Mexican Art,* 23–26. New York: Museum of Modern Art.

———. 1992. *Reyes y reinos de la Mixteca.* 2 vols. México: Fondo de Cultura Económica.

Castro Leal, Alberto. 1940. Introduction to *Twenty Centuries of Mexican Art,* 14–17. New York: Museum of Modern Art.

Causey, C. Andrew. 1997. "Getting More Than They Bargain For: Toba Batak Wood Carvers and Western Travellers in a Utopic Marketplace." Ph.D. diss. University of Texas at Austin.

Cerny, Charlene, and Suzanne Seriff, eds. 1996. *Recycled, Re-seen: Art from the Global Scrap Heap.* New York: Museum of International Folk Art/Harry N. Abrams.

Cervantes, Roberto T. 1963. "Miseria y artesanía." *Tlatoani* 17 (Dec. 1963): 6–11.

Charpenel, Mauricio. 1970. *Las miniaturas en el arte popular mexicano.* Latin American Folklore Series No. 1. Austin: University of Texas.

Chase, Stuart. 1931. *Mexico: A Study of Two Americas.* Illustrated by Diego Rivera. New York: MacMillan.

Christian, William A., Jr. 1981. *Local Religion in Sixteenth-Century Spain.* Princeton, N.J.: Princeton University Press.

CIESAS (Centro de Investigaciones y Estudios Superiores en Antropología Social). 1989. *Religión y sociedad en el sureste de México.* Vol. 5 by Patricia Fortuny Loret de Mola. México: CIESAS.

Clifford, James. 1988. *The Predicament of Culture: Twentieth Century Ethnography, Literature, and Art.* Cambridge, Mass.: Harvard University Press.

Cline, Howard F. 1972. "The Relaciones Geográficas of the Spanish Indies, 1577–1648." In *Handbook of Middle American Indians.* Vol. 12, *Guide to Ethnohistorical Sources,* Part 1, 183–242. Volume edited by Howard F. Cline. Austin: University of Texas Press.

The Codex Borgia. 1993. Edited by Gisele Díaz and Alan Rodgers. New York: Dover.

The Codex Nuttall: A Picture Manuscript from Ancient Mexico. 1975. The Peabody Museum facsimile edited by Zelia Nuttall. New York: Dover.

Codex Vaticanus 3773 (Codex Vaticanus B). 1993. Vol. 2. *Manual del adivino: Libro explicativo del llamado Códice Vaticano B.* Edited by Ferdinand Anders and Maarten Jansen. Madrid: Sociedad Estatal Quinto Centenario and México: Fondo de Cultura Económica.

Coe, Michael D. 1970. "Figurines." In *Pre-Columbian Mexican Miniatures,* by Anni Albers, n.p. New York: Praeger.

———. 1984. *Mexico.* 3rd ed. rev. New York: Thames and Hudson.

Cohen, Jeffrey H. 1999. *Cooperation and Community: Economy and Society in Oaxaca.* Austin: University of Texas Press.

Colloredo-Mansfield, Rudi. 1999. *The Native Leisure Class: Consumption and Cultural Creativity in the Andes.* Chicago: University of Chicago Press.

Cook, Scott. 1993. "Craft Commodity Production, Market Diversity, and Differential Rewards in Mexican Capitalism Today." In *Crafts in the World Market,* edited by June Nash, 59–83. Albany, N.Y.: State University of New York Press.

Cook de Leonard, Carmen. 1953. "Los popolocas de Puebla." In *Huastecos, totonacos y sus vecinos,* edited by Ignacio Bernal and E. Dávalos Hurtado. *Revista Mexicana de Estudios Antropológicos* 13, nos. 2 and 3 (1953): 423–45.

———. 1961. "The Painted Tribute Record of Tepexi de la Seda." In *A William Cameron Townsend en el 25 aniversario del Instituto Lingüístico de Verano,* 87–107. México.

Cooper-Hewitt Museum. 1983. *Miniatures.* The Smithsonian Illustrated Library of Antiques. Washington, D.C.: Smithsonian Institution.

Coronel Rivera, Juan. 1996. *Mexican Traditional Toys and Miniatures.* Exhibition catalog with an introductory essay by Coronel, "Toys and fantasies." Translated by Karina Bailey. Mexico: Secretaría de Relaciones Exteriores.

Cortés, Hernán. [1522]1975. *Cartas de relación.* 8 ed. Mexico: Porrúa.

Cortés Ruiz, Efraín, ed. 1996. "Tejiendo la naturaleza: La cestería en cinco regiones de México." México: Museo Nacional de Antropología. Typescript.

———, Catalina Rodríguez, and Donaciano Gutiérrez. 1989. *Actualidad de la cestería en México: Una tradición en las áreas rurales.* México: INAH, Museo Nacional de Antropología, Subdirección de Etnografía.

Covarrubias, Miguel. 1940. "Modern Art." In *Twenty Centuries of Mexican Art,* 137–41. New York: Museum of Modern Art.

———. 1957. *Indian Art of Mexico and Central America.* New York: Alfred A. Knopf.

———. 1991. *The Genius of Miguel Covarrubias.* Exhibition catalogue, Milagros Gallery, San Antonio, Texas. Taxco, Guerrero: Alberto Ulrich.

Curcio Nagy, Linda A. 1994. "Giants and Gypsies. Corpus Christi in Colonial Mexico City." In *Rituals of Rule, Rituals of Resistance,* edited by William H. Beezley, Cheryl English Martin, and William E. French, 1–26. Wilmington, Del.: Scholarly Resources.

Dahlgren, Barbro. [1954]1990. *La mixteca: Su cultura e historia prehispánicas.* México: UNAM.

Danly, Susan, ed. 2002. *Casa Mañana: The Morrow Collection of Mexican Popular Arts.* Albuquerque: Published for the Mead Art Museum, Amherst College, by the University of New Mexico Press.

Díaz del Castillo, Bernal. 1956. *The Discovery and Conquest of Mexico, 1517–1521.* New York: Farrar, Straus, and Cudahy.

Dörner, Gerd. 1962. *Mexican Folk Art*. Munich: Wilhelm Andermann.

Dorst, John D. 1989. *The Written Suburb: An American Site, an Ethnographic Dilemma*. Philadelphia: University of Pennsylvania Press.

Durán, Fray Diego. 1971. *Book of the Gods and Rites and the Ancient Calendar*. Translated and edited by Fernando Horcasitas and Doris Heyden. Norman: University of Oklahoma Press.

Echeverría Zuno, María Esther. 1993. "FONART, el modelo mexicano para el fomento del arte popular." *Revista del CIDAP* (Ecuador, Centro Interamericano de Artesanías y Artes Populares) no. 41–42 (Nov. 1993): 67–75.

Egan, Martha J. 1991. *Milagros: Votive Offerings from the Americas*. Foreword by Marion Oettinger, Jr. Santa Fe: Museum of New Mexico Press.

———. 1993. *Relicarios: Devotional Miniatures from the Americas*. Santa Fe: Museum of New Mexico Press.

Ehlers, Tracy Bachrach. 2000. *Silent Looms: Women and Production in a Guatemalan Town*. Rev. ed. Austin: University of Texas Press.

Enciso, Jorge. [1947]1980. *Sellos del antiguo México*. México: Editorial Innovación.

Errington, Shelly. 1998. *The Death of Authentic Primitive Art and Other Tales of Progress*. Berkeley: University of California Press.

Esparza Liberal, María José. 1994. "El siglo XIX. Retrato del pueblo y de sus hombres ilustres." In *La cera en México: Arte e historia,* by María José Esparza Liberal and Isabel Fernández de García-Lascuráin, 53–137. México: Fomento Cultural Banamex.

———, and Isabel Fernández de García-Lascuráin. 1994. *La cera en México: Arte e historia*. Prólogo de Teresa Castelló Yturbide. México: Fomento Cultural Banamex.

Espejel, Carlos. 1972. *Las artesanías tradicionales en México*. SepSetentas 45. Mexico: Secretaría de Educación Pública.

———. 1978. *Mexican Folk Crafts*. Photographs by F. Catala Roca. Barcelona: Blume.

Evans, Marie Padgett. 1952. "Mexican Miniatures: A Study of the Educational Contributions of Miniatures in Revealing Customs, Habits and Cultures of Mexico." Thesis, M. Ed. University of Florida.

Fainges, Marjory. 1994. *The Encyclopedia of Regional Dolls of the World*. Kenthurst, Australia: Kangaroo Press.

Feld, Steven, and Keith H. Basso, eds. 1996. *Senses of Place*. Santa Fe, N.M.: School of American Research.

Fernández Ledesma, Gabriel. 1930. *Juguetes mexicanos*. México: Talleres Gráficos de la Nación.

———. 1971. "Los juguetes." In *Lo efímero y eterno del arte popular mexicano*. Tomo I. México: Fondo Editorial de la Plástica Mexicana.

Firth, Raymond. 1973. *Symbols, Public and Private*. Ithaca, N.Y.: Cornell University Press.

Fortuny Loret de Mola, Patricia. 1989. *Religión y sociedad en el sureste de México*. Vol. 5. México: CIESAS.

Foster, George M. 1960. *Culture and Conquest: America's Spanish Heritage*. Chicago: Quadrangle.

———. 1967. "Contemporary Pottery and Basketry." In *Handbook of Middle American Indians,* Vol. 6, Social Anthropology. Volume edited by Manning Nash. London: University of Texas Press.

Franco, Felipe. 1946. *Indonimia geográfica del Estado de Puebla*. Puebla: Estado de Puebla.

Frazer, James George. 1922. *The Golden Bough: A Study in Magic and Religion*. New York: MacMillan. Available at http://www.bartleby.com.

Gamio, Manuel. 1924. "Posibilidades del arte indígena en México." *Boletín de la Unión Panamericana* (Washington, D.C.) (1924): 889–905.

García Canclini, Nestor. 1993. *Transforming Modernity: Popular Culture in Mexico*. Translated by Lidia Lozano. Austin: University of Texas Press.

———. 1995. *Hybrid Cultures: Strategies for Entering and Leaving Modernity*. Minneapolis and London: University of Minnesota Press.

García, Martha. n.d. "Origen de Santa María Chigmecatitlán, Edo. Puebla." Photocopy.

———, and Marco Antonio Hernández. 1986. "Práctica de campo realizada en abril de 1986, en Santa María Chigmecatitlán, Edo. de Puebla." Escuela Nacional de Antropología e Historia, México. Photocopy.

Gerhard, Peter. 1986. *Geografía histórica de la Nueva España, 1519–1821*. 1st pub. Cambridge University 1972. México: UNAM, Instituto de Investigaciones Históricas, Instituto de Geografía.

Giffords, Gloria Fraser. 1991. *The Art of Private Devotion: Retablo Painting of Mexico*. Fort Worth: InterCultura; and Dallas: Meadows Museum.

Gill, Robert R. 1976. "Ceramic Arts and Acculturation at Laguna." In *Ethnic and Tourist Arts,* edited by Nelson Graburn, 102–13. Berkeley: University of California Press.

Gilmore, David D. 1990. *Manhood in the Making: Cultural Concepts of Masculinity*. New Haven: Yale University Press.

Glassie, Henry. 1993. *Turkish Traditional Art Today*. Bloomington and Indianapolis: Indiana University Press.

Goffman, Erving. 1959. *The Presentation of Self in Everyday Life*. Garden City, N.Y.: Doubleday.

Golden, Arthur. 1996. "Baja in Struggle to Preserve a Multitude of Native Tongues." *San Diego Union-Tribune* (Dec. 2, 1996): A–1.

González y González, Luis, Eduardo Matos Moctezuma, Guillermo Tovar de Teresa, Virginia Armella, Jorge F. Hernández, and Martha Del Río Grimm. 1993. *Juegos y juguetes mexicanos*. México: Dina Camiones.

Gorenstein, Shirley. 1971. "Archaeology, History, and Anthropology in the Mixteca-Puebla Region of Mexico." *American Antiquity* 36(3): 335–43.

Gormsen, Erdmann. 1977. "La artesanía mexicana como factor de desarrollo regional." *Comunicaciones* (Proyecto Puebla-Tlaxcala, México) 14: 23–27.

Graburn, Nelson H. H., ed. 1976. *Ethnic and Tourist Arts: Cultural Expressions from the Fourth World*. Berkeley: University of California Press.

Harnoncourt, René d'. 1928. "Pancho el Juguetero. Pancho the Toy Maker." *Mexican Folkways* 4, no. 2 (Apr.–June 1928): 109–15.

Hernández, Francisco Javier. 1950. *El juguete popular en México: Estudio de interpretación*. México: Ediciones Mexicanas.

———. 1969. *El juguete mexicano*. Artes de México 16, no. 125 (1969). Edited by Teresa Castelló Yturbide.

———. 1981. "El juguete popular." In *Cuarenta siglos de arte mexicano,* edited by Xavier Moyssén, 292–305. México: Editorial Herrero.

The Holy Bible. n.d. New Revised Standard Version. New York and Oxford: Oxford University Press.

Hoppe, Walter A., and Roberto J. Weitlaner. 1969. "The Chocho." In *Handbook of Middle American Indians*. Vol. 7. Ethnology, Part 1, pp. 506–15. Austin: University of Texas Press.

——, Andrés Medina, and Roberto J. Weitlaner. 1969. "The Popoloca." In *Handbook of Middle American Indians*. Vol. 7. Ethnology, Part 1, pp. 489–98. Austin: University of Texas Press.

Horcasitas, Fernando. 1978. "Mexican Folk Art." *National Geographic* 153, no. 5 (May 1978): 648–69.

Huitrón, Antonio. 1962. *Metepec: Miseria y grandeza del barro*. México: UNAM.

INEGI (Instituto Nacional de Estadística, Geografía e Informática). 1990. XI Censo general de población y vivienda, 1990. Aguascalientes, Aguascalientes: INEGI.

——. 1993. La población hablante de lengua indígena en México. XI Censo general de Población y Vivienda, 1990. Aguascalientes, Aguascalientes: INEGI.

——. 1995. *1995 Anuario estadístico del estado de Puebla*. Aguascalientes, Aguascalientes: INEGI/Gobierno del Estado de Puebla.

——. 1996. *Puebla. Conteo de Población y Vivienda 1995*. Tomo I-III. Aguascalientes, Aguascalientes: INEGI.

Ingham, John M. 1986. *Mary, Michael, and Lucifer: Folk Catholicism in Central Mexico*. Austin: University of Texas Press.

Irvine, Madeline. 1997. "Toys and Joys from Mexico." *Austin American-Statesman* (April 2, 1997): E–8.

Jäcklein, Klaus. 1974. *Un pueblo popoloca: San Felipe Otlaltepec*. México: Instituto Nacional Indigenista.

——. 1978. *Los popolocas de Tepexi (Puebla): Un estudio etnohistórico*. Wiesbaden, Germany: Steiner.

Jacobs, Flora Gill. 1953. *A History of Doll Houses: Four Centuries of the Domestic World in Miniature*. New York: Charles Scribner's Sons.

Jiménez Merino, Alberto. 1995. "Pierde la mixteca poblana 40 toneladas de suelo por ha. al año." *La Jornada* (Mexico) Año 3, Núm. 33 (Jan. 5, 1995).

Josserand, J. Kathryn. 1983(1982). "Mixtec Dialect History." Ph.D. diss. 1983 (submitted 1982), Tulane University. Benson Latin American Collection, Film 17,798.

Kaplan, Flora S. 1993. "Mexican Museums in the Creation of a National Image in World Tourism." In *Crafts in the World Market,* edited by June Nash, 103–25. Albany, N.Y.: State University of New York Press.

——. 1994a. *A Mexican Folk Pottery Tradition: Cognition and Style in Material Culture in the Valley of Puebla*. Carbondale and Edwardsville: Southern Illinois University Press.

——, ed. 1994b. *Museums and the Making of "Ourselves": The Role of Objects in National Identity*. London and New York: Leicester University Press.

Kassovic, Julius S. 1996. "Reinventing the Wheel, the Tin Can, and the Bottle Cap: Folk Recycling in Mexico." In *Recycled, Re-seen,* edited by Charlene Cerny and Suzanne Seriff, 102–17. New York: Museum of International Folk Art/ Harry N. Abrams.

Kearney, Michael. 1996. *Reconceptualizing the Peasantry: Anthropology in Global Perspective*. Boulder, Colo.: Westview.

Lackey, Louana M. 1982. *The Pottery of Acatlán: A Changing Mexican Tradition*. Norman: University of Oklahoma Press.

León, Imelda de. 1984. *Artesanías tradicionales de México*. Drawings by Alberto Beltrán. México: Fonart/SEP.
———. 1988. *Calendario de fiestas populares*. México: SEP, Subsecretaría de Cultura,
  Dirección General de Culturas Populares.
———. 1996. "Miniaturas: Obsesión de coleccionistas." *México en el Tiempo* 11:
  64–71.
Lévi-Strauss, Claude. 1966. "The Science of the Concrete." *The Savage Mind*, pp.
  1–33. Chicago: University of Chicago Press.
Linati, Claudio. [1828]1956. *Trajes civiles, militares y religiosos de México*. Edited and
  translated by Justino Fernández. México: UNAM.
Lo efímero y eterno del arte popular mexicano. 1971. Tomo I. México: Fondo Editorial
  de la Plástica Mexicana.
López Domínguez, María Emilia. 1983. "Juguetes populares para nuestros niños."
  México Desconocido 74 (Jan. 1983): 12–15.
McAuley, Andrew. 1999. "Entrepreneurial Instant Exporters in the Scottish Arts
  and Crafts Sector." *Journal of International Marketing* 7, no. 4 (April 1999):
  67–82.
McDade, Barbara E. 1998. "Entrepreneurial Characteristics and Business Success in
  Artisan Enterprises in Ghana. In *African Entrepreneurship: Theory and Real-
  ity,* edited by Anita Spring and Barbara E. McDade, 199–215. Gainesville:
  University Press of Florida.
MacNeish, Richard S., Antoinette Nelken-Terner, and Irmgard W. Johnson. 1967.
  The Prehistory of the Tehuacán Valley. Vol. 2. Nonceramic Artifacts. Austin
  and London: University of Texas Press.
Manrique, Leonardo. 1964. "Notas sobre la población de Santa María Chigmecati-
  tlán." *Anales del INAH* 16 (1964)[1963]: 199–225.
Marín de Paalen, Isabel. 1976. *Historia general del arte mexicano. Etno-artesanías y
  arte popular*. 2 vols. México: Hermes.
Martínez Peñaloza, Porfirio. 1972. *Arte popular y artesanías artísticas en México: Un
  acercamiento*. Mexico: Secretaría de Hacienda y Crédito Público.
———. 1980. *Tres notas sobre el arte popular en México*. Colección Aniversario, 2.
  México: Miguel Angel Porrúa.
———. 1981. *Arte popular de México: La creatividad artística del pueblo mexicano a
  través de los tiempos*. México: Panorama.
———. 1982. *Artesanía mexicana*. México: Galería de Arte Misrachi/Cámara Nacional de Comercio de la Ciudad de México.
Masuoka, Susan. 1990. "Calavera Miniatures: Political Commentary in Three Dimensions." *Studies in Latin American Popular Culture* 9: 263–79.
Matos Moctezuma, Eduardo. 1993. "Juegos y juguetes en el México antiguo." In
  Juegos y juguetes mexicanos, by Luis González y González et al., 10–45. Méxi-
  co: Dina Camiones.
Medina, Andrés. 1975. Introduction. In *Santa Apolonia Teacalco,* by María Luisa
  Zaldívar Guerra, 9–12. México: Departamento de Investigación de las Tradi-
  ciones Populares, Dirección General de Arte Popular, SEP.
Medina San Román, María del Carmen. 1997. "Votive Art: Miracles of Two Thousand
  Years." In *Folk Art of Spain and the Americas,* edited by Marion Oettinger,
  Jr., 107–27. New York: San Antonio Museum of Art/Abbeville Press.
Mendoza, Vicente T., and Virginia R. R. de Mendoza. 1991. *Folklore de la región cen-
  tral de Puebla*. México: CENIDIM (Centro Nacional de Investigación, Docu-
  mentación e Información Musical "Carlos Chávez").

Los mexicanos pintados por sí mismos. [1854–55]1974. Reproducción facsimilar de la edición de 1855. México: Librería de Manuel Porrúa.

Miller, Arthur G. 1975. Introduction to *The Codex Nuttall*, edited by Zelia Nuttall, vii–xxii. New York: Dover.

Moedano, Gabriel. 1970. "Prólogo." In *Las miniaturas en el arte popular mexicano*, by Mauricio Charpenel. Austin: Center for Intercultural Studies in Folklore and Oral History, University of Texas.

———, ed. 1988. *Atlas cultural de México: Gastronomía*. México: SEP/INAH/Planeta.

———, ed. 1996. *"Soy el negro de la costa": Música y poesía afromestiza de la Costa Chica*. Compact disk INAH-033. Recording and liner notes by Gabriel Moedano. Mexico: INAH.

Monaghan, John. 1995. *The Covenants with Earth and Rain: Exchange, Sacrifice, and Revelation in Mixtec Sociality*. Norman: University of Oklahoma Press.

Montellano, Francisco. 1994. *C. B. Waite, fotógrafo: Una mirada diversa sobre el México de principios del siglo 20*. México: Grijalbo.

Montenegro, Roberto. 1940. "Folk Art." In *Twenty Centuries of Mexican Art*, 109–10. New York: Museum of Modern Art.

———. 1948. *Museo de Artes Populares*. Colección Anáhuac de Arte Mexicano, 6. México: Ediciones de Artes.

Morales-Moreno, Luis Gerardo. 1994. "History and Patriotism in the National Museum of Mexico." In *Museums and the Making of "Ourselves,"* by Flora S. Kaplan, 171–91. London and New York: Leicester University Press.

Motolinía, Toribio. 1973. *History of the Indians of New Spain*. Edited by Elizabeth Andros Foster. Westport, Conn.: Greenwood Press.

Moyssén, Xavier, ed. 1981. *Cuarenta siglos de arte mexicano*. México: Editorial Herrero.

Murdock, George P., and Caterina Provost. 1973. "Factors in the Division of Labor by Sex: A Cross-Cultural Analysis." *Ethnology* 12: 203–25.

Museo Nacional de Culturas Populares. 1995. "¡Echate ese trompo a la uña! La miniatura en México." (julio-octubre 1995). México: Museo Nacional de Culturas Populares. Exhibition brochure.

Nash, June, ed. 1993. *Crafts in the World Market: The Impact of Global Exchange on Middle American Artisans*. Albany: State University of New York Press.

Nebel, Carl. [1836]1963. *Viaje pintoresco*. México: Librería de Manuel Porrúa.

Noguera, Eduardo. 1939. "Corpus Christi Day." *Esta Semana en México* 5, no. 22 (June 1, 1939): 22–24.

Novelo, Victoria. 1976. *Artesanías y capitalismo en México*. México: SEP/INAH.

———. 1993. *Las artesanías en México*. Tuxtla Gutiérrez, Chiapas: Gobierno del Estado de Chiapas/Instituto Chiapaneco de Cultura.

———, ed. 1996. *Artesanos, artesanías y arte popular de México: Una historia ilustrada*. México: Consejo Nacional para la Cultura y las Artes.

Novo, Salvador. [1932]1989. "Nuestras artes populares." *Nuestro México* 1, no. 5 (1932): 54–56, 74. Reprinted in *La cultura popular vista por las élites*, edited by Irene Vázquez Valle, 415–18. México: UNAM.

Nuttall, Zelia, ed. 1975. *The Codex Nuttall: A Picture Manuscript from Ancient Mexico*. The Peabody Museum facsimile edited by Zelia Nuttall. New York: Dover.

Ochoa, José Antonio. 1993. "Las bandas de viento en la vida de los mixtecos de Santa María Chigmecatitlán." Tesis para obtener el título de Licenciado en Etnología. Escuela Nacional de Antropología e Historia, México, D.F.

Oettinger, Marion, Jr. 1990. *Folk Treasures of Mexico: The Nelson A. Rockefeller Collection*. New York: Harry N. Abrams.

———. 1992. *The Folk Art of Latin America: Visiones del pueblo*. New York: Dutton Studio Books and Museum of American Folk Art.

———, ed. 1997. *Folk Art of Spain and the Americas: El alma del pueblo*. New York: San Antonio Museum of Art/Abbeville Press.

Oles, James. 1993. *South of the Border: Mexico in the American Imagination, 1914–1947*. Washington, D.C.: Smithsonian Institution.

———. 2002. "For Business or Pleasure: Exhibiting Mexican Folk Art, 1820–1930." In *Casa Mañana,* edited by Susan Danly, 11–29. Albuquerque: Published for the Mead Art Museum, Amherst College, by the University of New Mexico Press.

Paisanos de Tequixtepec. 1994. *Tequix* 4. Tequixtepec, Oaxaca.

Panyella, August, ed. 1981. *Folk Art of the Americas*. New York: Harry N. Abrams.

Parsons, Elsie Clews. 1930. "Ritos zapotecas de Año Nuevo. Zapotecan Prayers at New Year." *Mexican Folkways* 6, no. 1: 38–46.

Peirce, Charles S. 1931–35. *Collected Papers of Charles Sanders Peirce*. Edited by C. Harteshorne and P. Weiss. Cambridge, Mass.: Harvard University Press.

———. 1958. *Values in a Universe of Chance*. Edited by Philip P. Wiener. New York: Doubleday.

Pellicer, Carlos. 1987. *El sol en un pesebre: Nacimientos*. México: INBA/Instituto de Cultura de Tabasco.

Pérez Turrent, Tómas. 1984. *Canoa: Memoria de un hecho vergonzoso. La historia, la filmación, el guión*. Puebla: Universidad Autónoma de Puebla.

Pettit, Florence H., and Robert M. Pettit. 1978. *Mexican Folk Toys, Festival Decorations and Ritual Objects*. New York: Hastings House.

Pomar, María Teresa. 1980. Introduction to *Las artes populares en México,* by Dr. Atl, VII-XI. México: Instituto Nacional Indigenista.

Porter, Katherine Anne. [1922]1993. *Outline of Mexican Popular Arts and Crafts*. Los Angeles: Young and McCallister. Reprinted in *Uncollected Early Prose of Katherine Anne Porter,* edited by Ruth M. Alvarez and Thomas F. Walsh. Austin: University of Texas Press.

———. 1970. *The Collected Essays and Occasional Writings of Katherine Anne Porter*. New York: Delacorte Press.

———. 1990. *Letters of Katherine Anne Porter*. Edited by Isabel Bayley. New York: Atlantic Monthly Press.

Poyo, Ruth. 1939. *Touring Mexico*. México: Publicaciones Fischgrund.

Presidencia Municipal, Chigmecatitlán, Puebla. [1995?]. "Visión general de la situación educativa de Chigmecatitlán, Puebla." Photocopy.

Ramos, Samuel. 1962. *Profile of Man and Culture in Mexico*. 1st pub. 1934. Translated by Peter G. Earle. Introduction by Thomas B. Irving. Austin: University of Texas Press.

Ravicz, Robert, and A. Kimball Romney. 1969. "The Mixtec." In *Handbook of Middle American Indians,* Vol. 7, Ethnology, Part 1, 367–99. Volume edited by Evon Z. Vogt. London: University of Texas Press.

Romero, Ignacio. 1993. "El Bazar Sábado." *Artesanías de América. Revista del CIDAP* (Centro Interamericano de Artesanías y Artes Populares, Ecuador) no. 41–42 (Nov. 1993): 100–102.

Rosquillas, Hortensia. 1986. *Huatlatlauca prehispánica en el contexto de la historia regional chichimeca*. Dirección de Restauración del Patrimonio Cultural, Cuaderno de Trabajo, 1. México: INAH.

Rubín de la Borbolla, Daniel F. 1963. *Arte popular de México*. Edición especial de *Artes de México*. México: Instituto Nacional Indigenista.

———. 1974. *Arte popular mexicano*. México: Fondo de Cultura Económica.

———. 1993. "El arte popular precolombino de México." In *Artesanías de América*. *Revista del CIDAP* (Ecuador, Centro Interamericano de Artesanías y Artes Populares) no. 41–42 (Nov. 1993): 13–33.

Rulfo, Juan. 1975. *Pedro Páramo*. 13 ed. (1 ed. 1955). México: Fondo de Cultura Económica.

Ryerson, Scott H. 1976. "Seri Ironwood Carving: An Economic View." In *Ethnic and Tourist Arts,* edited by Nelson Graburn, 119–36. Berkeley: University of California Press.

Sahagún, Fray Bernardino de. 1969. *Florentine Codex*. Edited by Charles E. Dibble and Arthur J. O. Anderson. Book 6, Part 7, Ch. 37, pp. 201–7. Santa Fe, New Mexico: University of Utah and School of American Research.

Sánchez Santa Ana, María Eugenia. 1991. *Los juguetes de Puebla*. Puebla: Gobierno del Estado de Puebla/Secretaría de Cultura/Comisión Puebla V Centenario.

———. 1992. *Muñecas mestizas. Catálogo de las colecciones etnográficas del Museo Nacional de Antropología*. México: CNCA - INAH - MNA.

Sayer, Chloe. 1990. *Arts and Crafts of Mexico,* pp. 105–28. San Francisco: Chronicle Books.

Scheffler, Lilian. 1982. *Juguetes y miniaturas populares de México*. México: FONART/FONAPAS.

SECOFI (Secretaría de Comercio y Fomento Industrial). [1991]. *Programa de Apoyo a la Actividad Artesanal 1991–1994*. México: SECOFI.

Secretaría de Gobernación y Gobierno del Estado de Puebla. 1988. *Los municipios de Puebla*. México: Secretaría de Gobernación y Gobierno del Estado de Puebla.

Seler, Eduard. 1963. *Comentarios al códice Borgia*. 3 vols. México: Fondo de Cultura Económica.

SEP (Secretaría de Educación Pública). 1927. *El sistema de escuelas rurales en México*. México: Talleres Gráficos de la Nación.

———. 1928. *Las misiones culturales en 1927: Las escuelas normales rurales*. México: SEP.

SEP/Comisión Nacional de los Libros de Texto Gratuitos. 1994. Libro integrado primer grado. 1 rev. ed. México: SEP.

———. 1995. *Libro integrado segundo grado recortable*. 1 ed. 1994, 1 rev. ed. 1995. México: SEP.

Seriff, Suzanne. 1997. "Babes in Toyland: The Globalization of the Folk Toy." Talk sponsored by the Center for Intercultural Studies in Folklore and Ethnomusicology, University of Texas at Austin, March 21, 1997.

Serna, Jacinto de la. [1892]1987. *Manual de ministros de indios. Para el conocimiento de sus idolatrías, y estirpación de ellas*. México: Imprenta del Museo Nacional, 1892. Facsimile reprinted in *El alma encantada*. México: INI/Fondo de Cultura Económica.

Snoddy Cuéllar, Elizabeth. 1993. "La cestería en México." *Artesanías de América*. *Revista del CIDAP* (Ecuador, Centro Interamericano de Artesanías y Artes Populares) no. 41–42 (Nov. 1993): 252–67.

Spores, Ronald. 1967. *The Mixtec Kings and Their People*. Norman: University of Oklahoma Press.

Starr, Frederick. 1897. "The Little Pottery Objects of Lake Chapala, Mexico." *University of Chicago Department of Anthropology Bulletin* 2. Chicago: University of Chicago Press.

———. 1899. *Catalogue of a Collection of Objects Illustrating the Folklore of Mexico*. Publications of the Folklore Society, 43. London: Published for the Folklore Society by David Nutt.

Stephen, Lynn. 1991. *Zapotec Women*. Austin: University of Texas Press.

Stewart, Susan. 1993. *On Longing: Narratives of the Miniature, the Gigantic, the Souvenir, the Collection*. Durham and London: Duke University Press.

Swift, Jonathan. [1735]1977. *Gulliver's Travels*. New York and Toronto: Oxford University Press. Available at http://www.freebooks.biz.

Tarazona Zermeño, Amanda, and Wanda Tommasi de Magrelli. 1987. *Atlas cultural de México: Artesanías*. México: SEP/INAH/Planeta.

Terry, T. Philip. 1923. *Terry's Guide to Mexico*. Boston: Houghton Mifflin.

Tezozómoc, Hernando Alvarado. 1878. *Crónica mexicana*. México: I. Paz.

Tice, Karin E. 1995. *Kuna Crafts, Gender, and the Global Economy*. Austin: University of Texas Press.

Toor, Frances. 1937. *Frances Toor's Guide to Mexico*. New York: McBride.

———. 1939. *Mexican Popular Arts*. Illustrated by L. Alice Wilson. México: Frances Toor Studios.

———. [1947]1985. *A Treasury of Mexican Folkways*. New York: Bonanza Books.

Torres Torres, Marvin Oriel. 1994. "Diagnóstico de salud, area de atención primaria, Santa María Chigmecatitlán." Benemérita Universidad Autónoma de Puebla, Escuela de Medicina. August 3, 1994. Typescript.

Tovar de Teresa, Guillermo, and Jorge F. Hernández. 1993. "Juegos y juguetes en el Virreinato de la Nueva España." In *Juegos y juguetes mexicanos,* by Luis González y González et al., 46–75. México: Dina Camiones.

Traven, B. 1990. "La canasta." *Traven para jóvenes,* pp. 15–32. México: Consejo Nacional para la Cultura y las Artes/INBA.

Turner, Victor, and Edith Turner. 1982. "Religious Celebrations." In *Celebration: Studies in Festivity and Ritual,* edited by Victor Turner, 201–19. Washington, D.C.: Smithsonian Institution.

Turok, Marta. 1988a. *Cómo acercarse a la artesanía*. México: Plaza y Valdés/SEP.

———, ed. 1988b. *Indice bibliográfico sobre artesanías*. México: SEP, Programa de Artesanías y Culturas Populares.

Twenty Centuries of Mexican Art. 1940. New York: Museum of Modern Art.

Vázquez Valle, Irene, ed. 1989. *La cultura popular vista por las élites*. México: UNAM.

Weckmann, Luis. 1992. *The Medieval Heritage of Mexico*. Translated by Frances M. López-Morillas. New York: Fordham University Press.

Weiser, Francis X. 1958. *Handbook of Christian Feasts and Customs*. New York: Harcourt, Brace.

Weston, Edward. 1973. *The Daybooks of Edward Weston*. Vol. 1. *Mexico*. Edited by Nancy Newhall. New York: Aperture.

Winn, Robert K. 1977. *Viva Jesus, María y José: Mexican Folk Art and Toys from the Collection of Robert K. Winn*. San Antonio: Trinity University Press.

Wolf, Eric. 1959. *Sons of the Shaking Earth*. Chicago: University of Chicago Press.

Zaldívar Guerra, María Luisa. 1975. "Modificaciones en el arte popular." *Boletín del*

Departamento de Investigación de las Tradiciones Populares, 2:53–63. México: Direccíon General de Arte Popular, SEP.

———. 1976. *Santa Apolonia Teacalco: Un pueblo canastero.* Estudios de Folklore y de Arte Popular 2. México: Departamento de Investigación de las Tradiciones Populares, Dirección General de Arte Popular, SEP.

———. 1982. *La cestería en México.* México: FONART/FONAPAS.

Index

clinic, 35; residents of, 113, 123
clothing, 30, 167
clown (palm figure), 99, 103, 163, *164*, 186n6
Codex Mendoza, 76
Codex Nuttall, *80*, *81*, 149, 175
Codex Vaticanus B, 73, *74*
Coe, Michael, 10
collecting crafts. *See* crafts: collecting
communications, 27–28
competitions, crafts, 147–48
Confederación Nacional Campesino (CNC), 59–60
consumers, 56; characterized by nationality, 163
Cook de Leonard, Carmen, 27, 77, 152, 154
Corpus Christi, 96, 185n15; altars, 126–30, 185n16; palm mules for, 158–59; toys for, 13
Cortés, Don Abraham (1907–1997), 57, 71; foundation narrative of, 150; on tentzo, 154
Cortés Ruiz, Efraín, 57, 69
Covarrubias, Miguel, *52*
Coxcatlán Cave, 73
coyulli beans, 57–*58*, 175
crafts: anonymity of, 167–69; collecting, 6–7, 18–19; exhibitions, 6–7; industrialization of, 62; national policy, 16; as national symbols, 4–7, 168, 178; *see also* artisans; designs; miniatures; palm weaving; selling
credit for artisans, 62–63

Day of the Dead, 95
designs: innovation of, 138–49; outside influence on, 142–45, 148–49, 185n1 (ch. 6); pre-Hispanic, 149
development projects, failure of, 179
Díaz, Manuel Bartlett (Puebla governor), 105–106
Dorst, John D., 118
Durán, Fr. Diego, 10–11, 130
dyes, 56–57
dye seller, 56–57, 154

economic conditions, 47–48, 62–66, 92–94, 99–100, 178
education, 29–30
emigration, 41–44, 46–47; crafts and, 66, 151, 165, 179
Escalante, Catalina. *See* Flores, José, and Catalina Escalante

Escamilla, Dolores (artisan, ca. 1906/1916–1997), 95, 129
Esparza Liberal, María José, 146
evangelist doctor, 33, 41, 111, 112–15; banishment of, 130–33; as craft buyer, 148
ex-votos, 119–22, 133–34; *see also* milagros

Felguérez, Luis, and Alicia Felguérez, 170; *see also* Miniaturas Felguérez
Fernández, Eligio, and Tomasa Rodríguez, 71, 88, 95, 182n3 (ch. 3)
Fernández Ledesma, Gabriel, 60–61, 69–70, 97–98, 174; on tourist influence on crafts, 148; on mulitas, 158
fieldwork: dates, xiii; research methodology, xiv–xv
fiestas, 27, 34–35, 41, 159–60; as days for selling, 159–60; Day of Guadalupe, 96, 161–62; Epiphany, 107; Fiestas Patrias, 86; Holy Week, 124; Nuestro Señor de la Paz, 160; Santo Jubileo, 128, 185n17
figurines, pre-Hispanic, 181n4
flora. *See* plants
Florentine Codex, 107
Flores, Jacinto (seller), 70, 95, 107, 147; biographical sketch, 58–60; designer, 146, 163; advocate of miniaturization, 98–100, 101–104, 177; modernization plan, 61–66; developer of museum, 85–87; seller in elite sphere, 162, 163–64; on "dressing the part," 167; on religion of sellers, 132; on support for retailers, 171
Flores, José, and Catalina Escalante (artisans), 51, 89–94, 98, 104, 138, 149
Flores, Pastor (artisan), 98, 155
Flores, Patricia (artisan), 27; interview, 142–45
flowers (palm figures), *45*, 83
FONAES, 63
FONART, 98, 147, 148, 165, 169, 186n4, 186n5
food, 26, 36–37
FOSOLPRO, 63
Foster, George, 69
foundation narratives, 21, 71, 72, 150; list of, 182n2 (ch. 3)
Fox, Vicente (Mexican president), 180
Frazer, Sir James, 7–8

middlemen. *See* intermediaries

milagros, 14; *see also* ex-votos

Miniaturas Felguérez, 169–70

miniatures: bibliography, 181n3
(intro.); collecting, 18–19; cultural
missions and, 8; in *Florentine Codex*,
10, 107; as a category of folk art,
7; magical use of, 7–8; in Mexico,
3; in Mixtec codices, 11; nuns and,
15; pre-Hispanic, 3, 9–11; sandals as
votive objects, 9; scarcity and, 17; in
Switzerland, 3–4, 17; virtues associated with, 16–18, 19

miniatures (Chigmecatitlán): animals,
72, 97–98, 99–100; as ex-votos,
119–22; history of, 95–98, 174; human characters, 98; leather sandals,
96–97; magical use of, 100; as
national symbols, 106; 164; prices,
41, 64–65, 91, 102–103, 156, 162–63;
ease of transport, 155–56

miniaturization of crafts, 89–108, 174

misterio (palm figure), 125

Mixteca, palm weaving in, 72

Mixteca-Puebla, xiv, 21, 44

Mixtec codices, 11, 73; list of, 181n6;
Codex Nuttall, 81, 175; *Codex Vaticanus B*, 73

Mixtec Indians: in Puebla, 21; pre-Hispanic, and the miniature, 11, 174;
reputation as traders, 152

Mixtec language, 28–30; loss of, 151;
terms for traders, 156; *see also*
language and ethnicity

Moctezuma, Don Francisco (cacique of
Tepexi), 78

models: architectural, 8; of Lake Texcoco, 4; of schools, 8

Moedano, Gabriel, xiii–xiv, 30–95

Monaghan, John, 83

Moncayo, Enrique (artisan), 82–83

Montenegro, Roberto, 6, 7; collection
of, 94, 174; 186n1

mule, as transport, 155

mule (palm figure), 51–*52*, 83, 158–59

Murdock, George P., and Caterina
Provost, 47

Murillo, Gerardo. *See* Atl, Dr.

Museum of Anthropology (Museo Nacional de Antropología e Historia,
Mexico City), 101, 162

museum of Chigmecatitlán crafts, 31,
40, 85–88, 105

musicians (palm figures), 91, *92*, 100,
143, 186n6

mysterious stranger, 142–45

nanotechnology, 15

Nash, June, 164

nationalism: and crafts, 4–7; miniatures
as symbols of, 173

nationalist designs, 145–49

Nativitas, Santa María, 69

nativity (palm figure), 104–105, 142,
167

nda'cho (basket), 73, *79*, 80, 95, 175

ndo'o (basket), *79*, 80

Nebel, Carl, 147

necklace (palm figure), 84, 105, 156,
159

Noguera, Eduardo, 158

Novelo, Victoria, 48–49, 55, 59, 66,
105; on national identity, 5, 178; on
popular and elite selling spheres,
156–57, 158

Ochoa, José Antonio, xiv, 122, 185n14

Oettinger, Marion, 137

Ojeda, Bernabé Pablo, 110, 124

old age: and mnemonic techniques, 70;
and weaving skill, 149–50

Oles, James, 181n1 (intro.)

outsiders: as innovators of designs,
142–45, 148–49, 185n1 (ch. 6);
treatment of, 115, 122–24, 130–33,
185n14

Painted Tribute Record of Tepexi, 76–77

palm plant, *24–25*; in *Codex Vaticanus
B*, 73, *74*

Palm Sunday, 119, 212–22; and crafts,
12, 157, 176, 184n13

palm weavers. *See* artisans

palm weaving: prehistory, 73; colonial
history, 74–78; history, 70–73, 88; in
the Mixteca, 72, 84

palm weaving production: likened to an
automobile plant, 60–61; household, 40–41, 49, 142; organized by
kinship, 61; as a microindustry, 65;
modes of, 48–52, 58–59; raw materials, 53–58; small capitalist workshop, 50–52; in wells, 51–52

palm weaving technique, 49–50, 53–54,
78–82, 103, 136, 138; learning,
135–42; adult learning, 139–40;

child learning, 137–38, 139, 151; as embodied knowledge, 140; forgetting, 137, 149–51
"Pancho el Juguetero," 18, 92–93
Parián, El, 144, 154–55
Parsons, Elsie Clews, 8–9
Pastorela, 31, *111*, 182n5 (ch. 1)
Paz y Sánchez, Fr. Mariano (priest in 1811), 109–10; testimony of, 109, 113, 114–15, 115–16, 117–18, 122, 123, 124, 125, 130, 131, 132–33
peacocks (palm figures), *45*
Peirce, Charles, 120–21
Pérez, León (artisan), 27, 103, 104, 119–20; interview, 142–45, 167
petates. *See* mats
Pettit, Florence H., and Robert M. Pettit, 122
pilgrimage, 160–62
Piña Olaya, Mariano (Puebla governor 1987–93), 104
piñera/piñero (palm figures), 91
plants, 23–25, 44, 68, 175, 181n3 (ch. 1), 182n1 (ch. 2)
plastic palm. *See* raffia
politics, 37, 105–106
Popoloca Indians, 150–51
population, 41–43, 47
Porter, Katherine Anne: on Mexican cultural renaissance, 5–6; 1922 popular art exhibit, 6; on outside influence on designs, 148
posadas, las, 116
PRI (Partido Revolucionario Institucional), 59, 106
prices: of crafts, 41, 64–65, 91, 102–103, 156, 162–63; of palm and raffia, 54
priest (1811). *See* Paz y Sánchez, Fr. Mariano
priest (elder). *See* Barragán, Fr. Abraham
priest (younger), 111, 112, 124–26; and banishment of evangelist doctor, 130–33
processions, 44, 116, 117, 118
Protestantism, 109, 124–25, 126, 133
Puebla (city), miniatures in, 155
Puebla (state), map, 22
Puig Casauranc, J. M., 8
pulque harvester (palm figure). *See* tlachiquero

raffia, 54–56, 175; market for, 157–58
Ramonato, 119, 184n10

Ramos, Samuel, 146
rattle, 57–58
Ravicz, Robert, and A. Kimball Romney, 153, 165
Regalos Hansen, 163
Relaciones Geográficas, 75–76
religion. *See* Catholic Church; Catholicism of town; Protestantism
Reséndiz, Edmundo (INI subdirector), 87–88
residence pattern, 140
Rivera, Diego, 147
robbers, 154
Rockefeller, Nelson, collection of, 94, 174
Rodríguez, Inocencio (artisan), 164–66
Rodríguez, Tomasa. *See* Fernández, Eligio, and Tomasa Rodríguez
Rosaldo, Renato, 18
Rosas, Benigno (artisan), 90, 95–96, 119, 183n5
Rubín de la Borbolla, Daniel F., 78

Sahagún, Bernardino de, 107
saints, statues of: San Antonio, 120; San Isidro Labrador, 44, 120; San Martín de Porres, 120; San Pascual Bailón, 14–15
Sanborns, 98
sandals, miniature, 96–97; as votive objects, 9
San Felipe Otlaltepec, 150, 151
sanitation, 34
San Pablo Anicano, 160, 161
San Pedro y San Pablo Tequixtepec. *See* Tequixtepec
Santa Catarina Tlaltempan, 21, 39, 82, 83–84; Corpus Christi altars, 129; residents as buyers of palm crafts, 96, 163; votive crafts in church, 120
Santo Jubileo, 128
SECOFI, 65–66, 179
sellers, 44; anonymity of, 167–69; competition among, 160; of miniatures, 115; Mixtec terms for, 156; numbers of, 156; relationship with artisans, 61–62, 162; San Martín Caballero as patron saint of, 154
selling palm crafts, 59–60; lack of in Chigmecatitlán, 152; elite sphere, 153, 156–57, 162–67, 175; history of, 155; in Mexico City, 143–44, 152, 162–67, 168–71; popular sphere, 153, 156–57, 158–62, *161*,

175; restrictions on, 170–71; social structure of, 156–58; list of towns, 159–60; votive art to increase, 121, 129–30
Serna, Jacinto de la, 130
shops, crafts, 148; La Carreta, 169; Casa Cervantes, 165–67; Miniaturas Felguérez, 169–70; Sanborns, 98
size categories, *90*, 104, 106, 134
soldier (palm figure), 83
Solidaridad, 46
souvenirs, 164, 169
Starr, Frederick, 121, 147, 155
statues, religious. *See* Christ, statues of; saints, statues of
Stewart, Susan, xiii, 41, 101, 104, 173
sugar mills, 90, 165
Swift, Jonathan, 101–102

teachers, 8; in Chigmecatitlán, 122–23
television, inflence on designs, 149
tentzo, 154, 185n3
Tepeaca, 76, 95, 106
Tepexi de Rodríguez (formerly de la Seda), 27, 70; colonial history, 75, 78, 110, 184n2; jail, 68–69; painted tribute record, 76–77; pre-Hispanic history, 182n5 (ch. 3)
Tequixtepec, San Pedro y San Pablo, 21–22, 29, 72, 88, 181n1 (ch. 1)
tlachiquero (palm figure), 83, 90, *91*, 95–96
Tlaltempan. *See* Santa Catarina Tlaltempan
Tonahuixtla, Santo Domingo, 29, 84, 184n11
Toor, Frances, 9
tourists: lack of in Chigmecatitlán, 40, 152; as crafts consumers, 173, 175; *see also* outsiders
toys, 72, 97–98, 107; pre-Hispanic, 181n5
travel, dangers of, 153–55

Traven, B., 66–67
Turner, Victor, and Edith Turner, 109
Turok, Marta, xiv, 48–49, 50, 121, 184n10

Universidad Nacional Autónoma de México (UNAM), 165

Vázquez, Sabino (buyer), 91–93
vegetation. *See* plants
Vidales, Agustín (artisan), 97, 103, 138–39
Vidales, Alberto (artisan), 96–97
Vidales, Fernando (ex-municipal president), 139, 140; victim of robbery, 154

Waite, C. B., 95, 147
wallets. *See* nda'cho
water petitioning ceremony, 44
weaving palm. *See* palm weaving
wells, weaving in, 51–52
Weston, Edward, 17–19, 177
woodpeckers on Corpus Christi altars, 128–29

Zaldívar Guerra, María Luisa, 179
Zamora, Celina (china/charro artisan), 49, 103
Zamora, Clara (seller), 87, 156, 170
Zamora, Imelda (seller), 87, 105, 156, 163, 167–68, 171
Zamora, Jesusa (artisan/seller), 96, 154
Zamora, Laura (china/charro artisan), 49, 103
Zamora, Luis (seller), 87, 150
Zamora, Tomás, and Luz María Guajardo (sellers), 155–56
Zapotec Indians, 8–9
Zócalo (Mexico City), xiii, 4, 91, 152, 170–71
Zona Rosa, 6, 169

About the Author

Katrin Flechsig is a cultural anthropologist, writer, and editor specializing in the material culture of Mexico. She received a master's degree in Latin American Studies from the University of California at Los Angeles and a doctorate from the University of Texas at Austin, where she has also taught cultural anthropology. In addition to her research with palm artisans, Dr. Flechsig has conducted fieldwork in Mexico on *chilte* miniatures from Talpa, Jalisco, that serve as souvenirs of pilgrimage; the regional cuisines of Puebla, Tlaxcala, and Hidalgo; and the Latin American "new song" movement. She has been employed by the Instituto Nacional de Bellas Artes, the Instituto Nacional de Antropología e Historia, and AmCham Mexico in Mexico City; and by the Tech Museum of Innovation in San Jose, California. She is co-author (with Karen Chester) of *Mi canto trabajador: Work Songs of Latin America* (Third World Teaching Resource Center, 1979) and contributor to *Atlas Cultural de México: Gastronomía* (SEP/INAH/Planeta, 1989). She received a Fulbright Grant for her research in Puebla and is currently working on an article about the foundation narratives of Chigmecatitlán, Puebla. She lives in Austin, Texas.